CAMBRIDGE CLASSICAL STUDIES

General Editors

M. I FINLEY, E. J. KENNEY, G. E. L. OWEN

TIMOLEON AND THE REVIVAL OF GREEK SICILY

344–317 B.C.

TIMOLEON AND THE REVIVAL OF GREEK SICILY

344–317 B.C.

BY

R. J. A. TALBERT

Lecturer in Ancient History
The Queen's University, Belfast

117832

CAMBRIDGE UNIVERSITY PRESS

Published by the Syndics of the Cambridge University Press
Bentley House, 200 Euston Road, London, NW1 2DB
American Branch: 32 East 57th Street, New York, N.Y.10022

© Faculty of Classics, University of Cambridge 1974

Library of Congress Catalogue Card Number: 74–16854

ISBN: 0 521 20419 4

First published 1974

Printed in Great Britain
at the University Printing House, Cambridge
(Brooke Crutchley, University Printer)

TO ZANDRA

CONTENTS

CONTENTS

PREFACE

In an earlier form this work was submitted to the University of Cambridge in April 1971 for the degree of Doctor of Philosophy. It seeks to discuss the evidence for Timoleon's career in Sicily and for the revival of the Greek zone of the island between 344 and 317 B.C.; relevant coin hoards buried up to c. 290 are also considered.

The nature of the surviving evidence has largely restricted previous treatments of Timoleon's career to discussion of literary source material. In this sphere the most valuable contribution has perhaps been made by Professor H. D. Westlake, even if some of his conclusions still seem open to argument. However an article by G. K. Jenkins in *CPANS* (1958) dated to Timoleon's time a sudden flow of Corinthian silver coinage into Sicily, thereby prompting a re-assessment of the relevant numismatic evidence and its significance. Meanwhile excavations conducted in Sicily since the Second World War shed fresh light on the revival of the Greek zone during Timoleon's day and afterwards. The importance of this archaeological evidence is especially well demonstrated in *Kokalos* 4 (1958).

Taking these new developments into account, I began my own work in the field by attempting a historical commentary on Plutarch, *Timoleon*. Later this project proved unsatisfactory, since my commentary on Plutarch's Life came to involve equally full treatment of almost all the other evidence for Timoleon's career. I likewise decided not to write a biography of Timoleon, because in my view there is too little evidence for such an approach to be rewarding. Instead the studies presented here aim to treat only those aspects of Timoleon's career for which there is some adequate evidence. This purpose has been kept in mind throughout the book, with the result that in Chapter 1, for example, I have discussed only Plutarch, *Timoleon*, and have not embarked on a general discussion of Plutarch's biographical technique, which would be inappropriate in this context. I do not claim professional expertise in either archaeology or numismatics, and my Chapters 8, 9 and 10 merely seek to appreciate the historical significance of evidence published by experts in these fields. Further information on archaeological discoveries may be sought through my bibliography: no such list of archaeological publications relating to the Timoleontic period has been attempted before, to the best of my knowledge.

My thanks are due to my successive supervisors, Professor F. H. Sandbach and Professor M. I Finley, and to my examiners, Professor H. W. Parke and Mr G. T. Griffith; to Mr A. G. Woodhead for advice on epigraphical publications; to Dr C. M. Kraay, for putting at my disposal his detailed notes on the contents of Sicilian coin hoards; to Mr G. K. Jenkins, for advice on coins and publications in the British Museum, London; to Professor E. de Miro and Dottoressa P. Pelagatti, for allowing me to see material in the possession of the Soprintendenze alle Antichità at Agrigento and Siracusa respectively; and finally to my colleagues in Belfast for their help and encouragement.

I am grateful to the Awards Branch of the Department of Education and Science for making me grants for two years' research and for a visit to Sicily in March and April 1970; and to The Queen's University, Belfast for grants towards research and towards another visit to Sicily in April 1972. The Faculty Board of Classics has honoured me by including this book in the series Cambridge Classical Studies, and the staff of the University Press have been most helpful in securing it a smooth passage to publication. At the same time the interval between the delivery of the script and publication has inevitably been a long one, with the result that it has been impossible to take into account the most recent work on some matters.

Belfast   R.J.A.T.

June 1974

NOTE ON TEXTS

For Plutarch, *Timoleon*, I have used the most recent edition, that of R. Flacelière and E. Chambry in the Budé series (*Plutarque Vies* 4, Paris 1966). For all other Lives I have used the Teubner edition (i.i–ii.i, K. Ziegler, Leipzig 1957–64; ii.ii–iii.ii, C. Lindskog and K. Ziegler, 1915–35).

For Diodorus I have used the Loeb Classical Library edition (16.66–90 is included in Vol. 8, ed. C. B. Welles, London 1963), together with the Teubner text edited by C. T. Fischer (Vol. 4, Leipzig 1906).

ABBREVIATIONS

The titles of the following publications are cited in abbreviated form:

Beloch, *GG²*
    K. J. Beloch, *Griechische Geschichte* (2nd edition, Berlin and Leipzig 1922)

Berve, *Die Tyrannis*
    H. Berve, *Die Tyrannis bei den Griechen* (Munich 1967)

Finley, *Ancient Sicily*
    M. I Finley, *A History of Sicily: Ancient Sicily to the Arab Conquest* (London 1968)

Sordi
    M. Sordi, *Timoleonte* (Palermo 1961)

Sordi, *Diodori Liber XVI*
    M. Sordi, *Diodori Siculi Bibliothecae Liber Sextus Decimus: Introduzione, testo e commento* (Florence 1969)
    (Note: In this book the views which Sordi expresses on Timoleon and on the history of Sicily during his time are substantially those put forward by her in 1961; they have not been revised in the light of later work.)

Westlake, *CHJ* 7 (1942)
    H. D. Westlake, 'Timoleon and the reconstruction of Syracuse', *Cambridge Historical Journal* 7 (1942), 73–100 (now reprinted in H. D. Westlake, *Essays on the Greek Historians and Greek History* (Manchester 1969), pp. 276–312).

Westlake, *Tyrants*
    H. D. Westlake, *Timoleon and his Relations with Tyrants* (Manchester 1952)

ABBREVIATIONS

The titles of the following periodicals and publications are cited in abbreviated form:

AIIN	*Istituto Italiano di Numismatica: Annali*
AJA	*American Journal of Archaeology*
AJP	*American Journal of Philology*
Arch. Cl.	*Archeologia Classica*
ASSO	*Archivio Storico per la Sicilia Orientale*
Ath. Mitt.	*Mitteilungen des Deutschen Archäologischen Instituts, Athenische Abteilung*
Atti e Mem.	*Atti e Memorie dell'Istituto Italiano di Numismatica*
BCH	*Bulletin de Correspondance Hellénique*
BMC Corinth	B. V. Head, *Catalogue of Greek Coins. Corinth, Colonies of Corinth, etc.* (British Museum, London 1889)
Boll. Circ. Num. Nap.	*Bollettino del Circolo Numismatico Napoletano*
CHJ	*Cambridge Historical Journal*
CPANS	*Centennial Publication of the American Numismatic Society*, ed. H. Ingholt (New York 1958)
CQ	*Classical Quarterly*
CR	*Classical Review*
CRAI	*Comptes Rendus de l'Académie des Inscriptions et Belles-Lettres*
*HN*²	B. V. Head, *Historia Numorum* (2nd edition, Oxford 1911)
IG	*Inscriptiones Graecae*
JHS	*Journal of Hellenic Studies*
JNG	*Jahrbuch für Numismatik und Geldgeschichte*
LSJ	H. G. Liddell and R. Scott, *A Greek–English Lexicon* (9th edition revised by H. S. Jones, Oxford 1940)
MAL	*Monumenti Antichi pubblicati per cura della Accademia Nazionale dei Lincei*
MAN	*Memorie dell'Accademia di Archeologia, Lettere e Belle Arti di Napoli*
MEFR	*Ecole Française de Rome: Mélanges d'Archéologie et d'Histoire*
NC	*Numismatic Chronicle*
NSc	*Notizie degli Scavi*
Ox. Pap.	*The Oxyrhynchus Papyri* (London 1898–)
RAL	*Rendiconti della Accademia Nazionale dei Lincei*
RE	*Real-Encyclopädie der classischen Altertumswissenschaft*
REG	*Revue des Etudes Grecques*
Rev. Arch.	*Revue Archéologique*
SEG	*Supplementum Epigraphicum Graecum*
SGDI	*Sammlung der griechischen Dialekt-Inschriften*, ed. H. Collitz (Göttingen 1899)
SIFET	*Bollettino della Società Italiana di Fotogrammetria e Topografia*
*SIG*³	W. Dittenberger, *Sylloge Inscriptionum Graecarum* (3rd edition, Leipzig 1920)
SNG	*Sylloge Nummorum Graecorum*
TAPA	*Transactions of the American Philological Association*

CHAPTER I

Timoleon and Plutarch

Plutarch's characterization of Timoleon

Plutarch's Preface to the Parallel Lives of Aemilius Paulus and Timoleon is an important piece of writing, which clarifies his aims in the Lives which follow, and informs us in general terms of what we can expect to learn from the Lives, and what we cannot. At the outset he claims that his purpose is to select from the πράξεις of his subjects τὰ κυριώτατα καὶ κάλλιστα πρὸς γνῶσιν (Pref. 2). 'What could be more effective πρὸς ἐπανόρθωσιν ἠθῶν?', he goes on to ask (Pref. 3). Timoleon is placed among τὰ κάλλιστα τῶν παραδειγμάτων (Pref. 5), and it must be admitted that Plutarch's selection of τὰ κυριώτατα καὶ κάλλιστα from his career leaves him a dull character. Certainly his upright, patriotic, level-headed, honest ἦθος is brought out through his πράξεις, but all the same he does not spring to life. There is hardly any relief afforded from the unceasing chorus of indiscriminate praise, either by the charming personal details which Plutarch introduces so ably elsewhere,[1] or by faults or emotions.

We are really told nothing distinctive about him at all, except that he emulated Epaminondas (36.1: a feature which would appeal to Plutarch as a Boeotian), that he went blind, as had other members of his family (37.7–8), that he spent much of his time in old age with his wife and children on the country estate presented to him by Syracuse (36.7; 38.2; Comp. 2.9), and that as an old man he went to the assembly in a cart (38.6–7). It is perhaps slightly unusual that there should be so few apophthegmata of Timoleon recorded, since Plutarch regarded the record of such sayings as an important indication of character. In this Life we are told that Timoleon spoke at Rhegium (10.1–2), and before the battles of Adranum (12.6) and the R. Crimisus

---

[1] For example, Agesilaus playing horses with his children, *Agesilaus* 25.11; Aemilius Paulus and his daughter Tertia, *Aem. Paul.* 10.6–8.

(27.9), but none of these occasions is of much interest, and the only apophthegmata as such are his replies to Laphystius and Demaenetus (37.2–3), his remarks about the parsley (26.3), and his observations on his own career (36.5).

His δικαιοσύνη (37.5; Comp. 2.1), ἀνδρεία (37.5) and πρᾳότης (Pref. 5; 37.5) are remarked upon. He is patriotic, and wishes αὐτοῦ τὴν πατρίδα πᾶσιν ἀνθρώποις ζηλωτὴν εἶναι (29.5). He is described directly as χρηστὸς ὢν καὶ φιλοίκειος (5.1), and at greater length as

φιλόπατρις δὲ καὶ πρᾷος διαφερόντως, ὅσα μὴ σφόδρα μισοτύραννος εἶναι καὶ μισοπόνηρος. ἐν δὲ τοῖς πολέμοις οὕτω καλῶς καὶ ὁμαλῶς ἐκέκρατο τὴν φύσιν ὥστε πολλὴν μὲν ἐν νέῳ σύνεσιν, οὐκ ἐλάττω δὲ γηρῶντος ἀνδρείαν ἐπιφαίνεσθαι ταῖς πράξεσιν (3.4–5),

all this in implied contrast to Timophanes.

Throughout almost the whole Life Timoleon is portrayed as a man who cannot put a foot wrong, who always takes the most correct and honourable course of action in any situation. He saves Timophanes' life in battle (4.1–3); at first he attempts to bring out Timophanes' good qualities, concealing his mistakes (3.8), but later he is so distressed by his brother's tyranny that he feels himself driven to murder (4.5–8). On the voyage to Sicily it is noticeable that the unpromising reports from the island bring to the soldiers δυσθυμίαν, but to Timoleon, who refuses to be disheartened, only πολλὴν ἀπορίαν (9.2); in the same way he is undismayed by the desertion of 1,000 mercenaries before the battle of the R. Crimisus, since τούτους ... κέρδος ἡγεῖτο πρὸ τῆς μάχης φανεροὺς γεγονότας (25.6). For the final battle in Syracuse against Hicetas he takes command of the sector where fighting is likely to be fiercest (21.2), and afterwards pulls down the citadel, thereby not making Dion's mistake (22.1–3). Naturally Timoleon grants ἄδεια to the man sent to kill him, on condition that the man makes a full confession (16.7–8), while in reply to the envoys of Hicetas and the Carthaginians he does not become heated like his own troops (9.7) and the Carthaginians (11.1–3), but speaks ἐπιεικῶς (10.1; cf. Comp. 2.12). He goes blind at Mylae, but perseveres to bring his campaign to a successful conclusion, rather than relinquish his command on the spot (37.7–10); later he bears his blindness without complaint (38.1), and endures nobly the attacks of Laphystius and Demaenetus (37.1–3).

Only twice is there an explicit hint of a less reputable quality, that of δεινότης (21.4; 37.5), though this is also brought out in Timoleon's deceit at Rhegium (10), and perhaps, too, by his ingenuity in averting the soldiers' δεισιδαιμονία and δυσελπιστία at the sight of parsley before battle (26.3). But only on one occasion do Timoleon's resolution and self-assurance seem to break down and to reveal a human being, and that is after his brother's murder, when

παντάπασι περίλυπος γενόμενος καὶ συνταραχθεὶς τὴν διάνοιαν ὥρμησε μὲν ὡς διαφθερῶν ἑαυτὸν ἀπέχεσθαι τροφῆς, τῶν δὲ φίλων οὐ περιιδόντων, ἀλλὰ πᾶσαν δέησιν καὶ πᾶσαν ἀνάγκην προσενεγκαμένων, ἔγνω ζῆν καθ' ἑαυτὸν ἐκ μέσου γενόμενος. καὶ πολιτείαν μὲν ἅπασαν ἀφῆκε, τοὺς δὲ πρώτους χρόνους οὐδὲ κατιὼν εἰς πόλιν, ἀλλ' ἀδημονῶν καὶ πλανώμενος ἐν τοῖς ἐρημοτάτοις τῶν ἀγρῶν διέτριβεν (5.3–4; cf. Comp. 2.11–12).

In order to show the power of τύχη and to enhance Timoleon's virtues, Plutarch is quick to stress the massive odds against the Corinthians. He says that Timoleon finally conquered the Carthaginians with τῆς τυχούσης στρατιᾶς (Comp. 1.4). In the Life itself he has Timoleon's men at Rhegium reflect on the impossibility of their overcoming both the Carthaginians, who had double the number of their ships, and Hicetas (9.8). Again, on Timoleon's arrival in Sicily, he stresses how very meagre were Timoleon's chances of success – χιλίων γὰρ αὐτῷ στρατιωτῶν καὶ τροφῆς τούτοις ἀναγκαίας πλέον οὐδὲν ὑπῆρχεν – not only because he had few resources, but also because of the difficulties of enlisting the friendship of the Sicilian cities (11.5–12.1). Timoleon's 1,200 troops beat the 5,000 of Hicetas at Adranum (12.4). After the arrival of his reinforcements Timoleon advances to Syracuse to fight Mago's vast horde (17.2) with only 4,000 men (20.1), and at the R. Crimisus he has only 6,000 soldiers against the Carthaginians' 70,000 (25.5). Later he has only a few soldiers when he finally defeats Hicetas at the R. Lamyrias (31.2).

It is noticeable that Plutarch seems to restrict Timoleon to passive participation in tortures and executions. While others murder Timophanes, he stands a little way off (4.8). The people of Messana execute Hippon (34.4); the executioner of Mamercus remains unspecified (34.7). And although Timoleon is blamed for allowing the execution of the wives and daughters of Hicetas and his friends, it is the Syracusans who actually do the deed (33.1). It might even be argued that in mentioning the punishments inflicted by Timoleon and his supporters, Plutarch displays a restraint which is not present when he deals with the punishments inflicted by enemies. ὡς τύραννοι καὶ προδόται κολασθέντες (32.2, of Hicetas, his son and Euthymus) might possibly conceal some gruesome punishment deliberately omitted by Plutarch, because he would not care for its brutality to be in any way connected with Timoleon. In the same way Plutarch does not specify Mamercus' punishment, but employs the paraphrase ἥνπερ οἱ λῃσταὶ δίκην ἔδωκε (34.7). On the other hand he does relate how the dead body of Mago was crucified by the Carthaginians (22.8), an action which confirms his description of them as κακίστους καὶ φονικωτάτους (20.7). Yet in *Dion* he does not conceal the cruelty of the Syracusans: he is ready to go into the closest details of how Philistus was tortured and finally put to death by them (*Dion* 35.4–6), and tells how they set out to exhume the body of Dionysius I and cast it out (*Dion* 53.1).

Plutarch's own attitude towards Timoleon is not quite consistent: at 33.2 he explicitly censures Timoleon's acquiescence in the execution of Hicetas' family and friends as τῶν Τιμολέοντος ἔργων ἀχαριστότατον, but at 36.2 he says that there is nothing in Timoleon's career to which it is not fitting to apply Sophocles' words of praise, except τὴν περὶ τὸν ἀδελφὸν ἀνάγκην. Thus in the latter case all deeds done by Timoleon of his own free will are approved, as the murder of Timophanes is regarded as an ἀνάγκη. In the final summing-up in the Comparison Timoleon is described as γενναῖα πράξας περὶ τὸν ἀδελφόν, but he is placed below Aemilius Paulus because he was unable to rid himself of his sorrow and repentance for as long as twenty years (Comp. 2.11–12).

I do not wish to belittle either Timoleon's achievements or

4

his nobility of purpose: Plutarch's portrait has impressed men of all ages, and indeed it may not be far from the kind of portrait which Timoleon would have wanted a biographer to present of himself (he was a more astute propagandist than is often realized), but it is not the portrait of a man. Plutarch wished to select τὰ κυριώτατα καὶ κάλλιστα from Timoleon's career in order to illustrate the workings of his ἦθος, to discern on a moral plane 'ὅσσος ἔην οἷός τε' (Pref. 2). He is not concerned by the fact that his selection inevitably introduces elements of distortion and idealization into the portrait, nor by the fact that both are magnified by his belief in the power of the supernatural in Timoleon's career, so that at one point, for instance, he has Timoleon rely more on his success and his good fortune than on his troops (20.1). Certainly it is not surprising that Plutarch's portrait of Timoleon is a generous one, when laudatory sources were probably the only ones readily accessible in his day; but the shortcomings of the portrait must still be appreciated by the historian who is forced, for want of much other source material, to use the biography for historical purposes, rather than for the 'ethical' purposes intended by Plutarch.

Plutarch's characterization of Hicetas and other figures in Timoleon

The same caution must be applied to the portrait of Hicetas. While Timoleon is the hero of the piece, Hicetas is undoubtedly the villain. His evil actions and motives are constantly set against the noble conduct of Timoleon.[1] Although few details are given of his character, his actions and motives are painted in the darkest colours, and in some places the opportunity is taken to narrate an incident in such a way as to balance the reader's judgement against him in favour of Timoleon.

Hicetas first appears in the Life as the chosen leader of the Syracusan exiles who wished to drive Dionysius from their city: but it is then at once noted that he was nevertheless no

---

[1] One of the clearest cases of Plutarch's use of σύγκρισις inside the Life; see also the comparison of Timoleon with other commanders of the time, at 36.1 and 4, and Comp. 2.2–7, and the antithesis of Timoleon and Timophanes.

better than any other tyrant, merely powerful enough to combat Dionysius (1.6). We are told plainly that he took the generalship in order to create a tyranny for himself, not to free Syracuse, and that he held secret talks with the Carthaginians, although openly supporting the Syracusans' appeal to Corinth at the same time. He expected Corinth to refuse the appeal, and he would then be able to use Punic help for his own ends (2.3–4). It was his letter to Corinth, which revealed his change of sides and his treachery, that prompted the Corinthians to dispatch Timoleon with renewed eagerness (7.3–6).

After his success against Dionysius and his enlistment of Punic aid, Hicetas plans to have Timoleon repulsed and to divide control of the island between himself and the Carthaginians (9.3–4): for this reason he sends envoys to Timoleon at Rhegium, who make the treacherous suggestion that Timoleon should send back his force and join Hicetas as σύμβουλος (9.5–6). For this reason, too, he is frightened by the news of Timoleon's arrival in Sicily, and therefore sends for a large number of Punic triremes (11.4).

His defeat at Adranum (12) induces him to initiate an unsuccessful assassination attempt against Timoleon, as well as preventing any food from reaching the garrison on Ortygia (16.5–11). The failure of the assassination attempt leads him to call in powerful Carthaginian forces, and Mago appears in the Great Harbour with 150 ships and 60,000 infantry (17). But even with Mago's help Hicetas fails to take Catania, and is unable to reach Achradina in the meantime (18). Mago becomes disturbed by rumours of disloyalty among the mercenaries, and cannot be persuaded by Hicetas to remain (20.11).

Plutarch's next two references to Hicetas are unclear: his narrative of Timoleon's final capture of Syracuse (21) is puzzling in that Hicetas seems on the one hand keen to retain the parts of the city in his possession, yet on the other hand puts up so poor a resistance in the fight that not one of Timoleon's troops is killed or even wounded. The second reference has been the subject of controversy too: although Timoleon is said to have made an expedition to Leontini, to have forbidden Hicetas to ally with Carthage, and to have made him agree to demolish

6

his acropolis and live as a private citizen in Leontini (24.1), there is no indication from the subsequent narrative that Hicetas ever did this.

Hicetas is next mentioned after the battle of the R. Crimisus, when he forms an alliance with Mamercus and the Carthaginians against Timoleon, εἴτε φθόνῳ τῶν κατορθουμένων ὑπὸ Τιμολέοντος, εἴτε φοβουμένων αὐτὸν ὡς ἄπιστον καὶ ἄσπονδον πρὸς τοὺς τυράννους (30.4). The two victories of the alliance are then mentioned (30.6). Hicetas is last mentioned in the section which opens with his defeat at the R. Lamyrias, after he had done much harm to Syracusan territory on a plundering raid (31.2–8). This defeat is followed by the capture of himself, his son and Euthymus (32.1). He and his son are put to death ὡς τύραννοι καὶ προδόται (32.2), while his wife and daughters and those of his friends are also put to death in revenge for his alleged murder of Arete, Aristomache and Dion's son (33).

The bad impression of Hicetas which Plutarch wishes to create in the reader's mind can be seen not only from this survey of the episodes where he is mentioned in the narrative, but also from a more detailed examination of certain passages. Plutarch's narrative of the battle of Adranum provides an example (12–13.1). Significant points are left out or passed over briefly: it is not made quite clear which route Timoleon took to reach Adranum from Tauromenium (we are merely told that he went through χαλεπὰ χωρία, 12.5); the narrative of the battle itself is unhelpfully short (12.5–8); and, most important of all, it is not explained why Hicetas should have been so completely unprepared. Plutarch seems to be most interested, not in the battle, but in the reaction of the god of Adranum, which is carefully described (12.9), and the propitious beginning this made for Timoleon's successes in Sicily (13.1). He brings out the importance of the god's support when he remarks at 12.2 that the god was highly revered throughout the whole of Sicily (rather than just locally in Adranum).

Chapter 17 has nothing to do with Timoleon personally, but it deals with the Carthaginians' response to Hicetas' request for aid. Details are given of the Carthaginian strength, but the main point, the barbarization of Sicily, is an emotional one put forward in such a way as to heighten the reader's good opinion of Timoleon, and to blacken Hicetas as the man who admitted the Carthaginians without the striking of a single blow. The point is stressed more strongly here than anywhere else in the Life; it is really made three times:

ὥστε πάντας οἴεσθαι τὴν πάλαι λεγομένην καὶ προσδοκωμένην ἐκβαρβάρωσιν ἥκειν ἐπὶ τὴν Σικελίαν. οὐδέποτε γὰρ Καρχηδονίοις ὑπῆρξε πρότερον μυρίους πολεμήσασι πολέμους ἐν Σικελίᾳ λαβεῖν τὰς Συρακούσας, ἀλλὰ τότε δεξαμένου τοῦ Ἱκέτου καὶ παραδόντος ἦν ὁρᾶν τὴν πόλιν στρατόπεδον βαρβάρων οὖσαν (17.2–3).[1]

So the narrative of chapter 17 comes to reflect badly on Hicetas, as the tyrant who called in the Carthaginians, but doubly well on Timoleon, who is thus forced to repulse both Hicetas and his Punic allies.

Plutarch's narratives of Timoleon's final capture of Syracuse from Hicetas (21), and of the victory of the alliance of Hicetas, Mamercus and the Carthaginians over Timoleon's mercenaries at Hierae (30.6) are both 'weighted' incidents, in that in neither case does Plutarch make any attempt to give a balanced account, but uses each incident to underline Timoleon's success. In 21 Plutarch is far more interested in praising the τύχη, ἀρετή and fame of Timoleon (especially in sections 5–7) than in describing the military aspects of this strange episode. In 30 Plutarch gives no account of the ambush, but is concerned solely with stressing the point that even in this significant defeat Timoleon's εὐτυχία displayed itself, since the mercenaries ambushed were spoilers of Delphi, who deserved punishment (30.7–10).

Perhaps Plutarch is most misleading of all in his picture of Hicetas when he fails to mention the policy pursued by him at the time of the Punic invasion. While Plutarch says nothing, Diodorus (16.77.5) says that Timoleon made peace with Hicetas and took over his troops, thereby considerably enlarging the size of his own force. We have no means of knowing whether

[1] Much the same point is also put forward elsewhere: 1.3, in the résumé of affairs in Sicily; 10.3, fears of the people of Rhegium; 20.7–9, speech of the mercenary of Timoleon, where Carthaginians are called κακίστους καὶ φονικωτάτους; 23.4, beneficial action of Corinth; 29.6, Sicily set free from the Carthaginians; 39.5, honorary decree of Syracuse.

Diodorus is correct or not, but his version is historically plausible, and, if he is right, it would seem that Plutarch has deliberately omitted this point so that his portrait of Hicetas may have no redeeming features. His omission of any agreement made between Hicetas and Timoleon before the battle also frees him from the need to explain how and why the agreement was broken afterwards. Plutarch's remark that Hicetas allied with Mamercus and the Carthaginians against Timoleon, φοβουμένων αὐτὸν ὡς ἄπιστον καὶ ἄσπονδον πρὸς τοὺς τυράννους (30. 4), might suggest that Hicetas realized after the battle that Timoleon would not honour the agreement made between them, duplicity on the part of Timoleon which Plutarch would prefer to conceal.

The vices of Hicetas and Timoleon's other opponents are to be contrasted with Timoleon's virtues. Plutarch regards all the Greek leaders in Sicily in Timoleon's time as corrupt, except for Dion (Comp. 2.2). His fullest picture is that of Hicetas, although all the references are incidental, since there is no direct character sketch. Those charitable to Plutarch and his sources might contend that Hicetas displays the characteristics of an ordinary human being, even if those less kind might reply that he is really no more than a 'stock' tyrant. The strongest indictment of him is in the speech of Timoleon's mercenary, where he is described as a man who was driving out the fathers of the island (i.e. the Corinthians) and leading enemies against his own country: he would not do this, εἰ λογισμὸν εἶχεν ἡγεμόνος (20.9). Certainly he does not display Timoleon's high moral purpose, but is seen as full of evil thoughts (9.6), self-seeking (2.3), treacherous (7.3) and envious (30.4), prepared to resort to duplicity (2.3–4) and assassination (16). He displays emotions unknown to Timoleon: he is gripped by fear (7.5; 11.4), once even by panic, when he and Mago συνταραχθέντες ἀνεχώρησαν, because of the news of the capture of Achradina (18.7).[1] He is described by Plutarch as ashamed of himself for his small and secret use of Punic help (17.1; cf. 13.3 for Dionysius' opinion that the defeat at Adranum was shameful), and in the last section where he appears, he is said to have taken much booty from Syracusan

---

[1] συνταραχθείς is used of Timoleon once, but after his brother's murder (5.3).

territory, and then, πολλὰ λυμηνάμενος καὶ καθυβρίσας, to have despised Timoleon (31.2). In contrast to this not one of Timoleon's actions is ever censured, except for his acquiescence in the execution of the wives and daughters of Hicetas and his friends (33); rather Plutarch believes that his generalship was conducted with ease (36.4).

The only other two opponents of Timoleon to make more than a fleeting appearance, Mamercus and Mago, display characteristics very similar to those of Hicetas. Mago is first shown as φοβερός because of the huge numbers of his forces (17.2), but soon he becomes worried, frightened and suspicious (20.2); finally his suspicions of treachery impel him to the disgraceful flight (20.10–11) of a coward (21.1). Mamercus is introduced as πολεμιστὴς ἀνὴρ καὶ χρήμασιν ἐρρώμενος (13.2), but becomes envious (30.4), and boastful (31.1), and in the end gives way to despair when the Carthaginians make peace with Timoleon (34.3). Most unusual is the definite compliment paid to Euthymus, when he makes his brief appearance and is described as ἀνὴρ ἀγαθὸς ὢν πρὸς τοὺς ἀγῶνας καὶ τόλμῃ διαφέρων (32.2); but he spoils these virtues with his insulting behaviour (32.3).

It is interesting to put against these references to Timoleon's opponents the flattering remarks made by Plutarch about Timoleon's supporters. We are told that Andromachus τῶν ἑαυτοῦ πολιτῶν ἡγεῖτο νομίμως καὶ δικαίως καὶ πρὸς τοὺς τυράννους φανερὸς ἦν διακείμενος ἀπεχθῶς καὶ ἀλλοτρίως (10.7). We also hear that Timoleon's reinforcements, on being asked to guard Thurii during their enforced stay in that city, guard it ὥσπερ πατρίδα καθαρῶς καὶ πιστῶς (16.3–4). The spoils which Timoleon sent to Corinth have inscriptions proclaiming, among other virtues, the justice of the victors' cause (29.6). When Corinth is asked by Timoleon to send out new settlers, the Corinthians οὐχ ἥρπασαν ... τὴν πλεονεξίαν οὐδὲ προσεποίησαν αὐτοῖς τὴν πόλιν (23.1), while their proclamations at the various games earned τὸν δικαιότατον καὶ κάλλιστον ἔπαινον καὶ ζῆλον (23.4). Indeed Plutarch's enthusiasm for Corinth leads him to portray the city as very democratic (2 and 3; 7.2), as always very concerned with her colonies' welfare, especially that of Syracuse (3.1), and as having waged most of her wars οὐχ ὑπὲρ ἡγεμονίας καὶ πλεονεξίας, ἀλλ' ὑπὲρ τῆς τῶν Ἑλλήνων ἐλευθερίας (2.2). These statements may be inaccurate, but at least they are not actually contradicted in *Timoleon* itself. However, facts in *Timoleon* do make Plutarch's enthusiastic account of the Corinthians' choice of Timoleon and his dispatch to Sicily seem uncritical. He states that the Corinthians first voted eagerly to help the Syracusans (3.1), that they voted eagerly to give the command to Timoleon (7.2), and that later, after the receipt of Hicetas' letter, they were even keener (7.7). None of these expressions is justified by the miserable force of seven ships (8.4) and 1,000 troops (11.5) which was finally gathered. Nor is Plutarch's statement that the task of leading the expedition was eagerly competed for among ambitious citizens at Corinth (3.2) borne out by the choice of Timoleon, an old man, with little military experience, who had been living in retirement for twenty years.

The nature of Plutarch's narrative in Timoleon

Part of Plutarch's purpose in writing Lives was to turn his readers' minds to the examination and emulation of the good (cf. *Demetrius* 1.6). It is to present his readers with the good that he describes himself as taking τὰ κυριώτατα καὶ κάλλιστα πρὸς γνῶσιν from the careers of Aemilius Paulus and Timoleon. He believes that his description of virtuous actions will inspire his readers to good conduct: ἥ γ' ἀρετὴ ταῖς πράξεσιν εὐθὺς οὕτω διατίθησιν, ὥσθ' ἅμα θαυμάζεσθαι τὰ ἔργα καὶ ζηλοῦσθαι τοὺς εἰργασμένους (*Pericles* 2.2; cf. *Aratus* 1.3–4). It is this desire to lead his readers to the good which distinguishes his attitude to the events of a man's career from that of a modern historian, and governs his selection of material. Naturally he would not omit the really important events of a man's life, but he would omit without apology or indication the record of incidents or even decades in which there occurred nothing relevant to his purpose.[1] Moreover this desire leads him to give an incomplete portrait

---

[1] For example, the twenty years in Timoleon's life after the murder of Timophanes. At 1.2 Plutarch says that Dion, having driven out Dionysius II, was assassinated εὐθύς; in fact these events are separated by three years.

not only of the subject of a biography, but also of the period in which he lived, and of the figures with whom he came into contact. Hicetas and Mamercus are little more than shadows in *Timoleon*, while almost nothing is heard of the achievements of Timoleon's many lieutenants, Euclides and Telemachus (13.4 only), Neon (of whom we know the most, 18.3), Isias (21.3 only), Deinarchus (21.3; 24.4), Demaretus (21.3; 24.4; 27.6) and Euthymus the Leucadian (30.6 only). Megillus, Pheristus and Gorgus, who led colonists to Sicily, are mentioned once and no more (35.2); the same applies to the legislators Cephalus and Dionysius (24.3). Because Plutarch relegates all Timoleon's helpers to the background, it is easy for us to ascribe to Timoleon himself work which may really have been done by his helpers.

As we have seen above,[1] significant points in some of Hicetas' dealings with Timoleon seem to have been omitted; there are further important omissions in other passages, where Plutarch is mainly concerned with Timoleon's ἦθος. Thus there is no more than a bare mention of the mysterious incident where Hicetas is forced to live as a private citizen at Leontini (24.1–2; it cannot have been insignificant, if true), of the defeat of 400 of Timoleon's mercenaries in the territory of Messana (30.6), of Timoleon's expedition to Calauria (31.2), of the capture of Hicetas, of Mamercus' defeat near the R. Abolus (34.1; although as many as 2,000 of Mamercus' troops were killed here), and of Timoleon's expedition against Messana by land and sea (34.4; cf. 37.9).

The narrative of some other episodes is unbalanced. When Plutarch describes Dionysius' handing over of the fortress of Ortygia to Timoleon (13.3–7), he offers no convincing motive for this extraordinary action by Dionysius, but in this short passage is more concerned to emphasize τὴν ἀνέλπιστον εὐτυχίαν of Timoleon (13.4) and to enumerate the large resources given up by Dionysius. Then after this short passage on a most important event, he spends the rest of chapter 13 (sections 8–10) on Dionysius' past life, and all of chapters 14 and 15 dilating on the μεταβολὴ τῆς τύχης (14) and on various apophthegmata of

[1] Pp. 5–10.

Dionysius (15), ending with a sentence excusing and justifying his long digression (15.11). He does not feel the narrative to be unbalanced (cf. *Dion* 21.9; *Pelopidas* 25.15).

Plutarch uses the attempt to assassinate Timoleon (16) to stress Timoleon's εὐτυχία. First he includes a reflection on τῆς τύχης τὴν εὐμηχανίαν (16.10), then he makes the point that the Corinthians gave a reward to the man who had killed one of the would-be assassins, because he put his πάθος δίκαιον at the disposal of τῷ φυλάττοντι δαίμονι τὸν Τιμολέοντα, and reserved his anger for the saving of Timoleon (16.11); finally Plutarch makes his most marked reference to Timoleon as ἱερός and to the divine aid given to his mission (16.12).

In chapters 18 and 19 Plutarch deals respectively with Neon's capture of Achradina and with Hanno's unsuccessful trick. Although neither of these incidents has anything to do with Timoleon personally, each can be regarded as an *exemplum* which serves to illustrate Timoleon's success, for in between the two incidents Plutarch inserts his opinion that in the first πρόνοια and ἀρετή might dispute with τύχη, while the second is due wholly to εὐτυχία (19.1).

Lastly Plutarch's account of Timoleon's defeat of Hicetas at the R. Lamyrias is unbalanced. Most of the short account is taken up with Timoleon's resolution of his officers' petty dispute. But the battle must have been more than a minor scrap, since 1,000 were killed on Hicetas' side (31.3–8).

Since Plutarch is not writing formal history, he does not feel the need to date events for their own sake, or to give any precise indication of the length of time between events. The indications of time which are given seem to be either figures introduced to make some special point, or figures preserved by chance from a fuller and better informed source. The clearest example of the latter type is Plutarch's dating of the battle of the R. Crimisus: he informs us that it was fought near the end of the month Thargelion, but he does not specify the year (27.1). His statement that Timoleon marched for eight days to the place where the mutiny occurred might provide another example (25.5). But really this figure is only mentioned by the dissatisfied mercenaries to stress the risk of fighting so far from home. Instances of figures introduced to make some special point are found more often. Timoleon is so μετανοίᾳ καὶ λύπη ταπεινωθείς that he lives in retirement for as many as twenty years (Comp. 2.11; 7.1). His success in taking over Dionysius' tyranny is stressed by the quotation of the number of years of the latter's rule (13.9). Timoleon was so lucky and successful that a mere fifty days elapsed between his arrival in Sicily and Dionysius' departure (16.2). There was so much Punic booty captured at the R. Crimisus that it was three days before a trophy could be erected (29.4). Finally it was ἐν οὐδ' ὅλοις ἔτεσιν ὀκτώ that Timoleon purged Sicily of its miseries and handed it over to its inhabitants (37.6). Otherwise dating is completely vague. When Timoleon is at Rhegium, we are told that he had been invited to go to Tauromenium πάλαι (10.6). The arrival of the powerful Punic army at Lilybaeum is dated solely by an ἐν τούτῳ (25.1); this army marched against the Corinthians εὐθύς (25.3).

Plutarch also tends to give no indication of how much time elapsed between important events. There is no indication of the intervals between the time when Timophanes began to seek power (3.6), when the battle was fought in which Timoleon saved Timophanes' life (4.1–3), and when Timophanes was murdered (4.6–8). We are also ignorant of the length of the period from Dionysius' departure to Timoleon's final capture of Syracuse, where the only chronological reference of any kind in the whole section is to τῇ δ' ὑστεραίᾳ (21.1; except for the information that the news of the capture of the city filled Sicily and Italy εὐθύς, and reached Corinth ἡμερῶν ὀλίγων, 21.6). Plutarch is vague, too, about the chronology of events after the battle of the R. Crimisus. No indication is given of when Hicetas was defeated at the R. Lamyrias (31.3), nor, except for an οὐ πολλῷ δ' ὕστερον at 32.1, of when he was finally captured. The expedition against Mamercus is fixed by no more than a μετὰ δὲ ταῦτα (34.1), whilst ἐκ δὲ τούτου (34.2) the Carthaginians made peace. Finally Plutarch's lack of interest in chronology leads him to portray Timoleon's colonization of Sicily as the work of a comparatively short time, whereas the embassies, appeals and settlements must have been spread over years (22.4–23.5; 35.2–3).

In his treatment of motive Plutarch sometimes does not choose to probe historical issues. When he records the appointment of Timoleon to lead the Sicilian mission (3.2–3), he shows no interest in why exactly Timoleon should have been preferred above all the others eager for the post, but is quite content to accept the explanation of 'divine inspiration' and to look no further. Similarly he does not choose to examine the reasons for the defeat of the mercenaries under Euthymus the Leucadian, but regards the men as justly punished by the gods (30.6–10). His story that Dionysius felt overwhelmed by despair and thus handed over Ortygia to Timoleon less than fifty days after the latter's arrival in Sicily is certainly dramatic (13.3; 16.2), but very unconvincing indeed. So, too, is his story of the final capture of Syracuse dramatic, but as it stands it is unconvincing that there should be a battle in which none of Timoleon's troops is killed or even wounded (21.2–5). Then Plutarch seems happy to accept that Euthymus, although worthy and brave, was put to death merely because of his alleged Euripidean insult to the Corinthians; he makes the remarkable generalization:

ὑπὸ λόγων μᾶλλον ἢ πράξεων πονηρῶν ἀνιᾶσθαι πεφύκασιν οἱ πολλοί· χαλεπώτερον γὰρ ὕβριν ἢ βλάβην φέρουσι. καὶ τὸ μὲν ἀμύνεσθαι δι' ἔργων ὡς ἀναγκαῖον δέδοται τοῖς πολεμοῦσιν, αἱ δὲ βλασφημίαι περιουσίᾳ μίσους ἢ κακίας γίνεσθαι δοκοῦσιν (32.4).

There is no suggestion that the real cause for Euthymus' death might have been perhaps that he was too dangerous an opponent to set free. An emotional motive is also given for the Syracusans' execution of Hicetas' wife and daughters, though it is a more plausible one than that for Euthymus' death (33). Finally Plutarch supplies purely emotional motives in two cases where Timoleon has dealings with Corinth. At 24.2 he has him send Sicilian tyrants into exile at Corinth so that they should live a humble life in their mother-city, without any mention of the value which his action might have as propaganda for the liberation of Sicily. A similar point applies at 29.5–6 also, where Plutarch gives only an emotional motive for Timoleon's sending of the finest spoils from the R. Crimisus to Corinth – that he wanted his city to be universally envied – and adds no such mundane motive as, for example, that he wanted to underline both his success and the end of the war in Sicily, in order to attract new settlers (cf. chap. 35). In both these cases the mundane reasons are avoided not just because Plutarch might have failed to see them, but also because they would hardly tally with his portrait of Timoleon as a ἱερὸς ἀνήρ.

Plutarch's lavish use of superlatives in *Timoleon*, and in many cases of two superlative adjectives together, has the effect of lending greater emphasis to some matters than they really deserve; it also means that the 'good' are over-praised and the 'bad' are bitterly condemned. It was οἱ βέλτιστοι καὶ γνωριμώτατοι of the Syracusans who appealed to Corinth (1.6). Dionysius' tyranny was τὴν μεγίστην τῶν πώποτε τυραννίδων (1.4; cf. 13.9 τυραννίδι τῇ πασῶν ἐπιφανεστάτῃ καὶ μεγίστῃ). Andromachus was πολὺ κράτιστος τῶν τότε δυναστευόντων ἐν Σικελίᾳ γενόμενος (10.7). The Carthaginians were κακίστους καὶ φονικωτάτους (20.7), while Greek mercenaries were later considered by them to be ἀνυποστάτους καὶ μαχιμωτάτους (30.5). The Corinthians' proclamations at the games won them τὸν δικαιότατον καὶ κάλλιστον ἔπαινον καὶ ζῆλον (23.4). Neon was able to capture Achradina, which was κράτιστον καὶ ἀθραυστότατον τῆς Συρακουσίων μέρος πόλεως (18.4). After the battle of the R. Crimisus the Punic spoils presented τὴν καλλίστην καὶ μεγαλοπρεπεστάτην ὄψιν around Timoleon's tent (29.3). Finally Timoleon arranged τὰ κυριώτατα καὶ κάλλιστα matters of the Syracusan constitution (24.3), inscribed the spoils sent to Corinth with καλλίσταις ἐπιγραφαῖς (29.6), and is considered in the summing-up to have performed μέγιστα καὶ κάλλιστα τῶν καθ' αὐτὸν Ἑλλήνων (37.4).

Plutarch's special interests

Plutarch's own special interests should be mentioned, although they obtrude less in *Timoleon* than in some other Lives. There are few digressions of any length. Indeed apart from the Preface and the outline of the state of affairs in Sicily before Timoleon's arrival in chapters 1 and 2, neither of which can strictly be called a digression, the only instances are chapter 6, philosophical reflections on Timoleon's reaction to the murder of Timophanes, and chapters 14 and 15, on Dionysius (such philosophical reflections as occur in chapter 6 are quite common: see *Aristides* 6 and *Comp. Aristid. and Cat.* 4).

Apophthegmata are not as numerous as in certain other Lives. In the narrative itself, apart from the dedication of Mamercus (31.1), the insult of Euthymus (32.3), and the quotations of a proverb about parsley (26.2) and of lines of Sophocles (from Timaeus, 36.2), there are only the replies of Timoleon to Laphystius and Demaenetus (37) and the saying of Teleclides (7.2; cf. *Lycurgus* 25.7). In the two digressions mentioned above, however, there appear the sayings of Phocion (6.5), Aristides the Locrian (6.6) and Dionysius in Corinth (15). The remark made by the people of Rhegium to the Carthaginians about τοῖς δι' ἀπάτης πραττομένοις (11.1) could also be classed as an apophthegm.

There is only a small number, too, of the anecdotes in which Plutarch so delighted. He has lavished most care on the speech of Timoleon's mercenary to the mercenaries of Hicetas as they fished for eels (20.3–9), an excellent case of a small incident having important repercussions (cf. *Dion* 26.7–10; *Pelopidas* 8.7–9). Further anecdotes which he will have enjoyed telling in this Life are those of Andromachus threatened by the Punic envoy (11.2–3), of Dionysius in Corinth (14), and of the unsuccessful trick of the Carthaginian commander who was supposed to prevent the passage of Timoleon's reinforcements (19.4–5). Lastly there are four striking vignettes, of the offer of a reward for news of Mago (21.1), of the preservation of Gelon's statue (23.8), of Hippon captured while trying to escape and tortured in the theatre before even schoolchildren (34.4), and of Timoleon, old and blind, going to the assembly in a cart (38.6).

Except for remarks on τύχη, very few broad generalizations by Plutarch are present in the Life. The reflections on the murder of Timophanes (6) and on Euthymus' insult to the Corinthians have already been mentioned; other than these it would seem that there are only the statements that Corinth was always concerned with the welfare of her colonies, especially Syracuse (3.1), and that every democracy must gain a συκοφάντης (37.1).[1]

Two more of Plutarch's special interests are quite prominent, however. Delphi is first mentioned at 8.2–4, where Timoleon visits the shrine and has a ribbon of victory fall on to his head accidentally ὡς δοκεῖν αὐτὸν ὑπὸ τοῦ θεοῦ στεφανούμενον ἐπὶ τὰς πράξεις προπέμπεσθαι. This remarkable incident is recorded by no other source. Delphi's second appearance is at 30.6–10, where Plutarch tells how the massacre of the 400 mercenaries under Euthymus the Leucadian was divine punishment for their raid on Delphi under Philomelus and Onomarchus (cf. D.S. 16.61–4).

Plutarch's interest in the appearance of omens at critical points is likewise quite prominent in the Life. The ribbon of victory which falls accidentally on to Timoleon's head at Delphi has already been mentioned (8.3), but there are two further sections on the omens foretelling his successes in Sicily. The first of these is 8.1–2, where the dream of the priestesses of Demeter and Kore in Corinth that the goddess and her mother are going to sail with Timoleon to Sicily prompts the Corinthians to equip a sacred trireme, and to name it after the two goddesses. The second is at 8.5 to 9.1, where the heavens open at night during the course of the voyage, and pour out a large and brilliant flame; out of this a torch rises and darts down towards the part of Italy which the helmsmen are making for.

The other omens in the Life all foretell Timoleon's success in battle. The doors of the temple of Adranum fly open of their own accord at the start of the battle outside the city, while the spear of the god trembles and sweat runs down his face (12.9). Before the battle of the R. Crimisus we are told of the parsley incident (26.1–5), and of the omen of the two eagles (26.6). Finally at the R. Lamyrias, when Timoleon shakes out from his cloak a seal-ring with the device of a trophy, his officers hail it as an omen of victory (31.4–6).

Plutarch's broad poetical and artistic interests are apparent in

---

[1] A good instance of Plutarch's dislike of democracy; see also *Theseus* 25; *Camillus* 36; *Marius* 28. Yet he seems to like Timoleon's democracy; *Tim.* 22.3.

the Life, but they are for the most part unobtrusive. Sophocles is quoted twice (Pref. 3; 36.2, from Timaeus); Democritus (Pref. 4) and Simonides (37.1) are alluded to once each. Plutarch decides that no work of Nature (φύσις) or Art (τέχνη) in the age can be compared with Dionysius' remarkable μεταβολὴ τῆς τύχης (14.3), and he likens the ease of Timoleon's generalship compared with the labour of other commanders, to the ease of the work of Homer and Nicomachus compared with the forced nature of that of Antimachus and Dionysius (36.3). Finally his artistic bent comes out in the delightful simile where he declares that no business was complete, which Timoleon μὴ προσάψαιτο μηδὲ κατακοσμήσειεν, ὥσπερ ἔργῳ συντελουμένῳ δημιουργὸς ἐπιθείς τινα χάριν θεοφιλῆ καὶ πρέπουσαν (35.4).

Plutarch's comparison of Timoleon and Aemilius Paulus

It is not clear why Timoleon is paired with Aemilius. Ziegler argued that like Aristides and the elder Cato, and Pericles and Fabius Maximus, Timoleon and Aemilius have little in common. He saw their comparison as no more than the superficial work of a rhetorician.[1] This view has been strongly attacked by Erbse,[2] who maintained that Plutarch paired men on the basis of their moral behaviour rather than on the basis of similar political careers.[3]

It may indeed be the case that Timoleon and Aemilius are paired on the basis of their moral behaviour – both are presented as men of exemplary virtue[4] – but this does not account for the weakness of the Comparison. As in the Comparison of Aristides and the elder Cato, Plutarch opens with a statement which might be interpreted as an acknowledgement of the superficial nature of the pairing: τοιούτων δὲ τῶν κατὰ τὴν ἱστορίαν ὄντων, δῆλον ὡς οὐκ ἔχει πολλὰς διαφορὰς οὐδ᾽ ἀνομοιότητας ἡ σύγκρισις. His view that there are so few differences between the two men

[1] K. Ziegler, *Plutarchos von Chaironeia* (Stuttgart 1949), col. 262.

[2] H. Erbse, 'Die Bedeutung der Synkrisis in den Parallelbiographien Plutarchs', *Hermes* 84 (1956), 398–424.

[3] H. Erbse, 'Die Bedeutung der Synkrisis', p. 401 n. 3, for example, with the quotation from Plut. *Pericles* 2.5.

[4] See, for example, *Tim.* Pref. 5–6; 36; 37.4–6. *Aem.* 2.6; 3.6–7; 28.10; 39.6–10.

immediately robs the Comparison of half its point.[1] It would seem that Plutarch feels himself compelled by his plan of work to write a Comparison of this pair, but does not much relish the task because there is so little of value to say. Not only is the piece short, but it is eked out by general statements,[2] and by a digression about the behaviour of Greek leaders in Sicily (Comp. 2.2–6). The few points made about Timoleon and Aemilius further the impression that Plutarch himself was not fully convinced of the value of the Comparison. In *Cimon*, where he had plenty to say, Plutarch remarks that he may not indicate all the resemblances between a pair, but that it will not be difficult to spot them from the narrative (3.3). Yet the first two of the points made about Timoleon and Aemilius, that their opponents were famous, and that their victories were celebrated (Comp. 1.2), make a very trite opening to the Comparison, and suggest that Plutarch lacked suitable matter. His mild criticism of Timoleon's acceptance of a house and estate from the Syracusans is such a minor one that he may have introduced it merely to repeat his view that statesmen should never accept gifts nor seek wealth (Comp. 2.9).[3] All in all *Timoleon* is one of the Lives where the spirit of σύγκρισις reveals itself more profitably within the Life (for example, in the contrast drawn between the merits of Timoleon and the shortcomings of Timophanes and Hicetas) than in the formal Comparison at the end of the pair.[4]

Ziegler has proved satisfactorily in my opinion that Plutarch himself placed *Aemilius* before *Timoleon*.[5] There are, in Ziegler's view, two other pairs where the Roman is placed before the

---

[1] Cf. *Phocion* 3.8–9; *Comp. Lycurg. and Num.* 1.1; and the discussion in S. Costanza, 'La synkrisis nello schema biografico di Plutarco', *Messana* 4 (1955), 127–56.

[2] *Comp.* 1.5; 2.9; 2.10 from ἐπεὶ δ', ὡς σώματος to συμφοραὶ ταπεινοῦσι; 2.12.

[3] See especially *Comp. Aristid. and Cat.* 4; and also, for example, *Comp. Per. and Fab. Max.* 3.5–6; *Comp. Nic. and Crass.* 1.3; *Comp. Coriol. and Alcib.* 3.1; 5.2.

[4] See D. A. Russell, 'On reading Plutarch's *Lives*', *Greece and Rome* 13 (1966), 150–1.

[5] K. Ziegler, *Die Überlieferungsgeschichte der vergleichenden Lebensbeschreibungen Plutarchs* (Leipzig 1907), pp. 29–32. Ziegler's arrangement has not, however, been followed in the Budé edition.

Greek.[1] But it would seem that Plutarch's usual practice was to pick a Greek first and then to find a suitable Roman as a parallel.[2] And even on the occasions when he definitely chose the Roman before the Greek (see, for example, *Theseus* 1.4), in the final arrangement the Greek nevertheless precedes the Roman. There seems no reasonable explanation of why Plutarch should depart from his usual practice in the case of Timoleon and Aemilius, and should place the Roman before the Greek. Although this striking difference is highly conspicuous, it is not referred to by Plutarch himself. It might suggest that he decided to write the life of Aemilius first, and could then find no more exact parallel than the little-known figure of Timoleon. We cannot tell for certain; but it may be that Plutarch's determination to include Aemilius among his Lives and his subsequent failure to find a really convincing Greek parallel both contribute to the weakness of the Comparison of Aemilius and Timoleon.

---

[1] *Coriolanus and Alcibiades*; *Sertorius and Eumenes*. See K. Ziegler, *Die Überlieferungsgeschichte*, pp. 26–9.

[2] See *Publicola* 1.1; *Nicias* 1.1; K. Ziegler, *Plutarchos*, col. 260.

CHAPTER 2

The literary sources for Timoleon's career

The sources for: Plutarch, Timoleon; *Nepos,* Timoleon; *Diodorus Siculus, the Sicilian narrative in Book 16, 65–90*

In this piece on the sources of the accounts of Timoleon by Plutarch, Nepos and Diodorus, the section devoted to Plutarch and Nepos consists of nothing more than a summary of the views put forward by H. D. Westlake, together with a statement of the few points on which I would differ from those views. I make no apology for the fact that I agree with Westlake's main arguments; the forced striving for originality which some writers on this topic seem to have exhibited[1] strikes me as valueless and indeed harmful. My section on Diodorus' sources is preceded by a summary of the views of N. G. L. Hammond on the subject, since a knowledge of his views and his terminology is essential for the understanding of my own section.

It seems fairly well established that Timaeus was the most important of the sources from whom Plutarch took material for his *Timoleon*. Plutarch cites Timaeus twice (4.6; 36.2), and attributes the story of the parsley omen (26.1–5) to him on one occasion in the *Moralia* (676D). He also gives a most generous description of Andromachus, whom he mentions as the father of the historian Timaeus (10.7). The observations of Polybius, who tirades against Timaeus' inappropriately lavish praise of Timoleon, are sufficient to indicate that Timaeus must have covered Timoleon's career in some detail,[2] while Timaeus'

[1] For example, T. S. Brown, *Timaeus of Tauromenium* (California 1958), pp. 84–5.

[2] Polyb. 12.23.1–7; 25.7; 25K.1–2; 26A.1–4. For the relation of a comparatively unimportant detail of the period by Timaeus, see Athenaeus 11.471F. Not too much weight should be put on this fragment as evidence for the fact that Timaeus treated Timoleon's career at length. Since Tauromenium was Timaeus' birthplace, he may well have paid greater attention to its affairs than to those of other minor Sicilian cities.

For a discussion of the difficult problem of how many books Timaeus devoted to Timoleon's career, see F. W. Walbank, *A Historical Commentary on Polybius*, Vol. 2 (Oxford 1967), p. 384.

uncritically generous treatment of Timoleon was well known in antiquity.[1]

Westlake maintains that Plutarch also used some kind of Peripatetic biography of Timoleon.[2] The starting point of his argument is his contention that the *Timoleon* of Plutarch and the *Timoleon* of Nepos have far more in common than would be reasonably expected of a somewhat lengthy, detailed and personal biography, and a very cursory biographical summary (p. 65). He shows that there are no events recorded by Nepos which are included by Diodorus and omitted by Plutarch, and that there are several events which are recorded both by Nepos and Plutarch, but not by Diodorus (for example, the crushing of Mamercus at Nepos 2.4) (p. 68). There are, however, points recorded by Nepos alone (for example, that Timoleon won all his victories on his birthday, 5.1), and there are details on which Nepos differs from Plutarch (for example, that Timoleon could have shared in the *regnum* of Timophanes, 1.3), but Westlake considers it possible to regard all these differences as inaccuracies on the part of Nepos. They are either inferences made by him or misunderstandings of his source (pp. 66–7 and 73).[3]

Westlake then argues that it would be easy to attribute both the *Timoleon* of Plutarch and the *Timoleon* of Nepos to one source, Timaeus (p. 67). But he considers that this is a doubtful attribution because it is unlikely that in almost every case the incidents chosen for record by Nepos were chosen by Plutarch also, in view of the length and detail of Timaeus' treatment of Timoleon and his work (p. 67 with notes 2 and 3, and p. 68).

Therefore Westlake argues that there existed, in addition to Timaeus' detailed account, a Peripatetic biography of Timoleon based on Timaeus. He considers that Nepos, who would have

---

[1] Cicero, *Ad Fam.* 5.12.7; Marcellinus, *Vit. Thuc.* 27; Suidas, *s.v.* 'Τίμαιος ὁ ἱστορικός'.

[2] H. D. Westlake, 'The sources of Plutarch's Timoleon', *CQ* 32 (1938), 65–74.

[3] Brown (*Timaeus of Tauromenium*, p. 84 and n. 39) is right in saying that Westlake's argument can neither be demonstrated nor refuted; and he is right, too, in concluding that an element of speculation is introduced by the fact that there are some slight differences between Nepos and Plutarch. But in my view these observations do not invalidate Westlake's contention that these differences are all due to Nepos himself.

found the account of Timaeus inconveniently long for the brief summary he intended to write, consulted only the Peripatetic biographer, whereas Plutarch consulted both the Peripatetic biographer and Timaeus, whose treatment of some of the greatest events in Timoleon's career will have been more detailed (p. 68).[1]

The type of Peripatetic biography which Westlake envisages was certainly written in Hellenistic times. Timoleon would have been a fairly attractive subject because of the ethical difficulties raised by the murder of a brother, the swift and unexpected success of an elderly man, and the number of amazing personal incidents (pp. 69–70). It is not surprising that Nepos and Plutarch should have used the same Peripatetic biography since the sources available to authors for consultation must have been few, not least because rather limited interest was usually shown in Timoleon by the ancient world (p. 69).

Lastly Westlake attempts, with due caution, to discern the use of a Peripatetic biographer in particular passages of Plutarch: he singles out 30.4 to 39 as a fair possibility. Timoleon's military activities after his spectacular victory over the Carthaginians are compressed into a very short space (whereas Timaeus will have presumably narrated the downfall of the tyrants in greater detail), while the account of Timoleon's old age is woven into a long, general eulogy of his character and work (whereas Timaeus is more likely to have presented the narrative of Timoleon's last years and then to have written a summing-up). Plutarch's quotation of a remark of Timaeus at 36.2 and his quotation of the honorary decree at 39.5 might both possibly have been taken from the Peripetetic biographer, who himself took them from Timaeus (pp. 71–2). In contrast Westlake suggests the description of the battle of the R. Crimisus and the events leading up to it as a passage where Plutarch may have used Timaeus rather than the Peripatetic biographer. The latter would probably have been less interested in military events than Timaeus. Even so, the narrative of the battle is still rather confused (p. 72).

[1] In a similar way L. Voit seeks to show that the Lives of Dion by Plutarch and Nepos are both based on the same Hellenistic biography ('Zur Dion-Vita', *Historia* 3 (1954/5), 171–92).

Westlake regards chapter 6, Plutarch's reflection on the behaviour of Timoleon after the murder of Timophanes, and chapters 14 and 15, on Dionysius II at Corinth, as Plutarch's own compilations (p. 73). In addition to chapters 6, 14 and 15, the Preface and the summary of affairs in Sicily before Timoleon's arrival (chaps. 1 and 2) are presumably Plutarch's original work.

In my view Westlake stresses Plutarch's knowledge of Peripatetic literature too much, and presents a rather weak case for the existence of a specifically Peripatetic biography of Timoleon. We have no evidence at all on the character of this biography. What is striking and indisputable is the close correspondence between the lengthy treatment of Plutarch and the brief summary of Nepos: the unexpected similarity of these two accounts is indeed excellent evidence for the supposition that some kind of short biography of Timoleon was written between the time of Timaeus and the time of Nepos. But nothing more may usefully be said about this biography, with the result that I refer to it by the vague term 'Hellenistic'.

Westlake's attempt to suggest specific passages where Plutarch may have used a particular source is an unprofitable exercise.[1] In general, however, it is possible that a Hellenistic biography of Timoleon based on the account of Timaeus was Nepos' only source, whereas Plutarch will have used this Hellenistic biography, Timaeus, and perhaps other sources. He cites Ephorus and Theopompus once each at 4.6 (the only composite citation in this Life), and Athanis twice (23.6; 37.9).[2] He may have read

[1] Westlake continues this dangerous attempt in 'The purpose of Timoleon's mission', *AJP* 70 (1949), 65–75. But it seems unduly rash to suggest, as he does here, that the genitive absolute in Plut. *Tim.* 2.1 'probably summarises a substantial excursus (ἐν τούτῳ) by Timaeus on Carthaginian plans to take advantage of Siceliot dissensions, ending with an account of the landing by Carthaginian forces in Sicily and the repressive measures undertaken by them in their own province, of which some details are preserved by Diodorus' (p. 69).

[2] The few surviving fragments of Athanis (or Athanas) of Syracuse are reproduced and discussed by F. Jacoby, *Die Fragmente der Griechischen Historiker*, Vol. IIIB (Nos. 297–607) (Leiden 1950), No. 562. Athanis may have been a προστάτης τοῦ δήμου whom Theopompus mentions for 357/6 or 356/5 with Heracleides (Steph. Byz. *s.v.* 'Δύμη'); the thirteen books of his work appear to have reached Timoleon's retirement and to have covered contemporary history in considerable detail (cf. D.S. 15.94.4;

these authors himself, or he may have copied the citations from a source: we do not possess evidence with which to decide this question.[1] Yet it would be rash to assert that he used nothing but the Hellenistic biographer and Timaeus. Plutarch's broad knowledge of historical works, his consuming interest in the past, and his powers of memory should not be underestimated.[2] Lastly we should bear in mind that we can seldom tell how closely Plutarch has followed his sources: it is possible that he altered his source material to suit his own purpose and interest at any particular point.[3] The frequent contrast drawn between the τύχη and ἀρετή of Timoleon, for example, may well be Plutarch's own work.[4]

The most important article on the sources of Diodorus' narrative of the career of Timoleon is by N. G. L. Hammond.[5] Hammond regards it as possible to divide the Timoleontic part of Diodorus' narrative into two sections:

Group 2 = 16.65 to 70, which gives a consecutive narrative for 346/5 to 343/2, beginning with the introduction of Timoleon and ending with the final expulsion of Dionysius II and the restoration of constitutional government at Syracuse by Timoleon.

Group 3 =   (i) 16.72.2 to 73 (under 342/1),
            (ii) 77.4 to 83 (under 340/39 and 339/8),
            (iii) 90.1 (under 337/6).

(Group 1 is not concerned with Timoleon's career.)

Athenaeus 3.98D). Our ignorance of Athanis and his work should be acknowledged frankly. There is no merit in attempts made on flimsy evidence to spot random passages for which he might have been the source.

[1] Cf. *CQ* 32 (1938), 72–3.

[2] His citation of a remark of Timaeus about Gylippus at Comp. 2.4 is presumably from memory.

[3] See P. A. Stadter, *Plutarch's Historical Methods: An Analysis of the 'Mulierum Virtutes'* (Harvard 1965), pp. 137–40.

[4] A suggested identity for Westlake's Peripatetic biographer is discussed in Note A, p. 195.

[5] 'The sources of Diodorus Siculus XVI. II: The Sicilian Narrative', *CQ* 32 (1938), 137–51. Cf. K. Meister, *Die sizilische Geschichte bei Diodor von den Anfängen bis zum Tod des Agathokles: Quellenuntersuchungen zu Buch iv–xxi* (Munich 1967), who lists clearly the different views which have been put forward on the sources of Diodorus' Sicilian narrative in Book 16, 65–90 (pp. 121–2). He takes the view that Diodorus used an unknown author, who had drawn together the account of Timaeus and that of another unknown historian (p. 129).

Hammond considers that Diodorus intends (i) and (ii) of Group 3 to be read as consecutive narrative, even though a year separates them. (iii) is also separated from (ii) by a year, and contains no link with it. He assumes that all Group 2 and all Group 3 are each from a single source, and that Diodorus has not changed sources within a Group.

Briefly, Hammond argues from the character of Diodorus' narrative in Group 2 and from the notice about the end of Theopompus' Sicilian Excursus at 71.3 that Theopompus is very likely to have been the main source for this Group (pp. 142–4). He suggests that Diodorus must have stopped using Theopompus after Group 2 for two reasons: first, Diodorus gives two summaries of Timoleon's legislation, one in each Group, copying the details from two different sources (pp. 140–1 and note 1); second, Theopompus' Sicilian Excursus ended with the expulsion of Dionysius II by Timoleon (pp. 142–3). From the similarity between Diodorus Group 3 and the corresponding section of Plutarch (22.4 to the end) Hammond argues that both authors used Timaeus as their common source for this Group (pp. 147–8).[1] In his view the identification of the source as Timaeus is supported by Diodorus' eulogy of Timoleon, a feature definitely present in Timaeus' work (pp. 139 and 144).

I wish to begin my own discussion of Diodorus' sources by examining Hammond's view that Timaeus was the source for Group 3.

In the first place, close examination of Group 3 reveals little sign of the eulogy mentioned above. Rather the attitude of the source of Group 3 is the same as that of the source of Group 2: Timoleon is praised 'highly, though not extravagantly', to use Westlake's words.[2] Diodorus presents Timoleon in a far more restrained manner than Plutarch. Timoleon is a man rather than an instrument of the gods. There are no hints of divine aid in Group 3 except for a single reference to the divine help of the weather at the battle of the R. Crimisus (79.5), and this refers to

---

[1] Westlake agrees with Hammond that Timaeus was the common source for Group 3, although he adds the caution that Timaeus was interpreted differently by the two authors. H. D. Westlake, 'The Sicilian books of Theopompus' *Philippica*', *Historia* 2 (1953/4), 301–2.

[2] *Historia* 2 (1953/4), 299.

the Greek army in general, rather than to Timoleon personally. In any event it is quite appropriate that divine aid should be mentioned at this point, since Diodorus has just remarked how after the parsley omen the soldiers προῆγον μετὰ χαρᾶς ὡς τῶν θεῶν προσημαινόντων αὐτοῖς τὴν νίκην (79.4). In Group 3 there is no other mention at all of divine aid or protection given to Timoleon. This would be fantastic if Diodorus was all the time copying from Timaeus, the historian who, according to the bitter Polybius, μείζω ποιεῖ Τιμολέοντα τῶν ἐπιφανεστάτων θεῶν (12.23.4).[1] The only other mention of divine intervention in Diodorus' account is the omens at sea in Group 2 (66.3–5). These are regarded as a sign not just to Timoleon himself, but to ὁ Τιμολέων καὶ οἱ συμπλέοντες, while they are just omens, not a case of divine aid (as Plutarch would interpret Timoleon's deliverance from assassination at chapter 16, for example).

That Timoleon is a man to Diodorus, not an instrument of the gods, is also brought out by the narration of incidents discreditable to Timoleon, without any attempt at disguise. Plutarch tends to omit information that does not reflect well on Timoleon, while such unfortunate incidents as are included are well camouflaged: the best example of this camouflage is the elaborate excuse put forward for the defeat of Timoleon's mercenaries under Euthymus, which is so twisted as to reveal Timoleon's good fortune (30.6–10). Diodorus, on the other hand, mentions the failure of Timoleon's attack on Leontini (72.2), and observes that Leptines had to be assailed with προσβολὰς συνεχεῖς (72.3) before he was frightened into submission (72.5). We are informed of the summary execution of fifteen Punic supporters at Entella by Timoleon (73.2), and of the execution of the Etruscan pirate Postumius in suspicious circumstances (82.3). Diodorus

---

[1] The extent to which the idea of Timoleon as the agent of the gods was already present in Plutarch's sources, and the extent to which Plutarch himself developed the idea, is unclear. Certainly there is no extant fragment of Timaeus in which Timoleon is explicitly portrayed as the agent of the gods, but the quotation at Plut. 36.2 and the general tone of that chapter would support the notion that the idea of Timoleon as the agent of the gods was present in Timaeus (see also Westlake, *Tyrants*, pp. 5–7). The passage at Polybius 12.24.5, where the work of Timaeus is accused of being ἐνυπνίων καὶ τεράτων καὶ μύθων ἀπιθάνων καὶ συλλήβδην δεισιδαιμονίας ἀγεννοῦς καὶ τερατείας γυναικώδους ἐστὶ πλήρης, would also support the idea.

reveals that Timoleon was still at war with Hicetas at the time of the threatened Punic invasion, but that he made peace with him and took over his troops, thereby considerably enlarging his forces (77.5); then in the next reference to Hicetas, after the victory of the R. Crimisus, Diodorus merely says that Timoleon defeated Hicetas and put him to death (82.4) – a sequence of events which might suggest that it was Timoleon who broke his treaty with Hicetas when the Punic threat was removed.

Moreover Diodorus makes no attempt to disguise Timoleon's difficulties when faced with the desertion of Thrasius and other mercenaries. He portrays the ταραχὴ καὶ στάσις (78.3) in a realistic manner, stressing Timoleon's desperate efforts to prevent large-scale desertion: τῶν δὲ μισθοφόρων ἀσμένως τοὺς λόγους (of Thrasius) δεχομένων καὶ νεωτερίζειν ἐπιχειρούντων μόγις πολλὰ δεηθεὶς αὐτῶν ὁ Τιμολέων καὶ δωρεὰς ἐπαγγελλόμενος κατέπαυσε τὴν ταραχήν (79.1). Plutarch, on the other hand, makes no attempt to bring out the panic and despair that Timoleon must have felt, however briefly, when faced both with the desertion of a sizeable part of his army and with a blow to the morale of the remainder; instead he merely reports the complaints of the mercenaries (25.5), and continues with nothing but: τούτους μὲν οὖν Τιμολέων κέρδος ἡγεῖτο πρὸ τῆς μάχης φανεροὺς γεγονότας (25.6). Further, Diodorus has Thrasius and his followers desert because they had not been paid (78.5–6), thereby implying that Timoleon was at fault; whereas Plutarch makes no mention of pay, but has the mercenaries desert because of their own cowardice: καθ' ὁδὸν ἀποδειλιάσαντες ἀνεχώρησαν (25.5).

Hammond (pp. 147–8) sees no differences of detail between Diodorus Group 3 and Plutarch 22.4 to the end serious enough to shake his idea that Timaeus was the common source for both narratives. But there are many differences which could not have arisen if both authors were following the same main source. For example, Plutarch places the arrival of the Corinthian legislator Cephalus between the capture of all Syracuse and the battle of the R. Crimisus (24.3), whereas Diodorus places his arrival after the battle of the R. Crimisus (82.7). Then Diodorus maintains that Thrasius was one of those who had plundered

Delphi with the Phocians (78.3–4), and that he and his fellow deserters were killed later by the Bruttians for their παρανομία (82.2). Plutarch mentions neither Thrasius nor the plundering of Delphi in this context (25.5–6; 30.2–3). Diodorus, on the other hand, does not mention the defeat of Euthymus at Hierae (Plut. 30.6–10).

A clear difference between the two historians occurs in the number given by each as the total of colonists who came to Sicily: Diodorus mentions a figure of 50,000 (82.5), whereas Plutarch reproduces the figure of 60,000, taken from Athanis (23.6).[1] When they come to the battle of the R. Crimisus, they agree substantially on the numbers of the Punic invading force, but they then disagree completely on the number of Timoleon's forces, Plutarch giving a total of 6,000 (25.5), Diodorus one of 12,000 (78.2). There is a difference, too, in the setting of events just before the battle: after his narrative of the mutiny Diodorus (79.2) remarks that the enemy are οὐ μακρὰν στρατοπεδεύοντας, whereas in Plutarch Timoleon encourages his men, and then κατὰ τάχος ἦγε πρὸς τὸν Κρίμισον ποταμόν, ὅπου καὶ τοὺς Καρχηδονίους ἤκουσε συνάπτειν (25.6), so that he marches to the R. Crimisus solely on the strength of a report. Diodorus mentions divine aid given to the Greeks in the form of a storm (79.5), yet all mention of divine aid is strangely and conspicuously absent from Plutarch's account of the battle, except in one reference to divine magnification of Timoleon's voice (27.9). Finally Diodorus represents Timoleon's peace with Carthage as a direct consequence of the victory at the R. Crimisus (81.4; 82.3), whereas Plutarch places a long series of events between the battle and the conclusion of peace (30–34.2).

When viewed together the difference in the treatment of tyrants by Diodorus and Plutarch is so great that it becomes hard to see how each could have selected incidents from a common source. Hicetas is mentioned by Diodorus at 72.2 (Timoleon's failure at Leontini), 72.4 (Hicetas' attack on Syracuse and his defeat by Timoleon), 77.5 (Timoleon's treaty with Hicetas before the battle of the R. Crimisus), and 82.4 (defeat and execution of Hicetas *after* Timoleon's peace with the Carthaginians);

[1] Hammond (*CQ* 32 (1938), 147) seems to regard these figures as the same.

whereas Plutarch mentions him in the difficult passage at 24.1 (Timoleon's apparent defeat of Hicetas), and at length in 30.4 (Hicetas' alliance with Mamercus and the Carthaginians) and 31.2 to 33.4 (Hicetas' defeat at the R. Lamyrias and his execution *before* Timoleon's peace with the Carthaginians). Both Plutarch and Diodorus refer to the expulsion of Leptines and the liberation of Apollonia (Plut. 24.2; D.S. 72.3 and 5; Diodorus does not mention Engyum), but Plutarch does not refer either to the Campanians on Etna, Nicodemus and Apolloniades (all at D.S. 82.4), or to Entella (D.S. 73.2; a city which Timoleon freed from the Carthaginians in fact, not from a tyrant). Lastly, in Group 3 Diodorus does not mention Mamercus, who is dealt with at some length by Plutarch (30.4; 31.1; 34; 37.9), nor does he ever mention Hippon at all (dealt with by Plutarch at 34.3–4; 37.9).

Any arguments based on differences of style are dangerous, as has been shown by Palm,[1] but there is one distinctive difference in the terminology employed by Diodorus and Plutarch, which deserves notice, even if it is not to be pressed too far. This is that Plutarch uses the term Κορίνθιοι rather indiscriminately, whereas it would appear that in Book 16, 65–90, Diodorus takes care to use the term solely in connection with actual citizens of Corinth (for example, at 66.1; 69.4; 82.3; 90.1). Otherwise he speaks, for instance, of Τιμολέων (66.3; 68.5 etc.), οἱ περὶ τὸν Τιμολέοντα (66.4; 68.6; 69.3; 80.1), ξένοι στρατιῶται (73.1) and μισθοφόροι (73.1; 78.2). For the battle of the R. Crimisus he speaks of Ἕλληνες (79.6; 80.1 and 5).

However, in Plutarch Κορίνθιοι is a looser term. It can include the Leucadians and Corcyreans who joined Timoleon's forces (8.4). Then at 17.4, 20.9 and 21.5, for example, it also includes the mercenaries whom Timoleon took over from Dionysius II (13.7). In the description of the battle of the R. Crimisus Κορίνθιοι is used to describe the whole of Timoleon's army, despite the high proportion of Syracusan and Sicilian allies in his forces (for example, 25.3; 27.3). Plutarch also uses Ἕλληνες, which seems to be interchangeable with Κορίνθιοι here (28.3; 28.6; 29.1). He certainly distinguishes between Κορίνθιος and

[1] J. Palm, *Über Sprache und Stil des Diodoros von Sizilien* (Lund 1955).

Συρακούσιος when recording something of an official nature (for example, 22.7; 23.2; 38.4; 39.5), but he rarely exhibits the care shown by Diodorus even over the minor matter of the distribution of the Punic booty:

τούτων δ' ὕστερον τὰ μὲν ἐν τοῖς ἐν Συρακούσσαις ναοῖς ἀνετέθη, τὰ δὲ τοῖς συμμάχοις διεμερίσθη, τινὰ δ' εἰς Κόρινθον Τιμολέων ἀπέστειλε προστάξας εἰς τὸ τοῦ Ποσειδῶνος ἱερὸν ἀναθεῖναι (80.6).

The care and consistency of Diodorus are interesting: the difference between his usage and that of Plutarch does not prove anything, but it might possibly be a result of the fact that each used a separate source.[1]

Naturally the accounts of Diodorus and Plutarch are similar at many points, but this is hardly surprising when both are meant to be narrating the same events! That is a trite point, but one which needs emphasis, as in my view it does not follow (as Hammond seems to imply on occasion) that if accounts are almost the same they are necessarily taken from the same source.[2]

Naturally there are bound to be differences between the accounts of Diodorus and Plutarch also, simply because Diodorus is concerned with a general historical picture (he even looks at matters from a Punic viewpoint at 81.2–4, for example), whereas Plutarch is concerned with Timoleon and with him alone. But this difference of emphasis, involving a different selection of material from more detailed sources, will not of itself account for all the differences between Diodorus and Plutarch in Group 3. Therefore I would put forward the conclusion that if Timaeus

[1] See Westlake, *Tyrants*, p. 33 n. 3, and D. Musti, 'Ancora sull' "Iscrizione di Timoleonte"', *La Parola del Passato* 87 (1962), 455.

[2] See Hammond (*CQ* 32 (1938), 147) on the omen of the parsley, the effects of the storm, and the record of the spoil; and *ibid.* p. 146, on the dream of the priestesses of the Maid, the naming of the trireme, the omen of the torch and its interpretation. In the latter instance it seems doubtful whether the accounts of Plutarch and Diodorus are sufficiently similar for them to be derived from one source, as Hammond maintains. For in Plutarch (8.2) a sacred trireme is equipped and named after Demeter and Kore before Timoleon leaves Corinth, whereas in Diodorus (66.5) it is Timoleon's best ship which is dedicated to Demeter and Kore during the voyage across the Ionian Gulf.

was Plutarch's main source for the events of Group 3, then Diodorus' source for Group 3 was not Timaeus.[1]

There is perhaps some value in seeking to identify the source which Diodorus did use for Group 3, although any conclusions must be very tentative. When I first investigated the problem I came to the view that Theopompus was the most likely source: Diodorus had followed him in Group 2, and simply continued to do so in Group 3 also. For reasons set out below I now question this opinion, but I think that it would still be useful to rehearse the arguments which once led me to favour Theopompus.

As mentioned above (p. 27), Hammond puts forward two arguments in support of his contention that Diodorus must have stopped using Theopompus after Group 2: first, that Diodorus gives two summaries of Timoleon's legislation, one in each Group, copying the details from two different sources (pp. 140–1 and note 1); second, that Theopompus' Sicilian Excursus ended with the expulsion of Dionysius II by Timoleon (pp. 142–3).

However, in my opinion Diodorus is correct in stating that Timoleon legislated twice, and that each occasion is quite different (70.5 under 343/2, and 82.6 under 339/8). The two reports seem by no means similar, and indeed I have argued below that each tallies well with what may have been the situation in Syracuse immediately after the expulsion of Dionysius II, and in the period after the battle of the R. Crimisus.[2] My view cannot be proved, but at least there seems to be no *need* to think that the two passages must imply a change of source. Then there seems to be no certainty that Theopompus ceased to deal with Sicilian affairs after he had finished his Excursus: the notice at 71.3 could mean just that he devoted no more separate books to Sicilian affairs.[3]

If Hammond's Groups 2 and 3 are based on Theopompus, are they consistent and similar in tone? I would suggest – against Hammond p. 139 – that they are indeed consistent and similar in tone. Throughout Timoleon is portrayed as a real man, not

[1] Further comments made by Hammond about the character of Diodorus' source for Group 3 are discussed in Note B, p. 196.

[2] See pp. 131–3.

[3] This point is suggested by C. B. Welles, *Diodorus Siculus*, Vol. VIII (Loeb, London 1963), p. 4.

as an instrument of the gods, and he is praised 'highly, though not extravagantly', as I have tried to show above. Hammond is wrong to suggest (p. 138) that Timoleon is eulogized throughout Group 2: Diodorus states plainly that he killed his own brother (65.4), and mentions the despair of his men (69.3). While Plutarch has Timoleon capture Ortygia and send Dionysius to Corinth within fifty days of his arrival in Sicily (16.2), Diodorus has a far longer period elapse between Timoleon's arrival in Syracuse (68.11, under 345/4) and the departure of Dionysius (70.1, under 343/2) – a version less favourable to Timoleon. The summaries of Timoleon's achievement at 65.9 and 90.1 are both more restrained than some passages in Plutarch (for example, 16.12; 36). Diodorus' use of terminology remains consistent, although this could be the result of his own care rather than of his use of a single source. His selection of incidents remains similar in Groups 2 and 3 in that Mamercus or Marcus, with whom Plutarch deals at some length, is mentioned only once in Group 2 (69.4), and never in Group 3, whilst Hippon is never mentioned in either Group, although there is a single reference to Messana in Group 2 (69.6). Further, Plutarch refers to seven of Timoleon's lieutenants on six separate occasions, but Diodorus never mentions any lieutenant in either Group.[1] Then Entella is mentioned in Group 2 (67.3) and in Group 3 (73.2) of Diodorus, but is never referred to by Plutarch. The same is true of the Campanians on Etna (Group 2, 67.4; Group 3, 82.4). Plutarch twice gives the name of Timoleon's father as Timodemus (3.2; 39.5), but Diodorus is also consistent in calling him Timaenetus, both at the start of Group 2 (65.2) and at the end of Group 3 (90.1). Hicetas is mentioned without comment or censure in Group 3 as well as in Group 2 (see Hammond p. 138). And as Hammond says (for Group 2, p. 138; Group 3, p. 139), there is abundant detail in both Groups. If Diodorus did use different sources for Groups 2 and 3, then he preserved a remarkable uniformity in his characterization of Timoleon and Hicetas, and in his selection of material. But it would seem that there are no differences of internal structure between the two Groups which

[1] For Timoleon's lieutenants, see p. 12 above. In fact Diodorus does refer to Demaretus once, but at 17.76.6.

would make it impossible for both to be drawn from the same source. Indeed certain similarities appear positively to support the contention that both were drawn from the same source. Thus the distinction between Group 2 and Group 3 seems arbitrary and misleading.

The view that Theopompus was Diodorus' source for Group 3 now strikes me as seriously open to doubt. No relevant fragment has survived, but that may not be very significant. More important is the belief that Theopompus would not have included a detailed narrative of Timoleon's career in the *Philippica* as a matter of course. The work was devoted to Philip of Macedon, as the title indicates, and it does not seem to have comprised sections of detailed Greek and Sicilian narratives side by side. There might have been a few paragraphs about Sicilian affairs from time to time, but hardly the lengthy narrative from which Diodorus' Group 3 must have been derived. The only point where Theopompus is known to have treated Sicilian affairs at length is the excursus which ended with the final expulsion of Dionysius II from Syracuse. As Westlake has stressed,[1] this choice of ending must imply that Theopompus wished to focus attention on Dionysius II: had he wished to describe Timoleon's achievements in detail, he would not have broken off his excursus before the most brilliant part of Timoleon's career.

Thus Theopompus seems unlikely to have been the source of Diodorus' Group 3. On the other hand I still believe that Diodorus used the same main source for Groups 2 and 3. If both these propositions are valid, then Theopompus cannot have been the main source for Group 2. Such a conclusion would undermine the carefully determined opinion of Hammond (pp. 142–4) and Westlake[2] that Theopompus was the source for Group 2; but there does seem to be some value in re-examining the point.

As mentioned earlier (p. 27), Hammond argues from the character of Diodorus' narrative in Group 2 and from the notice about the end of Theopompus' Sicilian Excursus at 71.3 that Theopompus is very likely to have been the main source for Group 2.

[1] *Historia* 2 (1953/4), 299; cf. 294.
[2] *Historia* 2 (1953/4), 301–2.

These are certainly valid arguments, but they need not show that Theopompus was Diodorus' *main* source in this Group; they merely show that Diodorus is likely to have been acquainted with Theopompus' narrative of these events. For example, he could have been following Theopompus when he moralizes about Dionysius' fall from power.[1] It remains unlikely that Theopompus will have been the main source for all Group 2. For if his Sicilian Excursus was devoted mainly to the Dionysii, and came to an end with the fall of Dionysius II, it seems strange that it should have devoted so much space to Timoleon's murder of his brother (65), his voyage to Sicily (66), and his early activities in the island (68.4–11), not to mention Carthaginian manoeuvres (67). None of these events concerned Dionysius closely, while such detailed narrative would only be expected from an author concerned with the whole of Timoleon's career in Sicily, not from one who was mainly interested in the tyrant, and who would say nothing further about Timoleon after the capture of all Syracuse. Finally, if Diodorus was following Theopompus' Sicilian Excursus with care, it is amazing that he should have omitted to mention the activities of Dionysius II between 355/4 and 347/6.

One small point leads me to suggest with the utmost caution that it was not Theopompus whom Diodorus followed when he described the murder of Timophanes. Plutarch's mention of the fact that Theopompus disagreed with Ephorus and Timaeus over the name of the seer who accompanied Timoleon (4.6) could suggest that these three historians wrote closely parallel accounts of the murder, differing from each other only in small details: Plutarch or his source could conveniently place the three accounts side by side, and spot the disagreement over the seer's name. In Diodorus, however, followers play no part, since Timoleon is himself the murderer, and it therefore becomes hard to see where any comment about a follower's name would fit into the account. If there were greater differences between the accounts of Theopompus and Ephorus/Timaeus than the name of a seer – major differences, for instance, over when the murder took place, or

[1] D.S. 70.1–3; cf. Polybius 12.4A.2 and Westlake, *Historia* 2 (1953/4), 303 n. 5.

who struck Timophanes – it is extraordinary that Plutarch should have reserved his only composite citation of sources in this Life for a minor quibble about a name. While I recognize that Plutarch often makes citations haphazardly, this particular citation of sources still leads me to suspect that Theopompus, Ephorus and Timaeus will all have written fairly similar accounts of the murder. Diodorus' description was derived from a completely different tradition.[1]

To sum up, I would suggest with due caution that for his whole narrative of Timoleon's career Diodorus used an unknown historian as his main source, and that he also referred to Theopompus' Sicilian Excursus for the fall of Dionysius II. As my next section tries to show, not enough is known about the various accounts of Timoleon's career to identify the unknown historian. Certainly he had a close knowledge of Timoleon's career in Sicily; Athanis, mentioned once by Diodorus (15.94.4), is therefore a possibility, but it should be remembered that he and Diodorus are known to disagree on numbers of colonists (cf. Plut. 23.6; D.S. 82.5), while Diodorus never mentions Timoleon's blindness, a point definitely covered by Athanis (cf. Plut. 37.9–10). Whether these two differences necessarily make it impossible for Diodorus to have followed Athanis is a matter for speculation. But my hypothesis that Diodorus based his Timoleontic narrative on a detailed and reasonable account by an unknown historian could at least help to show that on occasion he may have been more discriminating in his choice of a main source than has sometimes been thought.

I have argued throughout as if I agreed substantially with Hammond's view that Diodorus' method of composition seems to have been to choose the historian whom he considered to be the best standard author of convenient length, and to derive his narrative from that one source.[2] Yet in his bibliographical notices Diodorus does mention the work of Ephorus and Diyllus (16.14.3–5; 76.5–6), and it is possible both that he read their

---

[1] For this point cf. N. E. Cappellano, *Sulla venuta di Timoleonte in Sicilia* (Catania 1903), pp. 16–17.

[2] *CQ* 32 (1938), 149; cf. N. G. L. Hammond, 'The sources of Diodorus Siculus XVI. I: The Macedonian, Greek and Persian Narrative', *CQ* 31 (1937), 79–81.

sections on Sicily, however cursorily, and that he perhaps
incorporated some points in his narrative which he recalled
from their work. He specifically mentions the fact that Diyllus
dealt with Sicily (16.14.5). It is possible, too, that the narrative
of the Thrasius episode came from Demophilus, as Hammond
suggests cautiously (p. 147 and references there). We cannot
tell. All the same it may be dangerous to ascribe all the points of
Diodorus' narrative in a section to just one source.[1]

It has been shown convincingly by Brown that the idea that
Diodorus drew most of his information for Book 11 from a
single, main source is untenable,[2] and this point should be
remembered in any examination of the Sicilian narrative in
Book 16, 65–90. Brown rightly says, with reference to Book 11,
that 'the Diodorus question cannot safely be reduced to a for-
mula' (p. 341). Certainly it would be amazing if Diodorus did
not at least read Timaeus' account of Timoleon's career. Diodorus
definitely used Timaeus at other stages of his work, and he must
surely have heard of what the ancient world acknowledged to
be the most famous account of Timoleon (see, for example,
Cic. *Ad Fam.* 5.12.7). Finally Diodorus' Sicilian background
and his special interest in the affairs of the island would suggest
that a Sicilian section of his work is more likely than any other
to embody the results of wide reading and even personal observa-
tion (for the latter, cf. perhaps 83.2; and 82.5 and 83.3 on
Agyrium).[3]

[1] This is argued by R. K. Sinclair, 'Diodorus Siculus and the writing of
history', *Proceedings of the African Classical Associations* 6 (1963), 40.

[2] T. S. Brown, 'Timaeus and Diodorus' Eleventh Book', *AJP* 73 (1952),
337–55.

[3] Sordi convincingly shows the inadequacy of one of Hammond's reasons
for dividing Diodorus' Timoleontic narrative into two distinct parts, each
based on a separate source (Sordi, pp. 47–8 and 102–4). But her own view
that both Plutarch's *Timoleon* and Diodorus' Sicilian narrative in 16.65–90
are based on Timaeus (*Diodori Liber XVI*, pp. xli–xlii) remains unattractive
while the many important differences between the two accounts go unexplained. Of the passages which in her view show the use of a common
source with particular clarity, two hardly seem to serve their purpose
(*Diodori Liber XVI*, p. 112, the murder of Timophanes; pp. xlii–xliv and
119–25, the fall of Dionysius II).

Timoleon's fame

If the Lives of Timoleon by Plutarch and Nepos are laid aside, together with Diodorus' Sicilian narrative at 16.65–90, the remaining ancient literature on Timoleon is tiny. Timaeus, Theopompus, Ephorus and Athanis certainly all dealt with Timoleon's career, in whole or in part, but their treatments are lost, except for a few fragments. It seems that Arrian wrote ὅσα Τιμολέοντι τῷ Κορινθίῳ κατὰ Σικελίαν ἐπράχθη, but nothing of this work has survived, and its existence is only known from a passing reference by Photius.[1] Duris, Demophilus and Diyllus may have covered at least part of Timoleon's career, but nothing is known of their treatments.[2] Then there was probably some Hellenistic biography of Timoleon, which Nepos and Plutarch used as a source, but the identity of the writer is unknown, while no fragments of the work have survived.[3] Finally, Plutarch or one of his sources (36.5) seems to have discovered a letter written by Timoleon, which is now lost. We do not know whether there was more such material available, or what use the ancient writers made of it.

Of surviving authors Polyaenus describes three stratagems of Timoleon[4] and mentions the Timoleonteium twice,[5] while

[1] *Bibl.* 93, p. 73.a.35.

[2] The works of Duris of Samos (F. Jacoby, *Die Fragmente der Griechischen Historiker*, Vol. II A, No. 76) were known to Diodorus (15.60.6 and 21.6.1–2), but there is no evidence to suggest that he covered Timoleon's career in detail, and thus he is hardly likely to be a main source for Diodorus' Sicilian narrative in 16.65–90, although Welles mentions this as a possibility (*Diodorus Siculus*, p. 473).

For Demophilus and Diyllus, see pp. 37–8 above.

[3] See pp. 23–5 above. There seems to be wholly insufficient evidence for the views put forward by Lauritano, first that Silenus covered Timoleon's career, and then that Silenus' narrative was used by Diodorus (R. Lauritano, 'Sileno in Diodoro?', *Kokalos* 2 (1956), 206–16). Yet these conjectures are supported by E. Manni, 'Da Ippi a Diodoro', *Kokalos* 3 (1957), 152, and E. Manni, 'Sileno in Diodoro?', *Atti Accad. Palermo* 18 (1957/8), 83. For a sensible discussion of the 'Silenus hypothesis', see F. W. Walbank, 'The historians of Greek Sicily', *Kokalos* 14–15 (1968/9), 488–97.

[4] *Strat.* 5.12.1, parsley omen; 5.12.2, execution of Mamercus; 5.12.3, speech of Timoleon before the battle of the R. Crimisus. Since Polyaenus' figure for the size of the Punic army at the battle of the R. Crimisus (5.12.3) differs considerably from the figures given by Plutarch (25.1 and 5) and

Pompeius Trogus mentions Timoleon's liberation of Sicily from the Carthaginians (Prologue to Book 21).[1]

Plutarch and Diodorus mention Timoleon in works other than the Life and the Sicilian narrative of 16.65–90 respectively. Plutarch mentions the day of the month on which Timoleon defeated the Carthaginians at the battle of the R. Crimisus (*Camillus* 19.7), and he refers to Timoleon's capture and execution of Hicetas and his family at *Dion* 58.10. In the *Moralia* he has brief references to Timoleon's part in the murder of Timophanes (808A), to the parsley omen (676D), and to Timoleon's erection of a shrine to Automatia (542E and 816F). He also mentions how Timoleon took with him to Sicily men who had plundered Delphi (552F).

In discussing the laws of Diocles Diodorus mentions how constitutional changes were made at Syracuse under Timoleon (13.35.3). When he narrates the early career of Agathocles, he refers to Timoleon's victory at the R. Crimisus and to his grant of Syracusan citizenship to those wanting it (19.2.8), and he also mentions the Timoleonteium (19.6.4). Later he tells how the people of Acragas remembered Timoleon's good conduct in Sicily (19.70.3).

The total absence of contemporary or near-contemporary references to Timoleon and his work is extraordinary. Plutarch says that on Timoleon's capture of all Syracuse οὐ γὰρ μόνον Σικελίαν πᾶσαν οὐδ' 'Ιταλίαν εὐθὺς ἡ φήμη κατέσχεν, ἀλλ'

Diodorus (77.4; 78.5), it might be reasonable to suggest that on this point at least Polyaenus followed a source ignored by our two main authorities. In addition only a single mule is mentioned in Polyaenus' story of the parsley omen, as opposed to a number of them in Plutarch (26.1) and Diodorus (79.3), but this difference of detail may not be of any significance.

⁵ *Strat.* 5.3.8; cf. Plut. 39.6.

¹ A number of ancient authors who mention Timoleon do so only because of their interest in Timaeus or in some other matter. Thus although Timoleon occurs in Suidas, he is only referred to in sections devoted to Μαρκελλῖνος (cf. Marcellinus, *Vit. Thuc.* 27) and Τίμαιος ὁ ἱστορικός (= Polyb. 12.23). There is no section on Timoleon himself. Fragments of Polybius' considerable discussion involving Timoleon have come down to us, but it is Timaeus in whom Polybius is interested here, not Timoleon (12.23.4–7; 25.7; 25K.2; 26A.1–4). Likewise Marcellinus (*Vit. Thuc.* 27) and Cicero (*Ad Fam.* 5.12.7) are both concerned with Timaeus on the occasions when they mention Timoleon.

ἡμερῶν ὀλίγων ἡ Ἑλλὰς διήχει τὸ μέγεθος τοῦ κατορθώματος (21.6; cf. *Dion* 52.2), but in fact neither this nor any other achievement of Timoleon is referred to by a contemporary Greek author.[1] Timoleon's success was certainly not ignored or belittled by the Sicilians themselves (cf. the praise of the Syracusans and of Timaeus), and there seems to be no good reason why it should have been ignored by the Greeks of the mainland, particularly since Timoleon actually carried out the kind of programme so long recommended by orators like Isocrates.[2] Isocrates spoke with reference to Persia rather than to Sicily, but Timoleon's programme was similar in outline. He faced the βάρβαροι and defeated them, and then linked together the cities of the Greek zone in an alliance which gave them peace, prosperity and autonomy. Further, Timoleon achieved his success at the time when city-states in Greece were falling to Philip of Macedon (cf. Plut. 36.8). No better example of the enterprise of independent city-states could have been given by (say) Athenian orators wishing to inspire their hearers than the victory over the Carthaginians won by Timoleon and the Syracusans, and their expulsion of all tyrants from Sicily.

The Greeks of the mainland will certainly have been told of Timoleon's success. Corinth was quick to take advantage of this success, and she advertised it at all the Greek festivals in her appeal for colonists to go to Sicily (Plut. 23.2). Many thousands felt sufficient confidence in Timoleon to leave Greece for Sicily. Timoleon himself proclaimed his victory over the Carthaginians at the R. Crimisus with one dedication at Corinth, and perhaps with another at Delphi.[3] Then the growth of trade with Sicily cannot have left the mainland Greeks ignorant of developments on the island.

[1] The nearest contemporary reference to Timoleon's work, that of the anonymous *Rhetorica ad Alexandrum* (Aristotle 8.1429b) is very vague, and does not mention Timoleon by name.

[2] Cf. Plut. *Tim.* 37.4–5. Fontana has made the plausible suggestion that Arrian was attracted by Alexander and Timoleon as suitable subjects for biography because both men were great liberators. The βάρβαροι of the East were defeated by Alexander, those of the West by Timoleon. We know that Arrian also wrote about Dion, another liberator. M. J. Fontana, 'Fortuna di Timoleonte: Rassegna delle Fonti Letterarie', *Kokalos* 4 (1958), 21.

[3] See pp. 49–50.

Unless all the Greeks of the mainland felt, like Polybius, that to seek fame in Sicily was to seek fame καθάπερ ἐν ὀξυβάφῳ (12.23.7), there seems no reasonable explanation of why they ignored Timoleon's achievements. Even if they saw him as no more than an aged, inexperienced commander of a motley band of mercenaries at first, they cannot have remained blind to the fact that he did achieve striking success in the end. Plutarch tells how visitors to Syracuse were taken to see Timoleon, and how a brilliant return to Greece was prepared for him (38.2–3).

The disregard for Timoleon shown by later writers is a little more understandable. Many may have felt, with Polybius, that he had been extravagantly over-praised by Timaeus, and was therefore not a suitable subject. Then, despite his skilful use of propaganda to further his own cause, Timoleon does not seem to have been able to build up a great legend about himself. Perhaps he did not want to. He certainly does not seem to have attracted the attention of those who sought anecdotes or apophthegms, in the way that Dionysius II, for example, attracted it.[1] So common a theme was Dionysius' change of fortune, that Διονύσιος ἐν Κορίνθῳ even seems to have become a proverbial expression of the inconstancy of fortune.[2] Yet Plutarch's Life contains very few apophthegms of Timoleon: since Plutarch considered that a man's sayings were an important indication of character (see *Cato the Elder* 7), this absence of apophthegms probably means that few of Timoleon's sayings had been preserved. Indeed it seems reasonable to draw the conclusion that Timoleon would not provide a vast amount of material for the biographer interested wholly in personality, rather than in politics or war. As shown above, few biographies of him are recorded: the varied material for many different treatments just was not available. Because little was known about Timoleon's personality, the Life of Plutarch contains very few personal details about him. For example, we hear of only two incidents in his life before his departure to Sicily (his rescue of Timophanes in

[1] See the long list of references to Dionysius at Corinth in Berve, *Die Tyrannis*, Vol. 2, p. 664.
[2] See Cicero, *Ad Att.* 9.9.1, and the commentary of W. W. How, *Cicero, Select Letters* (Oxford 1926), Vol. 2, pp. 349–50.

battle, and the murder of Timophanes), while his wife and children are only mentioned once in passing (36.7).

Although Timoleon's work was warmly appreciated by Sicilians in his own day, and was remembered for a certain time afterwards (cf. D.S. 19.70.3), his political settlement was swept away by Agathocles within twenty years of his death. In mainland Greece and in the East so many events of the greatest importance took place within those twenty years that the attention of biographers and historians was not drawn to Sicily. Thus the memory of Timoleon faded, even if the prosperity which he had brought about still continued. After Timaeus had written about him it is possible that few considered that they could either add anything to his treatment, or discover evidence with which to modify his generous opinion of Timoleon. Nevertheless the complete disregard shown for Timoleon's achievements by his own contemporaries still remains strange.

CHAPTER 3

The chronology of Timoleon's career in Sicily

The chronology of Timoleon's career centres around the date of the battle of the R. Crimisus, and controversy has raged over this point.[1] Diodorus relates the battle under the archonship of Theophrastus in 340/39 (77.4–81.2), while Plutarch (*Camillus* 19.7; *Tim.* 27.1) informs us that it was fought on the 24th Thargelion. He does not specify the year, but from his narrative it would be natural to assume the year after the capture of all Syracuse by Timoleon.

With regard to this last event, Diodorus (70.1) and the anonymous Oxyrhynchus chronographer agree that Dionysius II departed for Corinth in 343, in the archonship of Pythodotus.[2] So Plutarch's statement at 22.8 that the Syracusans πολὺν πόλεμον ἐκ Λιβύης προσεδέχοντο, πυνθανόμενοι τοὺς Καρχηδονίους ... συνάγειν μεγάλην δύναμιν ὡς ἔτους ὥρᾳ διαβησομένους εἰς Σικελίαν, might suggest that the Punic invasion came in 342, a year after the departure of Dionysius. But the many events in Plutarch's narrative between the departure of Dionysius and the arrival of the Punic invasion make it more probable that at least two years intervened. The Carthaginians could well have taken two years over their preparations: they clearly spent a considerable time preparing for the invasion of 396 (D.S. 14.54.4–5), and as many as three years preparing for that of 480, according to Diodorus (11.1.5). Finally we should bear in mind that at Plutarch 22.8 342 is no more than the *expected* date of the invasion: we have no certain knowledge that the invasion did actually come at the expected time.

[1] The only useful discussion of the chronological problems of Timoleon's career is contained in Beloch, *GG*[2] III.2, pp. 380–5, paragraphs 155–8, although his chronology of events between the battle of the R. Crimisus and Timoleon's retirement seems speculative. No firm evidence exists.

[2] *Ox. Pap.* I.12, col. 2: κατὰ τὸ δεύτερον ἔτος (Ol. 109; 343/2) Διονύσιος ὁ δεύτερος τῆς Σικελίας τύραννος ἐκπεσὼν τῆς ἀρχῆς κατέπλευσεν εἰς Κόρινθον καὶ ἐκεῖ κατέμεινε γράμματα διδάσκων.

Thus from Plutarch and Diodorus it is a little hard to see where the battle of the R. Crimisus should be placed. Those who investigate the problem today would probably all agree that 342 is an unsatisfactorily early date. The battle must almost certainly be later than that: how far on is it to be shifted? 341 is the date which could be inferred from Plutarch's narrative, but there is a temptation to shift the date as late as 339, in order to follow Diodorus' view. Among those who argue for 339, Sordi stresses that there are many events to be included between Dionysius' departure and the arrival of the Punic invasion.[1] In this space we hear of colonization (Plut. 22.7–23.7), of changes in the constitution of Syracuse (Plut. 24.3; D.S. 70.5–6), of the formation of an alliance of Greek cities (D.S. 73.2; cf. 77.5), and of attacks by Timoleon on Leontini (Plut. 24.1; D.S. 72.2), on Apollonia (Plut. 24.2; D.S. 72.5) and on Engyum (D.S. 72.3). Then Hicetas launched an unsuccessful counter-attack on Syracuse (D.S. 72.4); and troops were sent to operate in the Punic sector of the island (Plut. 24.3–4; D.S. 73.1–2). In her discussion Sordi stresses the likelihood of these events being spread over four years, as Diodorus would suggest, rather than over one, two or three years.

This is an attractive argument, but it falls down on one main point, as Westlake mentions briefly.[2] If Sordi considers that those who place the battle in 341 are cramming the events between Dionysius' departure and the Punic invasion into too short a space, then those who support 341 would certainly consider that Sordi's date leaves too little time for all the events between the battle and the retirement of Timoleon. Sordi agrees with most modern scholars in placing the retirement in 337/6.[3] But it is hard to see how Timoleon's major colonization programme (Plut. 35; D.S. 82.3 and 5; 83.1–3), his changes in the Syracusan constitution (D.S. 82.6–7), the two defeats of his troops (Plut. 30.4–6), his expedition to Calauria (Plut. 31.2), the battle of the R. Lamyrias (Plut. 31.3–7), the final crushing of Hicetas (Plut. 32–3; D.S. 82.4), the battle of the R. Abolus (Plut. 34.1), the peace with Carthage (Plut.

[1] Sordi, pp. 109–12. [2] CR 12 (1962), 269.
[3] Sordi, p. 86; D.S. 90.1.

34.2; D.S. 82.3), the expedition against Messana (Plut. 34.4), and the final crushing of Hippon (Plut. 34.4), Mamercus (Plut. 34.5–7), and indeed all the tyrants except Andromachus (D.S. 82.4), may all be squeezed into the period from June 339 to the date of Timoleon's retirement. This presumably came at the end of the campaigning season in 337 (or very early in 336), since we are informed that he laid down his command as soon as he returned to Syracuse after the capture of Messana (Plut. 37.9–10).[1]

It may be difficult to see how the events from Dionysius' departure to the Punic invasion all fit into summer 343 to summer 341 – although I do not find it particularly difficult – yet it is certainly impossible that the events between the battle of the R. Crimisus and Timoleon's retirement should be squeezed into the space June 339 to autumn 337/early spring 336. It is possible that Timoleon's attacks on Leontini, Apollonia and Engyum, and Hicetas' counter-attack on Syracuse all took place in the campaigning season of 342: the distances between the towns are not vast, and the campaigns will probably have been short. Certainly Timoleon himself need not have been absent from Syracuse for more than a few weeks on the Crimisus campaign, for example. We know that his army marched for eight days (Plut. 25.5), and not long afterwards fought the decisive battle. He then returned to Syracuse a few days after the victory (Plut. 30.1; cf. 29.4). The changes in the constitution of Syracuse may be assigned to late 343/early 342, and the operations in the Punic sector to late 342/early 341, while arrangements for colonization will have continued throughout the period.

So in my view the date given by Diodorus for the battle of the R. Crimisus, and favoured by Sordi, is unlikely, and perhaps even impossible. It seems most probable that Diodorus' mistake arose from his annalistic arrangement of material. This has led to a peculiar structure at this point, whereby he describes the Carthaginians' preparations under Sosigenes in 342/1 (73.3), makes no mention at all of Sicilian affairs under Nicomachus in 341/0 (74–6), and then resumes his treatment of Sicilian affairs with a narrative of the Punic invasion and the battle of the

[1] M. I Finley (*Ancient Sicily*, p. 97) mentions 338 as a possible date for Timoleon's retirement. This seems much too early.

R. Crimisus under Theophrastus in 340/39 (77–81). He ignores the campaign fought later by Gisco against Timoleon (Plut. 30.4–34.1), and represents Timoleon's treaty with the Carthaginians as a direct consequence of the battle of the R. Crimisus (82.3; cf. Plut. 34.2). Thus it is possible that for some reason he relates the battle and the treaty (end of 340/39 – beginning of 339/8) at the time when the treaty alone was made, instead of separating the battle and the treaty by about two years.

Altogether 341, the date for the battle inferred from Plutarch's narrative, is more probable than 339, although it is only an inference, and depends on acceptance of 343 as the date of Dionysius' departure.[1]

The chronology of events from the Syracusans' appeal to Corinth to the departure of Dionysius II needs treatment as a whole. It is by no means clear, and Diodorus is our only guide. He places the appeal of the Syracusans under Archias in 346/5 (65.1). Then under Eubulus in 345/4 he places events from the start of Timoleon's mission to Timoleon's dash to Syracuse after his victory at Adranum (66.1–68.11). Under Lyciscus in 344/3 he places events up to Timoleon's capture of all Syracuse except Ortygia (69.3–6). Under Pythodotus in 343/2 he places the surrender and departure of Dionysius II (70.1–3).

If the Syracusans made their appeal in 345, it seems reasonable that Timoleon should set sail in 344 after the necessary arrangements and preparations had been made. We have no absolute check on this date: yet Diodorus mentions that when Timoleon retired he had been commanding troops for eight years (90.1), while Plutarch says that he liberated Sicily ἐν οὐδ᾽ ὅλοις ἔτεσιν ὀκτώ (37.6). Diodorus places the retirement in 337/6, so that it is possible for Timoleon to go to Sicily in 344 in his scheme.

The sequence of events between the victory of Adranum and the departure of Dionysius II, quite apart from the chronology, is confused. The chronological point which has caused most trouble is Plutarch's remark that Timoleon ἐπιβὰς γὰρ Σικελίας ἐν ἡμέραις πεντήκοντα τήν τ᾽ ἀκρόπολιν τῶν Συρακουσῶν παρ-

[1] For discussion of a possible inconsistency in Diodorus' narrative mentioned by Sordi, see Note C, p. 197.

ἔλαβε καὶ Διονύσιον εἰς Πελοπόννησον ἐξέπεμψεν (16.2). That the events from Timoleon's arrival in Sicily to the departure of Dionysius II should be crammed into fifty days seems impossible. Both Diodorus' narrative (68.11–70.1) and Plutarch's own narrative show that Timoleon's capture of Ortygia will have been a slow business in whatever way it was in fact accomplished. For example, Plutarch relates how 400 of Timoleon's men entered Ortygia κρύφα καὶ κατ' ὀλίγους after an arrangement had been made with Dionysius (13.4): these moves cannot have been the work of a day. It might therefore be best to ignore Plutarch's statement that Dionysius departed within fifty days of Timoleon's arrival in Sicily. Westlake's assumption that Plutarch means that Timoleon had made contact with Dionysius within fifty days of his landing in Sicily cannot be confirmed, as Westlake himself recognizes.[1] We may only say with certainty that Timoleon began his siege of Syracuse after the battle of Adranum in 344, either by taking the outlying parts of the city (Diodorus' version), or by sending his men into Ortygia (Plutarch's version).

Mago will have presumably arrived in Syracuse to help Hicetas at the opening of the sailing season in 343, after Timoleon had been threatening the city for some months (Plut. 17.1–2; D.S. 69.3).[2] But in the same season he departed (Plut. 20.11; D.S. 69.5), and allowed Timoleon to capture all Syracuse very soon afterwards (D.S. 69.6; on the next day, according to Plut. 21.1). So Diodorus and the Oxyrhynchus chronographer would seem

---

[1] H. D. Westlake, *Tyrants*, p. 24; see also pp. 106–7.

[2] It is perhaps reasonable to believe that a sizeable fleet would not normally set sail during winter. Nicias implies in a speech that all sea communication between Sicily and Greece would be suspended during the four most wintry months (Thuc. 6.21.2), but this remark seems to reflect common Greek prejudice against winter sailing, rather than actual practice. Although such winter sailing would undoubtedly have been hazardous, we do hear of ships sailing in the winters of 415/14 and 414/13, for example from Sicilian Naxos and Syracuse to Athens (Thuc. 6.74.2 and 7.10), from Catania to Carthage and Etruria (Thuc. 6.88.6), from Syracuse to Corinth (Thuc. 6.88.7), and from Athens to Syracuse (7.16.2). Yet while these references show that messengers (7.10), or even an advance party (7.16.2), would set sail in winter, it is clear from Thucydides' narrative that a sizeable fleet would not normally expect to set sail during the winter, but would await the coming of spring (7.17.1; cf. Plato *Ep.* 7.345D).

to be right in placing the end of the struggle over Syracuse under Pythodotus, in the second half of 343.

The movements of the reinforcements dispatched to Timoleon from Corinth seem to fit well into Diodorus' scheme too. Presumably it was news of Timoleon's first success shortly after his arrival in Sicily in 344 (Plut. 16.2–3) which encouraged the Corinthians to raise reinforcements. These men will have set out to Thurii at the earliest convenient sailing season, in other words spring 343. They will have stayed a considerable time in South Italy – in Thurii (during a campaigning season), Bruttium and Rhegium – as we are informed by Plutarch (19.2–3). Then they will have crossed over to Sicily (Plut. 19.6), and will have joined Timoleon's march on Syracuse in the second half of 343 (Plut. 20.1).

Since Diodorus does not give a detailed treatment of the events in Sicily from the battle of the R. Crimisus to Timoleon's retirement, but merely makes some remarks under 339/8 alone (82–3), it is impossible to construct any useful chronology for this period. He places Timoleon's retirement in 337/6 (90.1). Timoleon probably died at some unknown date during the next few years.[1]

Most scholars who discuss the date of the battle of the R. Crimisus have worked only from Diodorus and Plutarch, and have left out of account two inscriptions which may throw light on the matter.

The first stone (now inv. 2280) was found at Delphi in 1887 and published by Pomtow in 1895.[2] He suggested the following restoration:

’Απὸ Κα]ρχαδονίων
Τιμολέ]ων τῶι ’Απόλλωνι

[1] Diodorus' summary account of Timoleon's death (90.1) has led some scholars to think that he died almost immediately after he had retired (see, for example, E. A. Freeman, *A History of Sicily from the Earliest Times* (Oxford 1894), Vol. 4, p. 337 n. 4). But the stories about the period of his retirement (Plut. 36.7–9; Nepos 3.4–4) and the separation of his retirement and death by Plutarch (37.10; 39.1) and Nepos (3.4; 5.4) show that some time must have elapsed between the two events.

[2] H. Pomtow, 'Ein sicilisches Anathem in Delphi', *Ath. Mitt.* 20 (1895), 483–94.

Then the ends of three proper names (?) on three separate lines.

ζ]εῦγος ἕσταθι

He maintained that this stone was a fragment of the dedication made by Timoleon at Delphi of one of the 200 chariots (ζεῦγος) captured from the Carthaginians at the battle of the R. Crimisus (D.S. 80.5; Plut. 29.2). The favour which Apollo was supposed to have shown to Timoleon (Plut. 8.2–3), and Timoleon's pursuance of piety and publicity all make Pomtow's restoration a plausible one.

The dedication perhaps assumes greater significance with the publication by Bousquet of a newly discovered list of those who had made contributions for the rebuilding of the temple at Delphi.[1] The relevant part of the stone (inv. 6372) records the contributions of three Syracusans (p. 353):

> [Αἰ]σχύλος Συ[ρακόσιος]　　3
> Κορινθίου δρ[αχμὰς τρεῖς].
> Εὐκλῆς Συρακό[σιος]　　5
> Κορινθίου δραχ[μὰς τρεῖς].
> Σώσιππος Συρακόσι[ος]
> Κορινθίου δραχμὰς τ[ρεῖς].
> τοῦτο ἀπεδόμεθα καὶ αἱ[γιναῖ]-
> ον ἐποήσαμεν δραχμὰς τέ[σσε]-　　10
> ρας χαλκοῦς ἐννέα.

The stone gains significance first from the fact that it is firmly dated by the mention of an archon (line 24): it records the sums contributed to the temple fund in the period before his term of office opened, that is, sums contributed in spring 340 (p. 350). Secondly it is written in exactly the same lettering as that of the dedication above (p. 355 n. 1).

That three Syracusans should appear together at Delphi in spring 340 and should make equal contributions to the temple fund in *Corinthian money*[2] is strange to say the least. And Bousquet was tempted to put forward the idea that these were the men who brought Timoleon's chariot from Syracuse to Delphi,

[1] J. Bousquet, 'Nouvelles Inscriptions de Delphes: III. Compte du IVᵉ Siècle', *BCH* 62 (1938), 348–57.

[2] That is, in the coinage widely used in Sicily during Timoleon's time. See pp. 161–3.

and made small private contributions to the temple fund while they were staying at Delphi (p. 355 n. 1). The dedication of the chariot and the list of contributors were both cut by the same mason, and therefore they were possibly made about the same time.

If Bousquet's suggestion is correct, then the battle of the R. Crimisus must have been before spring 340, and most probably in June 341. Certainly it cannot have been fought in 340 or 339.

The suggestion is hedged about with difficulties. We have no evidence which specifically links the dedication and the list, except the unhelpful fact that both were cut by the same mason. It is possible that the three Syracusans on the list were exiles, living in Greece, who happened to be visiting Delphi. According to Plutarch (*Dion* 22.7), there were at least 1,000 Syracusan exiles at the time of Dion's expedition.

Then it is hard to see why Timoleon's dedication should only have been made at Delphi six months or so after the battle, when Plutarch mentions that spoils were sent to Corinth ἅμα δὲ τῇ φήμῃ τῆς νίκης (29.5): the news of the victory is hardly likely to have taken six months to reach Corinth. Even if Plutarch's statement here is an exaggeration, and the spoils were sent some time after the first news of the battle, the interval between the battle and the dedication still remains peculiarly long.[1] It seems best to draw no firm conclusions from the inscriptions.[2]

[1] No precise figure may be given for the time which we might expect a ship to take on a voyage from Sicily to the Peloponnese, when the speed of a sailing ship is entirely determined by its build and by the force and direction of the wind. Apollonius of Tyana sailed the 300 nautical miles from Syracuse to the mouth of the R. Alpheus in six days (Philostratus, *Vit. Apoll.* 8.15), a voyage which Casson (L. Casson, 'Speed under sail of ancient ships', *TAPA* 82 (1951), 140), considers slow, since the wind ought to have been favourable. Certainly Dion, travelling in the opposite direction from Zacynthus to C. Pachynus, took thirteen days against adverse winds (Plut. *Dion* 25). But any generalization with regard to sailing times is impossible when wide differences in speed were common: for example, Apollonius had the good fortune to reach Puteoli on only the fifth day after leaving Corinth (Philostratus, *Vit. Apoll.* 7.10), whereas Pyrrhus' fleet in 278 B.C. apparently took as many as ten days to go from Tarentum to Locri (D.S. 22.8.2).

[2] Bousquet re-examined inv. 2280 and suggested that the last word was ἐστάθη, not ἔσταθι. He also hoped to publish a further study of the stone (p. 355 n. 1), but he has not yet done so.

CHAPTER 4

Military studies

Relations between Syracuse and Corinth from 415 to 344 B.C.

In describing the appeal made by the Syracusan exiles (2–3.3) Plutarch gives the impression that relations between Corinth and Syracuse were close, and that Corinth had frequently given generous help to Syracuse (esp. 2.2 and 3.1). This impression is somewhat misleading. Although Corinth was in a position to control the sailing routes from the Peloponnese to the West, and although she always acknowledged with pride the fact that she was the μητρόπολις of Syracuse, she helped Syracuse little in the seventy years or so before Timoleon's expedition (or, indeed, earlier in the fifth century).

In 415/14, during the Athenian siege of the city, Syracuse appealed to Corinth for help κατὰ τὸ ξυγγενές; measured in terms of men and ships Corinth's response was not lavish,[1] but nevertheless she did show some enthusiasm, and was especially useful to Syracuse in pressing Sparta to send aid (Thuc. 6.73.2 and 6.88.7–10).

During the first half of the fourth century Corinthian aid to Syracuse dwindled to nothing. This is not surprising, since it seems certain from our meagre evidence that Corinth's position as a great trading power was destroyed during the Archidamian War, not least because Athenian operations in the West of Greece will have hampered trade with Italy and Sicily. In 433 Corinth could assemble a fleet of ninety ships (Thuc. 1.46.1), while as late as 418 she could send 2,000 hoplites to fight at the battle of Mantinea (Thuc. 5.57.2); but five years later, in 413, King Agis only expected Corinth to furnish a mere fifteen ships for the Peloponnesian fleet (Thuc. 8.3.2), ten fewer than the number contributed by both Sparta and Boeotia.[2] Then the

---

[1] Fourteen ships (Thuc. 6.104.1) and later 500 hoplites (Thuc. 7.17.3; 7.19.4).

[2] On the decline of the Corinthian economy during the Peloponnesian War, see D. Kagan, *Politics and Policy in Corinth, 421–336 B.C.* (Ohio 1958), pp. 63–5.

confusion and disorder which persisted after the end of the Peloponnesian War did not permit the economy of the city to revive significantly by the time of the King's Peace.[1] It was probably only in the years after the King's Peace that Corinth was able to revive. She could gain revenue from trade, from the tolls which she must have levied on ships being hauled across the Isthmus, and from the very fact that she was situated at a meeting of ways.[2] From the Demosthenic speech *In Neaeram* (esp. sections 18–32) it seems that in the fourth century Corinth continued to be noted for her prostitutes: huge sums of money were spent on fashionable courtesans.[3]

It must have been Corinth's convenient position which led Philip of Macedon to choose the city as the meeting place for his 'League of Corinth' in 338–7. But Broneer bears out the view that fourth-century Corinth remained only a shadow of what she had been before the Peloponnesian War, when he says of the South Stoa, probably built to accommodate League delegates: 'It is difficult to suggest any other time during the fourth century when Corinth would have felt the need of a public building of such size and sumptuous appointments.'[4] The South Stoa seems to have been the first important building erected at Corinth during the fourth century.

Since Corinth will have had no money to spend on foreign ventures during the fourth century, it is easy to see why she did not respond to Syracusan appeals. In 406 Dionysius mentions that Syracuse might request help from Italy and the Peloponnese, but only to brush the idea aside (D.S. 13.92.5). Then in 404 we hear of a Corinthian Nicoteles, who is described as ἀφηγούμενος τῶν Συρακοσίων, but we do not know if he was actually sent out to Sicily by Corinth (D.S. 14.10.3).[5] Dionysius appealed

---

[1] On this matter see G. T. Griffith, 'The union of Corinth and Argos (392–386 B.C.)', *Historia* 1 (1950), 240–1.

[2] Cf. Strabo 8.6.20.

[3] Cf. Strabo 8.6.20; 12.3.36; and the words κορινθιάζομαι and κορινθιαστής in *LSJ*, p. 981. For the exorbitant sums demanded by one of the two famous courtesans named Lais (both of whom established themselves in Corinth), see Aulus Gellius, *Noct. Att.* 1.8.

[4] O. Broneer, *Corinth*, Vol. 1, Part 4: *The South Stoa and its Roman Successors* (Princeton 1954), p. 98.

[5] There is no evidence to support Stroheker's presumption that Nicoteles

to Corinth among other cities in 396 (D.S. 14.62.1). Diodorus
does not state the answer to this request, but some Corinthians
are mentioned as serving Dionysius at Syracuse later in the same
year (14.75.5). Finally Dion appealed to the Corinthians for
help in overthrowing Dionysius II (D.S. 16.6.5; cf. Nepos,
Dion 5.1–3), but, as far as we know, he received nothing at
first. The Corinthian government presumably recognized
Dionysius as ruler of Syracuse, and wished to play no active
part in unseating him. After Dion had gained control of Syracuse,
some σύμβουλοι καὶ συνάρχοντες did come out from Corinth
(Plut. *Dion* 53.2–3), but their mission could have been sponsored
by Dion himself rather than by the Corinthian government.

Although Corinth had not helped Dion in his expedition to
overthrow Dionysius, she did later prove willing to interfere
in the domestic affairs of Syracuse by dispatching Timoleon,
in response to an unofficial appeal from Syracusan exiles in
Leontini. It is not at all clear why she unexpectedly decided to
involve herself in the troubled situation in Sicily at this juncture,
especially when the force sent was such a weak one.[1]

Altogether the meagre evidence for relations between Corinth
and Syracuse in the seventy years or so before Timoleon's
expedition shows quite clearly that there was no special relationship between the two cities in this period, but that Corinth was
usually unhelpful. At this time she was not rich enough to send
aid to Syracuse. The formal ties between mother-city and colony
were maintained, but the relationship was no more than a formal
one. There is no evidence to suggest that Corinth had any
authority over Syracuse at the time of Timoleon's expedition: no
sign of such authority appears in the fifth century, and, as shown
above, there is no fourth-century occasion known to us when
Corinth might have gained such authority.[2] It was only when

was sent out by Corinth like Timoleon. See K. F. Stroheker, *Dionysios I:
Gestalt und Geschichte des Tyrannen von Syrakus* (Wiesbaden 1958), p. 56.

If the fragment of Heracleides Ponticus (= *Aristotelis Fragmenta* 611.62,
ed. V. Rose) which mentions a Κορινθίων στόλος does belong to a work on
Locri, it might be correct to date the incident recorded in it to the period
415–344. But certainty is impossible here. Professor G. L. Huxley kindly
drew my attention to this bizarre passage.

[1] On the exiles' appeal, see pp. 122–3; on the size of Timoleon's force,
see p. 57.   [2] See pp. 123–7.

Timoleon was unexpectedly successful that Corinth again took a real interest in Syracuse.[1]

The armies of Timoleon and his opponents

This section attempts to bring together such information about the armies of Timoleon and his opponents as is related to us by our sources, and to estimate Timoleon's talent as a commander of mercenaries. Neither Plutarch nor Diodorus was particularly interested in giving an accurate account of the size and composition of the forces led by Timoleon and his opponents, even if the necessary information was available. Yet while my account is inevitably made scrappy by the lack of evidence, it is possible to say something of the various forces from the information which has come down to us.

Timoleon's recruitment of a mercenary force after his election as leader of the Sicilian expedition is mysterious. Plutarch represents the Corinthians as eager to help the Syracusans (3.1), eager to give the command to Timoleon (7.2), and even more eager to dispatch a force after the receipt of Hicetas' letter (7.7). But Plutarch's statement that the task of leading the expedition was keenly competed for among ambitious citizens (3.2) is not borne out by the choice of the aged Timoleon. Nor is Plutarch's statement that the Corinthians were eager to send a force borne

---

[1] See p. 126. M. Scheele stresses the small help afforded to Syracuse by Corinth in ΣΤΡΑΤΗΓΟΣ ΑΥΤΟΚΡΑΤωΡ: *Staatsrechtliche Studien zur griechischen Geschichte des 5. und 4. Jahrhunderts* (Leipzig 1932), pp. 49–50.

In his unreliable section on the relations between Corinth and Syracuse J. Seibert overemphasizes the strength of the ties between the two cities, and believes that Corinth had authority in Syracuse during Timoleon's time (*Metropolis und Apoikie: Historische Beiträge zur Geschichte ihrer gegenseitigen Beziehungen* (Würzburg 1963), pp. 109–21, especially pp. 118–21).

A. J. Graham discusses the relations between Corinth and Syracuse briefly. His statement that Corinth showed little interest in Timoleon's expedition (p. 145) is not quite correct: Corinth showed little interest at first, but she became far more interested once Timoleon was successful (*Colony and Mother City in Ancient Greece* (Manchester 1964), pp. 144–5).

Wentker's discussion 'Timoleon in Syrakus' (pp. 14–18) should be disregarded. Wentker overemphasizes the strength of family ties between the nobility of Corinth and the nobility of Syracuse (H. Wentker, *Sizilien und Athen* (Heidelberg 1956)).

out by the final dispatch of a mere seven ships (8.4) and 1,000 men (11.5): only the ships were actually supplied by Corinth.

Later Plutarch remarks that Timoleon recruited mercenaries who had taken part in the Phocian sack of Delphi in 356:

ἦσαν μὲν γὰρ οὗτοι τῶν μετὰ Φιλομήλου τοῦ Φωκέως καὶ 'Ονομάρχου Δελφοὺς καταλαβόντων καὶ μετασχόντων ἐκείνοις τῆς ἱεροσυλίας. μισούντων δὲ πάντων αὐτοὺς καὶ φυλαττομένων ἐπαράτους γεγονότας, πλανώμενοι περὶ τὸν Πελοπόννησον ὑπὸ Τιμολέοντος ἐλήφθησαν ἑτέρων στρατιωτῶν οὐκ εὐπορῦντος (30.7–8; cf. *De Ser. Num. Vind.* 552F).

But his view that Timoleon found it impossible to recruit any mercenaries, except despoilers shunned by everyone else, because there was a shortage of mercenaries, cannot be correct, since Timoleon searched for men after the Peace of Philocrates in 346. Isocrates, in his oration *Philippos*, written shortly after this peace, makes it clear that there existed a dangerously high number of Greeks willing to become mercenaries.[1] If Timoleon had been prepared to pay such men the low wage which was customary in the mid fourth century,[2] he should have had no difficulty in recruiting a good force at a time when the supply of mercenaries far exceeded the demand. That he took men shunned by everyone else must indicate either that more suitable mercenaries sensibly doubted his chances of success, or that he did not offer an acceptable wage. In all probability he offered little or no payment (μισθός) at the outset, but was compelled by Corinthian meanness to offer just rations, or money for rations (σιτηρέσιον),[3] together with the prospect of booty. Such a dim prospect, combined with the age and inexperience of the leader, and the distant campaign (cf. D.S. 16.62.2), did not attract the best mercenaries. However, it was common practice for mercenaries who were unable to gain other employment to serve without *misthos* under a commander who held out the prospect of booty. Indeed in Timoleon's time Phalaecus took his mercenaries, who

---

[1] Oration 5, sections 96, 120, 121.

[2] See G. T. Griffith, *The Mercenaries of the Hellenistic World* (Cambridge 1935), pp. 296–7.

[3] On the terms μισθός and σιτηρέσιον, see G. T. Griffith, *Mercenaries o, the Hellenistic World*, pp. 264–71. σιτηρέσιον would sometimes represent as much as half a mercenary's total emoluments.

could find no employment because they had plundered Delphi, from Corinth towards Italy and Sicily, νομίζων ἐν τούτοις τοῖς τόποις ἢ καταλήψεσθαί τινα πόλιν ἢ τεύξεσθαι μισθοφορίας (D.S. 16.61.4). It is possible that Timoleon recruited his mercenaries from Phalaecus' force, but neither Plutarch nor Diodorus makes this point clear, nor is it certain when Phalaecus set out for Italy and Sicily.[1]

According to Diodorus (16.66.2) Timoleon recruited 700 mercenaries before setting out from Corinth. Plutarch refers to the collection of mercenaries by Timoleon at Corinth (7.3; 8.1; 30.8), but gives no figure for Timoleon's total force until he reaches Tauromenium, when he mentions 1,000 men (11.5). The discrepancy between the 700 of Diodorus and the 1,000 of Plutarch might indicate that Timoleon picked up 300 men at Leucas and Corcyra.[2]

According to Diodorus Timoleon had 1,000 men at the battle of Adranum (68.9), that is, presumably, 700 men recruited in Corinth, and 300 recruited variously from Leucas, Corcyra and Tauromenium. Plutarch gives the figure of 1,200 for Timoleon's total force (12.4), with the result that he must envisage Timoleon recruiting 200 men at Tauromenium. Neither author mentions the casualties incurred by Timoleon's force in the battle, but it seems likely that they were slight, because Hicetas' army was caught unprepared.

According to Plutarch Dionysius handed 2,000 mercenaries over to Timoleon (13.7; cf. Justin 21.5.2), while Corinth dispatched 2,000 infantry and 200 cavalry to Timoleon as reinforcements (16.3; Diodorus merely mentions ten ships – 69.4). There is no suggestion that Corinth had any difficulty in assembling these reinforcements, whose total number was greater than that of the original force. Although the prospect of booty for these men was greater now that Timoleon had a fair chance of success,

---

[1] Westlake assumes that Timoleon did take men from Phalaecus' force. In my view this remains no more than a possibility. See H. D. Westlake, 'Phalaecus and Timoleon', CQ 34 (1940), 44–6.

[2] See D.S. 66.2; Plut. 8.4. We hear of a Leucadian officer, Euthymus, at Plut. 30.6. That some Corcyrean troops served under Timoleon at the battle of the R. Crimisus may also be inferred from the victory monument at Corinth: there seems to be no doubt about the restoration of the word Κορκυραῖοι. See p. 76.

it seems likely that Corinth paid them properly, unlike Timoleon's original force.[1] For these reinforcements carried money
(D.S. 69.4), and guarded Thurii faithfully during their long
voyage to Sicily (Plut. 16.4). If they were dishonest men who
had not been paid, they might have been discouraged by the
Punic blockade (Plut. 16.3; 19.2), and tempted both to take the
Corinthian money and to seek loot in South Italy, in the way
that the men who deserted Timoleon before the battle of the
R. Crimisus later attempted to ravage Bruttium (D.S. 82.2;
cf. Plut. 30.3).

When his reinforcements finally crossed over to Sicily, Timoleon marched on Syracuse from Messana with an army of 4,000
men (Plut. 20.1). If the narrative and the figures related by
Plutarch are correct, 2,200 of this army will have been Timoleon's
reinforcements. The rest of the army will have been composed
of the force with which Timoleon fought at Adranum, and of
other allies. It would be reasonable to assume that the force of
1,000 or 1,200 with which Timoleon fought at Adranum could
contribute no more than 300 men. By this stage 400 had entered
Ortygia with Euclides and Telemachus (Plut. 13.4) and a few
more with Isias (Plut. 21.3), while perhaps as many as 300 were
dead or wounded. Thus Timoleon's allies between them would
only be contributing about 1,500 out of a total of 4,000, an
unimpressive figure, but one that perhaps shows the effect which
decades of disorder had worked on the population and resources
of most Sicilian cities. All the same, the small number of allies is
strange when we know that Tauromenium (Plut. 10.6; D.S.
68.9), Adranum (Plut. 12.9; D.S. 69.3), Catania (Plut. 13.2;
D.S. 69.4), Tyndaris (D.S. 69.3) and πολλὰ τῶν φρουρίων
(D.S. 69.4) had all joined Timoleon by this time.[2] Then Diodorus
says that Adranum and Tyndaris provided στρατιώτας οὐκ

[1] Corinth's lack of resources in the first half of the fourth century may be
gauged from the fact that no army as large as Timoleon's reinforcement
force is known to have been assembled by her since 394, when 3,000 Corinthian hoplites fought at the battle of Nemea (Xen. *Hell.* 4.2.17). On the size
of Corinthian military and naval contingents from 492 to 344, see D. Kagan,
Politics and Policy in Corinth, pp. 135–7.
[2] And when we consider that the unimportant city of Galeria was able
to send as many as 1,000 men to the relief of Entella shortly before Timoleon's arrival in Sicily (D.S. 67.3).

ὀλίγους (69.3), and that Mamercus δύναμιν ἀξιόλογον ἔχων προσέθετο τῷ Τιμολέοντι (69.4). Mamercus is not likely to have been poverty-stricken, like some of the smaller allies, since Plutarch describes him as χρήμασιν ἐρρωμένος (13.2).

It is far harder to gauge the number of Timoleon's forces after his capture of all Syracuse.[1] Diodorus (73.1) says that Timoleon sent 1,000 men with his best officers into the Punic zone, whereas Plutarch merely says that he sent to the Punic zone τοὺς περὶ Δείναρχον καὶ Δημάρετον (24.4): if by this Plutarch means the whole force brought by these two commanders, then 2,200 men will have departed to the Punic zone, rather than just 1,000.

Diodorus and Plutarch differ significantly over the size of Timoleon's army at the battle of the R. Crimisus. Diodorus says that before the battle Timoleon was εἰς ὀλίγους στρατιώτας συνεσταλμένος, but that οὐ μετρίως ηὔξησε τὴν ἰδίαν δύναμιν by taking over Hicetas' forces (77.5). He says finally that Timoleon set out for the campaign with 12,000 men altogether, comprising mercenaries, Syracusans and allies (78.2). 1,000 mercenaries deserted with Thrasius, leaving 11,000 men to fight the battle (79.1).

Plutarch, on the other hand, says that the Syracusans were so terrified by reports of the size of the Punic expedition that only 3,000 citizens accompanied Timoleon (25.4).[2] He mentions that there were 4,000 mercenaries in Timoleon's force, of whom 1,000 deserted (25.5), with the result that Timoleon's total

[1] Plutarch makes the strange statement that none of Timoleon's forces was killed or even wounded in the capture of all Syracuse (21.5).

There seems to be little support for Stier's view that, according to Diodorus 70.4, Dionysius' mercenaries were dismissed after the capture of all Syracuse (RE 2.VIA s.v. 'Timoleon', col. 1281). On this point see Westlake, CHJ 7 (1942), 80 n. 38. Westlake rightly considers that Stier is wrong in translating τοῖς φρουρίοις in this passage as 'mercenaries', rather than as 'fortresses'.

[2] His statement that they were 3,000 ἀπὸ τοσούτων μυριάδων is just sheer exaggeration, and may arise because he wishes to stress the Syracusans' fear, and because he seems to date the start of the colonization programme before the battle, rather than after it. The low figure of 3,000, which was probably not the full levy of those citizens fit to go, possibly bears out Warmington's point that it was difficult for a Greek city to muster a full levy unless the city itself was directly threatened. Warmington notes that less than 4,000 Syracusans went to aid Himera against the Carthaginians in 409 (D.S. 13.59.9): B. H. Warmington, Carthage (London 1964), p. 93.

force was 6,000. Of this total 5,000 were infantry and 1,000 were cavalry (25.5).

Plutarch seems to have gone badly astray in reporting the size of Timoleon's army. It is true that Timoleon had suffered reverses and therefore losses to his army (D.S. 72.2–3) since the capture of Syracuse. But his gain of Ortygia and its subsequent demolition will have released the men guarding it for service elsewhere. (Originally these had comprised 400 of the original force under Euclides and Telemachus, and 2,000 of Dionysius' mercenaries.) Then he had also gained many minor allies (D.S. 73.2).[1]

Plutarch's figure for Timoleon's army may be smaller than that of Diodorus because he fails to note either the help afforded Timoleon by Hicetas, or the size of the contribution made by the allies (he mentions the allies only at 27.7). Yet he does make it clear that Deinarchus and Demaretus had not returned to Syracuse before the Punic force landed (25.3), and he does not seem to include their forces in the number with which Timoleon set out from Syracuse. While he never mentions that Timoleon joined up with Deinarchus and Demaretus, he does think that these men's forces were present at the battle, since he portrays Demaretus as commander of the cavalry (27.6). So if about 2,000 men under Deinarchus and Demaretus, together with an unknown number of men contributed by Hicetas and other allies, are added to Plutarch's total of 6,000, the discrepancy between the 6,000 of Plutarch and the 11,000 of Diodorus may not be as great as it might appear at first sight.

While it is impossible for us to be certain of the number who fought under Timoleon at the battle of the R. Crimisus, Diodorus' figure of 11,000 is more likely to be the truth than the 6,000 of Plutarch. From the figures discussed elsewhere in this section it can be seen that the combined forces of Timoleon, Hicetas and the other Sicilian allies would have exceeded 6,000. Further, it is an army of 11,000, not one of 6,000, which is more likely to have first withstood the fierce Punic resistance, and then to have inflicted immense casualties on the Punic army. In any

[1] The victory monument shows that Corcyreans fought for Timoleon at the battle, with perhaps Leucadians, Ambraciots and Apollonians too. See pp. 76–7.

event Timoleon's army was outnumbered by the Punic forces (cf. Polybius 12.26A.1). No source provides separate figures for the number of hoplites who made up the phalanx (cf. D.S. 79.5), and the number of light-armed troops, who pursued the defeated Carthaginians (Plut. 28.9).

There seems no reasonable explanation of Diodorus' statement that Timoleon was εἰς ὀλίγους στρατιώτας συνεσταλμένος before the battle (77.5), especially as he earlier describes Timoleon as αὐξομένου τῇ τε δυνάμει καὶ τῇ κατὰ τὴν στρατηγίαν δόξῃ (73.2), and as he does not seem to think that Timoleon already had a force in the Punic zone when the Punic expedition landed (78.1–2).

Unfortunately neither Plutarch nor Diodorus mentions the numbers lost on Timoleon's side at the battle of the R. Crimisus. It is quite likely that the Greeks incurred heavy casualties in the early stages of the battle, when the Carthaginians held their ground (Plut. 28.1; D.S. 80.1). After the battle it took three days to gather the Punic spoils because there were so few Greeks to strip so many Carthaginians (Plut. 29.4; cf. D.S. 80.5–81.1). That it took three days to gather the spoils might indicate the greed of Timoleon's mercenaries, but on the other hand it might indicate that the Greek army had indeed been sadly depleted in the battle. Yet Plutarch's account would suggest that there were sufficient men remaining to hand 5,000 captives εἰς κοινόν, and to secrete away many more (29.2).

We have almost no information about Timoleon's forces after the battle of the R. Crimisus. As soon as he returned to Syracuse he dismissed the 1,000 mercenaries who had deserted him before the battle; these men were killed by the Bruttians (Plut. 30.2–3; D.S. 82.1–2). His other mercenaries he left to plunder the Punic zone, according to Plutarch (30.1).

Later we hear of the loss of 400 mercenaries near Messana (Plut. 30.6), and of the ambush of an unknown number at Hierae in the Punic zone (30.6). For some reason Timoleon only had a few soldiers when he besieged Calauria (Plut. 31.2). But he had enough soldiers at the battle of the R. Lamyrias to leave 1,000 of Hicetas' men dead on the field (Plut. 31.8). Then at the battle of the R. Abolus over 2,000 of Mamercus' men were killed (Plut. 34.1).

The numbers of the armies opposing Timoleon are even harder to gauge than the numbers of Timoleon's own forces. Difficulty is caused not merely because the numbers of Punic forces are probably exaggerated, but also because Plutarch gives a muddled account of the aid afforded Hicetas by the Carthaginians.

At some point shortly before Timoleon's arrival in Sicily the Carthaginians came to the island with a large force according to Plutarch (2.1; this is presumably the force mentioned by Diodorus 67.2). At first Hicetas collaborated with these Carthaginians secretly (2.3), but later openly (7.4). It is not clear whether the many Punic triremes which aid him (Plut. 9.5; 11.4–5; 13.4; 19.2; cf. D.S. 68.5) are ships detached from this force, or whether they are others. Nor is it clear whether Mago brings to Syracuse a completely new force, or the force which had landed before Timoleon's arrival in Sicily (Plut. 17.1–2). It seems likely that the only Punic forces operating in Sicily up to the time of the battle of the R. Crimisus were those which had landed shortly before Timoleon's arrival in the island, but this cannot be proved.

According to Diodorus the Carthaginians had landed in Sicily with 150 battleships, 50,000 infantry, 300 war chariots, and over 2,000 extra teams of horses (67.2). Nothing is known of the numbers who helped the defenders of Entella against the Carthaginians, except that the city of Galeria dispatched 1,000 hoplites, all of whom were killed by the Carthaginians (67.3).

Meanwhile Hicetas besieged Dionysius in Syracuse with ἀξιόλογος δύναμις (D.S. 68.1; cf. Plut. 1.6). When it came to a pitched battle, more than 3,000 of Dionysius' mercenaries were killed by Hicetas' army (D.S. 68.3). Plutarch and Diodorus agree that Hicetas' army numbered 5,000 at the battle of Adranum; according to Diodorus these men were Hicetas' best soldiers (68.9; Plut. 12.8). Certainly Hicetas must have left behind a sizeable part of his army to continue the siege of Syracuse. Plutarch and Diodorus also agree that Timoleon's army killed 300 of Hicetas' force and captured 600 (Plut. 12.8; D.S. 68.10).

Plutarch says that Mago arrived to help Hicetas at Syracuse with 150 ships and 60,000 men (17.2); Diodorus, too, gives a figure of 150 ships, but mentions only 50,000 men (69.3). It is likely that both writers have over-estimated the number of men, possibly because they have used the total number of Carthaginians serving in Sicily at the time.[1] We cannot tell whether the figure of 150 ships is an exaggeration or not. Certainly the near-contemporary writer of the *Rhetorica ad Alexandrum* (Aristotle 8.1429b) gives the same figure, but we have no guarantee that his testimony is accurate.[2]

According to Plutarch Dionysius had 2,000 soldiers (13.7), whom he handed over to Timoleon, together with the horses and the armour in Ortygia. The armour was sufficient for 70,000 men (13.6).

Of the period between Timoleon's capture of all Syracuse and the battle of the R. Crimisus, Diodorus says that Timoleon was repulsed in his attempt to capture Leontini because Hicetas had retreated there with δύναμις ἀξιόλογος (72.2). Later Hicetas lost many men when he led out his whole force (72.4).

Diodorus and Plutarch agree substantially on the size of the Punic army at the battle of the R. Crimisus. Diodorus (77.4; cf. 78.5) says that the Carthaginians had altogether, including their forces already in Sicily, more than 70,000 infantry; cavalry, chariots and extra teams of horses amounting to 10,000; 200 battleships; and more than 1,000 freighters. Plutarch (25.1 and 3) agrees for the most part, mentioning 70,000 men, 200 warships and 1,000 freighters. But he gives these figures as the total of the invading force alone, not as the total of the invading force and the troops already in Sicily.[3] Of the 70,000 infantry the Sacred Band comprised 10,000 according to Plutarch (27.4), but only 2,500 according to Diodorus (80.4).

Diodorus says that all 2,500 of the Sacred Band were killed during the battle, together with 10,000 other soldiers. 15,000 soldiers were captured (80.4–5). Plutarch describes how the

[1] See Westlake, *Tyrants*, p. 30 n. 1.
[2] Aelian (*VH* 4.9) also mentions 150 ships, but he may have been copying from the *Rhetorica ad Alexandrum*.
[3] This is consistent with his narrative at 20.11 (cf. 22.8), where he says that Mago sailed to Libya from Syracuse. Diodorus' narrative is also consistent: he says that when the Carthaginians abandoned the siege of Syracuse they returned εἰς τὴν ἰδίαν ἐπικράτειαν (69.5), and therefore he believes that there were still Punic forces in Sicily at the time of the R. Crimisus campaign.

400 men who made up the first rank of the Punic army were all wiped out (28.8), and later says that of the 10,000 killed, 3,000 were from the Sacred Band (28.10). According to him, most of the captives were stolen away by Timoleon's soldiers, but 5,000 were handed εἰς κοινόν (29.2). We have no means of gauging the accuracy of the figures given for the size of the Punic army and for its losses, but it would seem probable that all the figures have been exaggerated, partly because accurate information is unlikely to have been available, partly in order to magnify the odds against Timoleon, and the glory of his victory. Indeed the conditions of Greek hoplite warfare were such that it would have been a physical impossibility for one army to beat in pitched battle another army almost seven times its size (that is to assume that the Greeks had 11,000 and that the Carthaginians had 70,000 men). The Punic army must have been smaller than Plutarch and Diodorus believe, although we have no evidence with which to estimate its real size. Polyaenus' figure of 50,000 is more reasonable than those mentioned above (*Strat.* 5.12.3).

We have little information about the size of the armies opposing Timoleon after the battle of the R. Crimisus. Diodorus gives us no figure for the troops under Gisco's command (81.3–4); neither does Plutarch, who merely says that Gisco came with 70 ships (30.5).[1]

At the battle of the R. Lamyrias Hicetas lost as many as 2,000 men (Plut. 34.1). Plutarch says that in this last battle a considerable proportion of the dead were Carthaginian auxiliaries sent to Mamercus by Gisco (cf. D.S. 81.4).

[1] Both Plutarch and Diodorus (81.4) agree that the Carthaginians used Greek mercenaries for the first time after the battle of the R. Crimisus, but they are probably mistaken over the point. So-called 'Siculo-Punic' silver coins, modelled on Greek types and often with legends such as 'the pay-masters', 'the camp', 'the people of the camp', had been minted in Sicily throughout the fourth century. They were almost certainly produced to pay Greek mercenaries in the service of the Carthaginians (see C. M. Kraay and M. Hirmer, *Greek Coins* (London 1966), pp. 280 and 300–1). The meagre literary evidence on the employment of Greek mercenaries by the Carthaginians before Timoleon's time is discussed by G. T. Griffith, *Mercenaries of the Hellenistic World*, pp. 209–10, and by H. W. Parke, *Greek Mercenary Soldiers* (Oxford 1933), p. 175 n. 1, with particular reference to D.S. 13.58.1 and 14.53.4.

Examination of the narratives of Plutarch and Diodorus shows Timoleon to have been a mercenary commander of unusual distinction. He seems never to have held an independent command before he set out for Sicily as an elderly man, to become a ξένος στρατιωτικός, the type of figure with which his brother Timophanes was always surrounded (Plut. 3.6).[1] As far as we know, he was also completely ignorant of Sicily. He took with him to the island a small, motley band of men, who were unable to gain employment because they were reputed to have taken part in the Phocians' raid on Delphi; these men were therefore probably prepared to accept booty in place of regular pay (μισθός).

Sicily itself had been suffering from the mercenaries of Dionysius I, Dionysius II and Dion for the previous half-century when Timoleon arrived in the island.[2] So great was the disorder in Sicily by 344, and so widespread the insecurity, that power could only be retained by those ruthless commanders who were backed by strong mercenary forces. In all probability Plutarch is hardly exaggerating when he writes of Sicily at this period: αἱ δὲ πλεῖσται πόλεις ὑπὸ βαρβάρων μιγάδων καὶ στρατιωτῶν ἀμίσθων κατείχοντο, ῥᾳδίως προσιεμένων τὰς μεταβολὰς τῶν δυναστειῶν (1.3).[3] In the military sphere there was no real difference between the forces of Timoleon and those of his Greek opponents: both sides relied heavily on mercenaries who were sometimes of a low standard. Both the similarity between the forces on each side, and the mercenary soldier's lack of interest in the cause for which he was fighting, are brought out in

[1] In the undated battle against the Argives and Cleonaeans Timophanes was τῶν ἱππέων ἡγούμενος, but Timoleon was merely ἐν τοῖς ὁπλίταις τεταγμένος (Plut. 4.1). On the other hand, while Timoleon may have lacked experience as a commander, his education as an aristocrat (Plut. 3.4–5; cf. D.S. 65.2) will have included training in hoplite warfare.

[2] The trouble caused by mercenaries in this period is well discussed by Parke, *Greek Mercenary Soldiers*, pp. 63–72 and 114–22.

[3] Compare Timoleon's later savage treatment of the Campanians on Etna (D.S. 82.4). For the situation in the island at the time of Timoleon's arrival there, see also D.S. 83.1. Mercenaries were prepared to take on the most desperate tasks for pay: it was two ξένοι whom Hicetas hired to assassinate Timoleon (Plut. 16.5). One of these men had been at Leontini for some time, and had committed murder there, a crime for which he had apparently remained unpunished (Plut. 16.9).

the fraternization between the mercenaries of Timoleon and the mercenaries of Hicetas at the siege of Syracuse (Plut. 20.4–11).[1]

We hear of further instances of disloyalty and lack of interest. 1,000 mercenaries deserted Timoleon before the battle of the R. Crimisus. In Diodorus' account of the incident these men can at least maintain that they are justified in deserting because they have not been paid their *misthos* (78.5–79.1), but in Plutarch's version this excuse does not appear, and the men desert merely out of cowardice (25.5). Sensibly Timoleon sent these deserters back to Syracuse to collect their *misthos*, rather than allowing them the opportunity to join the enemy. Hicetas' mercenaries actually hand over their employer to Timoleon themselves (Plut. 32.1), while Mamercus' followers – it is not stated specifically whether they were mercenaries or not – betray Catania to Timoleon, having mutinied on their voyage to Italy (Plut. 34.3): these men saw no hope of further employment from Hicetas and Mamercus respectively, and so turned to Timoleon. After the battle of the R. Crimisus most of the Punic captives were secreted away, rather than handed εἰς κοινόν, a probable case of mercenary greed (Plut. 29.2). Parke[2] suggests that the greed of the mercenaries, who were so intent on gaining loot that they did not leave off gathering it for three days (Plut. 29.4), prevented Timoleon from following up his victory and annihilating the Punic remnants as they retreated in disorder, but this explanation may not be correct. Other factors may have persuaded Timoleon not to pursue the defeated Carthaginians.[3]

[1] Possibly it was Hicetas' mercenaries, rather than those of the Carthaginians, with whom Timoleon's mercenaries fraternized. Westlake comes to this conclusion (*Tyrants*, p. 31 n. 1), but Sordi disagrees (*Diodori Liber XVI*, p. 123).   [2] *Greek Mercenary Soldiers*, p. 174.

[3] The Greek army will have been exhausted after its long march and will have suffered considerable losses in the battle. These losses, combined with bad weather, and the assurance that the Punic army had already been dealt a crippling blow, may have persuaded Timoleon not to pursue the fleeing Punic remnants. Further, Timoleon will probably have been as keen to gather booty as his own mercenaries, since Syracuse was so desperately poor at this time (cf. Plut. 23.7–8). Finally Timoleon will not have been eager to attack a fortified place like Lilybaeum. Quite apart from the fact that he will have had no siege equipment, he was not always successful in siege warfare. His unusual tactics gained him Syracuse, but his employment of conventional siege methods against Leontini ended in failure

The payment of mercenaries will have been one of Timoleon's constant worries. It seems likely that his original force was paid little *misthos* at the outset, or possibly nothing at all;[1] and even if the men were paid, it would appear from Plutarch's account that Timoleon's resources were soon exhausted. He states that when Timoleon reached Tauromenium: χιλίων γὰρ αὐτῷ στρατιωτῶν καὶ τροφῆς τούτοις ἀναγκαίας πλέον οὐδὲν ὑπῆρχεν (11.5). So he gives the impression that Timoleon had difficulty even in feeding his men at this stage, not to mention paying them any *misthos*. The victory of Timoleon's forces at Adranum will not have provided much booty, although we are told that Hicetas' camp was captured (Plut. 12.8; D.S. 68.10). However, Timoleon's reinforcements brought money from Corinth (D.S. 69.4), while Neon took good supplies of corn and money from Achradina (Plut. 18.5).

The final liberation of Syracuse was fairly peaceful, with the result that there will have been little opportunity for looting. Certainly Syracuse was very poor, and would at first have been unable to contribute much towards the cost of Timoleon's mercenary forces. Thus Plutarch's statements about Timoleon's eagerness to gain booty are in no way surprising: he tells how Timoleon was eager for his mercenaries to go to enemy territory (Plut. 24.3), and how he sent a force to the Punic zone, which raised money for the war, as well as living in plenty itself (24.4).[2] Substantially the same version of events is given by Diodorus (73.1), who says that Timoleon now paid his mercenaries *misthos* εἰς πλείω χρόνον, although before he had had no money with which to make such a payment. Yet in Diodorus (78.5–79.1), though not in Plutarch, 1,000 mercenaries later desert Timoleon before the battle of the R. Crimisus because their *misthos* is in arrears.[3] That some men's *misthos* was in arrears could be borne out by the generous allowance of booty which Timoleon made

(D.S. 72.2). Engyum may not have been captured even after repeated assaults (D.S. 72.3), while Messana was surrendered by its citizens, not taken by direct attack (Plut. 34.4; cf. 37.9).

[1] See Plut. 30.8, and the discussion earlier in this section, pp. 56–7.

[2] Plutarch recognizes the overriding importance of war expenditure at 23.7, where this is the one expense which he specifies in the anecdote of the auction of the statues at Syracuse.

[3] On this point, see also p. 29 and Note C, p. 197.

his troops after the battle (D.S. 81.1). It was certainly a common practice of commanders to withold *misthos* due in order to ensure the loyalty of their mercenaries,[1] but it may be that before the battle Timoleon could not conveniently find sufficient resources with which to pay all the money due.

It is possible that in the period after the victory at the R. Crimisus Timoleon will have used citizen levies in order to decrease the number of his mercenaries. As Parke suggests,[2] he may have granted land to those mercenaries who wished to remain in Sicily after their discharge. It was certainly important that this large number of men should either be expelled, or be given the land and the security with which to become law-abiding citizens. If they had been allowed to remain in the island without the means to earn a livelihood, they would have turned to brigandage.

Despite the sources' lack of interest in Timoleon's subordinates, it is clear that he had excellent lieutenants, either sent out to him (like Deinarchus and Demaretus), or presumably selected by him, men who took the opportunities to display initiative which were presented to them. Deinarchus and Demaretus, who brought reinforcements to Timoleon from Corinth (Plut. 21.3), successfully enlisted the friendship of the Thurians (Plut. 16.3–4), took their force through the hostile territory of Bruttium to Rhegium (Plut. 19.2–3), and finally crossed over to Sicily (Plut. 19.6). Both men took part in the capture of all Syracuse (Plut. 21.3), and then led a profitable plundering expedition to the Punic zone (Plut. 24.4; cf. D.S. 73.1 μετὰ τῶν ἀξιολογωτάτων ἡγεμόνων). Demaretus commanded Timoleon's cavalry at the battle of the R. Crimisus (Plut. 27.6). Both he and Deinarchus had highly successful careers after they left Timoleon's service.[3]

Of Timoleon's other lieutenants we hear less. But we know that Euclides and Telemachus were able to infiltrate 400 mercen-

---

[1] See the anecdotes in Aristotle, *Oeconomica* 2, and the discussion in G. T. Griffith, *Mercenaries of the Hellenistic World*, pp. 268–71.

[2] *Greek Mercenary Soldiers*, p. 176.

[3] See H. Berve, *Das Alexanderreich auf prosopographischer Grundlage*, Vol. 2 (Munich 1926), No. 248 Deinarchus; No. 253 Demaretus. Neither these two lieutenants nor any others are mentioned by name in Diodorus' narrative of Timoleon's career. However, Diodorus does mention Demaretus at 17.76.6.

aries into Ortygia, while it was being blockaded by Hicetas (Plut. 13.4). Then a later commander of the forces in Ortygia, Neon, boldly took advantage of the absence of Mago and Hicetas to sally out and capture Achradina (Plut. 18.3–5). Another lieutenant, Isias, presumably took in further troops to Achradina at some stage.[1]

Despite his age and lack of experience Timoleon seems to have made an excellent commander of mercenaries. His forces were frequently outnumbered by those of the enemy. Yet his swift movement, his audacity, and his willingness to employ unorthodox tactics frequently made his numerical weakness of no account.[2] Except on one occasion he seems to have been able to retain the loyalty of his troops and to satisfy their demands for pay. On the one occasion known to us when he was faced with large-scale desertion, before the battle of the R. Crimisus, he seems to have acted with such speed and fortitude that he only lost 1,000 out of 7,000 mercenaries, and raised the morale of the remaining troops sufficiently to inspire them to beat the huge Punic army (see especially Plut. 25.6–26; D.S. 79.2–5). Plutarch is certainly justified in praising him because:

πολλοὺς μὲν τυράννους, μεγάλην δὲ τὴν Καρχηδονίων δύναμιν ἀπὸ τῆς τυχούσης στρατιᾶς ἐνίκησεν, οὐχ ὥσπερ Αἰμίλιος ἀνδράσιν ἐμπειροπολέμοις καὶ μεμαθηκόσιν ἄρχεσθαι χρώμενος, ἀλλὰ μισθοφόροις οὖσι καὶ στρατιώταις ἀτάκτοις, πρὸς ἡδονὴν εἰθισμένοις στρατεύεσθαι (Comp. 1.4).

The site of the battle of the R. Crimisus and Timoleon's march to it[3]

Although our evidence is so meagre that it seems impossible to determine the exact site of the battle of the R. Crimisus, we may

[1] See Plut. 21.3, where Isias is ordered to attack *from* Achradina. On the other hand Isias might have been one of Neon's original force.

[2] Plutarch's narrative of the battle of Adranum (12.6–8) provides an excellent illustration of Timoleon's resourcefulness and his use of unorthodox military tactics. For his lieutenants never seem to have dreamt of a surprise attack on the enemy. They were about to encamp for the night, presumably with the intention of facing Hicetas the next day, when Timoleon hurriedly persuaded them to advance without delay. He led the charge himself, as he did at the battle of the R. Crimisus.

[3] In connection with this section reference may be made to *War Office Map, South Italy* 1:50,000, sheets 257 and 258 (second edition 1943).

nevertheless suggest the general area in which the battle was fought. Of many discussions of the question, perhaps the most exhaustive are those by Chisesi[1] and Aloisio.[2]

Since no Sicilian river bears the name Crimisus today, the problem hinges on the identification of the ancient R. Crimisus with a modern river. The site of the battle must also be in a mountainous area, as Plutarch's description especially makes clear (26.1; 27; 28.3; cf. D.S. 79.5; Polyaenus 5.12.3): and the absence of mountains rightly leads Aloisio to reject the suggestion that the battle was fought on the R. Delia to the north-east of Mazara and the north-west of Selinus (pp. 62–4).

Some scholars have identified the ancient R. Crimisus with the Fiume Freddo, which enters the sea near Castellammare del Golfo.[3] Beloch, for example, thought that the Carthaginian force, having landed at Lilybaeum (Plut. 25.1; cf. D.S. 81.2), marched towards the main Punic centre in Sicily, Panormus, but that it was caught by Timoleon's force at the Fiume Freddo between Calatafimi and Alcamo.

This seems impossible for four reasons. First, Timoleon is known to have marched through the territory of Akragas on his way to the Punic zone (D.S. 78.3); and this is the logical route for him to have taken with the knowledge that the Punic invading force had landed at Lilybaeum, rather than at Panormus. Since he knew nothing more than the Carthaginian landing place, it would be most sensible of him to make for that area, and to search for the enemy there. When the Carthaginians had landed at Lilybaeum Timoleon would hardly make for Panormus, and if he had done so, he would almost certainly not have passed through the territory of Akragas.[4] Then the Carthaginians would

---

[1] F. Chisesi, 'Entella, il Crimiso e la battaglia di Timoleone', *RAL* 5 (1929), 255–84. For a review of Chisesi's article, which cites further mediaeval evidence in support of his identification of the ancient R. Crimisus with the modern R. Belice Sinistro, see C. A. Garufi, *Archivio Storico Siciliano* 52 (1932), 445–8.

[2] F. Aloisio, *Rocca di Entella: note storico-critiche* (Mazara 1940).

[3] For example, K. J. Beloch, *GG*² III.1, pp. 585–6; L. Giuliano, *Storia di Siracusa Antica* (Milan 1911), p. 316; R. Flacelière and E. Chambry, *Plutarque Vies* 4 (Budé), p. 44 n. 1.

[4] It is not clear what Diodorus means when he refers to the territory of Akragas. But it is likely that he considered Akragas to have influence over

be unlikely to march to Panormus after landing at Lilybaeum. Their army was large, their equipment heavy; their forces would have moved so slowly over the difficult terrain of western Sicily that if they had wanted to go to Panormus from the outset, they would have sailed directly there, instead of landing at Lilybaeum, and then marching to Panormus. Further, if the battle were fought on the Fiume Freddo between Calatafimi and Alcamo, it is a little strange that the Carthaginians retreated to Lilybaeum, rather than to Panormus (D.S. 81.2). If they had been marching to Panormus they might still have attempted to reach that city after their defeat.[1] Finally the road between Calatafimi and Alcamo does not cross the Fiume Freddo at a point closely surrounded by mountains.

It seems better to identify the R. Crimisus with a section of the R. Belice, which enters the sea near Selinus.[2] This identification fits well with the fact that Timoleon marched from Syracuse through the territory of Akragas, presumably on his way to search for the Carthaginians in the area of Lilybaeum, where they were known to have landed. He found them one day in late May or early June (Plut. *Tim.* 27.1; *Camillus* 19.7). They were crossing a river which had sufficient water in it at that season to

the territory between the R. Platani in the west and the R. Salso in the east. Neither of these rivers will have formed a definite boundary at all times. We know that Akragas sometimes laid claim to land further west than the R. Platani (cf. D.S. 15.17.5), and that Monte Eknomos, west of the R. Salso, was held by Akragas and Gela at different times (Akragas: Plut. *Dion* 26.4; Gela: D.S. 19.104.3). On the extent of the territory of Akragas, see P. Griffo, 'Sull'identificazione di Camico con l'odierna S. Angelo Muxaro a nord-ovest di Agrigento', *ASSO* 7 (1954), 68–70.

[1] The crossing of the Fiume Freddo between Calatafimi and Alcamo is also slightly nearer Panormus than Lilybaeum, but the 5.4 km difference in distance is not significant.

Since ancient routes are not fully known, no estimate of the road distance from one place to another can be particularly accurate. In calculating modern road distances I have used the maps of the Touring Club Italiano (*Carta Automobilistica* 1:200,000 (Milan 1966); Sicily is covered by Fogli 25, 26, 27).

Marsala to Fiume Freddo crossing, via Salemi, Vita and Stazione di Calatafimi: 61.1 km.

Fiume Freddo crossing to Palermo, via Alcamo, Partinico and Monreale: 55.7 km (Foglio 25).

[2] This is the opinion of A. Holm, *Geschichte Siciliens im Alterthum* (Leipzig 1874), Vol. 2, pp. 208 and 470.

present an obstacle to their army, and in particular to split the phalanx (Plut. 27.6). Apart from the R. Belice there is no river known to me in southern Sicily, west of the R. Platani, which would have presented such an obstacle at this hot time of year: the R. Delia, for example, is only a 'fiumicello', as Aloisio remarks (p. 63).

Certainly climatic conditions in Sicily are not the same today as they were in ancient times. There is little accurate information on the matter, but since Arab times at least Sicily has probably become drier in general.[1] However, even if Sicilian rivers did carry more water in ancient times, there still seems to be no river in south-western Sicily, except the Belice, which would have been any obstacle to an army in late May or early June.[2]

The identification of the ancient R. Crimisus with the modern R. Belice fits well with the possible intentions of the Punic invaders. A force which had landed at Lilybaeum and was intent on avenging the damage done by Timoleon's troops in the Punic zone (Plut. 25.3; cf. D.S. 73.1–2) might well make for Entella, a strongly fortified city (cf. D.S. 14.48.5) in the Punic zone east of Lilybaeum. Entella's strength made it a valuable acquisition. The city had been loyal to Carthage,[3] but had been captured by Dionysius I in 368/7 (D.S. 15.73.2). According to Diodorus the Carthaginians then tried to regain it in 345/4: no reinforcements reached the city from other parts of Sicily,

[1] See, for example, D. Mack Smith, *Mediaeval Sicily*, p. 183; *Modern Sicily*, pp. 271 and 379 (London 1968).

[2] The difference between the Belice and the lesser rivers of the area is brought out by G. di Lampedusa in his account of journeys between Partanna and Montevago in late June (p. 42) during the early years of this century: 'We were moving at walking pace, for the slope down towards the Belice river was now starting ... Then we were across the Belice, a real and proper river for Sicily – it even had water in its bed – and began the interminable ascent at walking pace' (G. di Lampedusa, *Two Stories and a Memory*, trans. A. Colquhoun (London 1966), p. 44).

According to the *Guida d'Italia del Touring Club Italiano: Sicilia* (Milan 1968), the two largest rivers in the south of Sicily are the R. Salso and the Platani, with basins extending over 2,000 sq. km and 1,785 sq. km respectively (p. 20). The basin of the R. Belice measures only 866 sq. km (p. 271).

On the sudden rising of the R. Belice Destro after heavy rainfall, see F. Aloisio, *Rocca di Entella*, p. 73.

[3] D.S. 14.48.4–5, under 397; 14.53.5; 14.61.5.

however (D.S. 16.67.3–4), and the Carthaginians almost certainly did capture the place, because a little later we are told that Timoleon gained it and put to death the fifteen strongest supporters of the Carthaginians (D.S. 73.2). Thus it is clear that both Timoleon and the Carthaginians recognized the strategic importance of Entella.

It seems possible, therefore, that the Punic invading force marched from Lilybaeum in the direction of Entella, and that it was caught by Timoleon on the R. Belice some time before it reached the city.[1]

Finally it is tempting to suggest an exact site for the battle, but there can be little value in pursuing this subject when there is so little evidence on it. Chisesi suggests that the battle was fought by Rocca d'Entella on the section of river which has Contrada Garcia and Contrada Renelli on the one bank, and Contrada Vaccara on the other (p. 283). Aloisio does not favour the area just south of the confluence of the two branches of the Belice, around Cusumano, Mandra di Mezzo, Carrubelle, Malacarne and Cavallaro (pp. 64–7), but puts forward a case for the R. Belice Destro crossing on the road from Poggioreale to Roccamena in Contrada Carbone (pp. 70–5; the road is not marked on the map cited in note 3 on p. 69). He maintains that this crossing lies on what would have been the most direct route from Lilybaeum to Entella (p. 71). Most recently Lojacono has argued that the battle was fought to the immediate north-west of Rocca d'Entella, with the Greeks drawn up between the R. Belice Sinistro and the R. Belice Destro, which he believes to have been the ancient Crimisus. No compelling reason is given for the choice of this site in preference to that suggested by Chisesi,

[1] It must be stressed that no ancient source portrays the Punic army making for Entella on its march from Lilybaeum: that this is only a modern conjecture is apparently not appreciated by Aloisio (*Rocca di Entella*, pp. 52 and 58–9) and Lojacono ('Entella ed il Crimiso', sect. 1, p. 1: see Note D, p. 198).

The ancient Entella may be the modern Rocca d'Entella, although this is by no means certain and is doubted by V. Tusa, 'Aspetti storico-archeologici di alcuni centri della Sicilia occidentale', *Kokalos* 4 (1954), 157–8. He favours M. Castellazzo, near modern S. Ninfa, to the west of Rocca d'Entella. However the exact site of ancient Entella does not affect my argument, since the ancient city will certainly have been in the region of present-day Rocca d'Entella.

for example, while it is puzzling that Lojacono should first maintain that the two rivers are only 1½ km apart at his chosen site for the battle (section 1, p. 2), although his own Figure 1 (section 2, p. 26) later makes it clear that the real distance between the rivers is actually much greater.[1]

Timoleon's march from Syracuse to the Punic zone seems to have been a considerable feat. It is impossible to make precise calculations about his speed, because we do not know either his exact route or the exact time he took. Diodorus says that the mutiny took place κατὰ τὴν 'Ακραγαντίνην (78.3): this is a vague term, but it does show that Timoleon went near Akragas at least, and in the following calculations I have assumed that he went through Akragas itself.

For his march from Syracuse to the territory of Akragas there were probably two main routes open to him as far as the area of Ragusa. He might either take an inland route via Palazzolo,[2] or a coastal route via Noto and Ispica.[3] We do not know which he chose: the inland route was perhaps the more difficult, but it was shorter and better placed for allied contingents to join the Syracusans as they passed. Despite its length the coastal route was easy, yet it ran through country which was most probably deserted at that time, and therefore unable to provide food and reinforcements for the Greek army.

Plutarch suggests that the mutiny took place after eight days' march (25.5). If it had taken place at Akragas itself, Timoleon would have had to march a little under 30 km each day, assuming that he took the coastal route.[4] Marching at the same

---

[1] For further discussion of N. Lojacono, 'Entella ed il Crimiso', see Note D, p. 198.

[2] See B. Pace, *Arte e civiltà della Sicilia antica*, Vol. 1 (Milan 1935), pp. 439–41; and G. Uggeri, 'La Sicilia nella "Tabula Peutingeriana"', *Vichiana* 6 (1969), 41–4.

[3] See B. Pace, *Arte e civiltà*, Vol. 1, pp. 441–2; T. J. Dunbabin, *The Western Greeks* (Oxford 1948), pp. 200–1; and G. Uggeri, 'Sull' "Itinerarium per maritima loca" da Agrigento a Siracusa', *Atene e Roma* 15 (1970), 107–17.

[4] Syracuse to Agrigento is 220.9 km by road via Noto, Ispica, Modica, Ragusa, Vittoria, Gela, Licata and Palma di Montechiaro (Strada 115) (Foglio 27). Timoleon's army would need to march 27.6 km each day, to cover 220.9 km in eight days.

pace it would have taken him a further four days at least to reach Entella.[1] This pace would not be remarkable if the whole march lasted only one or two days. But to sustain the same pace for twelve days or more over difficult country in a hot season, and then to fight a battle with no opportunity for rest beforehand, is a considerable feat for an army which was made up partly of Syracusan citizens and allied levies (who would not have been as fit as professional mercenaries), and which suffered a serious blow to its morale because of the mutiny.[2]

The mutineers' speech in Plutarch (25.5) might suggest that the battle took place eight days' march from Syracuse. But this can hardly be right, since it would require Timoleon's army to march impossibly fast, and since immediately after the speech Plutarch shows that Timoleon was not aware of the whereabouts of the Punic army (τοὺς δ᾽ ἄλλους ἐπιρρώσας κατὰ τάχος ἦγε πρὸς τὸν Κρίμισον ποταμόν, ὅπου καὶ τοὺς Καρχηδονίους ἤκουσε συνάπτειν – 25.6).

Diodorus' version of events could suggest that the battle took place in the territory of Akragas or very near it. He says that after the mutiny Timoleon τοὺς ἄλλους ... προῆγεν ἐπὶ τοὺς πολεμίους οὐ μακρὰν στρατοπεδεύοντας (79.2). But this impression may have arisen because Diodorus is writing an abbreviated account of events. There seems no doubt that the battle did take place in the Punic zone (Plut. 30.1; cf. D.S. 78.1).

[1] The route from Akragas to Entella or thereabouts is unknown. However, to give some idea of the distance to be covered, I have assumed that Timoleon went from Agrigento to Sciacca (69 km), and from Sciacca to Santa Margherita di Belice (29.2 km). His route from Santa Margherita di Belice to Rocca d'Entella cannot even be guessed, yet the distance in a straight line is 13 km. This is the minimum distance. Clearly the actual distance to be covered between two places in such a mountainous area is greater. So to reach Entella from Akragas Timoleon would have had to go at least 111.2 km, which would require four days' marching at a pace of 27 to 30 km a day (Fogli 27, 25).

[2] On the distances covered in one day by ancient and modern armies, see, for example, R. D. Milns, 'Alexander's pursuit of Darius through Iran', *Historia* 15 (1966), 256; and C. Neumann, 'A note on Alexander's march-rates', *Historia* 20 (1971), 196–8.

Timoleon's victory monument

Excavations at Corinth have brought to light two fragments of what appears to be a victory monument set up by Timoleon and the representatives of the Greek cities which helped him. Both fragments were examined by Kent, who proposed the following restoration:

[Κορίνθιοι, Συρακούσιοι, Σικελ]ιῶται, Κο[ρκυ]ραῖο[ι, ᾽Α]πο[λ]λώ[νιοι,
    Λευκάδιοι, καὶ]
[Τιμολέων ὁ στρατηγὸς ἀπὸ τῶν] πολεμίων ἀ[ν]έθηκαν.
[Ταίδε πόλεις θεραπεύσαντες] κτιστῆρα Κόρινθον
[24   ] χρησάμεναι
[19   ἐλευ]θερίας ἐπέβησαν   5
[ἐκ Καρχηδονίων ὅπλα θεοῖσι] τάδε.[1]

Kent's restoration of the first two lines of the inscription has been challenged by Musti, who proposes:

[Κορίνθιοι Λευκάδιοι ᾽Αμβρακ]ιῶται Κο[ρκυ]ραῖο[ι
   ᾽Α]πο[λ]λω[νιᾶται καὶ
[Τιμολέων στρατηγὸς ἀπὸ τῶν?] πολεμίων ἀνέθηκαν   vac.[2]

This reconstruction is certainly more satisfactory. The monument is thus one set up by Corinth and her dependencies alone, with the dependencies, incidentally, listed in order from south to north. Musti thinks that Kent's restoration is unacceptable because at this stage, immediately after the battle of the R. Crimisus, Sicilian cities are not likely to appear in a dedication which includes the words κτιστῆρα Κόρινθον (p. 463). The fact that Plutarch mentions only Κορίνθιοι καὶ Τιμολέων ὁ στρατηγός (29.6) might also suggest that no Sicilian city appeared in the inscription.

J. and L. Robert rightly view Musti's restoration with caution, although they think that the substitution of Ambraciots for

---

[1] J. H. Kent, 'The victory monument of Timoleon at Corinth', *Hesperia* 21 (1952), 13. See also *SEG* 11, No. 126A, which follows Kent, except that in line 3 νομίσουσαι is conjectured instead of θεραπεύσαντες. νομίσουσαι is also printed by J. and L. Robert (*REG* 66 (1953), Bulletin Epigraphique No. 69, p. 136).

[2] D. Musti, 'Ancora sull' "Iscrizione di Timoleonte"', *La Parola del Passato* 87 (1962), 462.

Siceliots seems justified.[1] Not enough of the inscription survives for any definite restoration to be made.

Kent believed that the Apollonians of line 1 were men from the Sicilian city of Apollonia (Plut. 24.2; D.S. 72.5), but Berve sensibly suggested that they were more likely to be men from the Corinthian dependency of Apollonia in Illyria. They will have joined Timoleon's forces at some stage, as did men from Leucas and Corcyra (Plut. 8.4; D.S. 66.2).[2]

From the cuttings which remain on the top surfaces of the blocks Kent deduced that above the inscribed base of this monument there was placed a bronze statue of Poseidon, perhaps the famous statue by Lysippus (pp. 16–17). This speculative idea cannot be fully discussed here. But I would mention that the text which Kent quotes in support of his guess that the statue was bronze gives no support in one respect (Lucian, *Zeus Tragoedus* 9: Hermes replies to Poseidon: ναί, ἀλλὰ σὲ μέν, ὦ ἐννοσίγαιε, χαλκοῦν ὁ Λύσιππος καὶ πτωχὸν ἐποίησεν, οὐκ ἐχόντων τότε τῶν Κορινθίων χρυσόν). For the period after the battle of the R. Crimisus was the one time in the fourth century when the Corinthians would have had gold (Plut. 29; D.S. 80.6). J. and L. Robert[3] suggest that the statue placed above the base could have been Corinthos, founder of Corinth, who perhaps appears in the accusative as the object of the dedication.

Plutarch (29.6) seems to give a paraphrase of the victory monument inscription. We do not know where he found a report about it; Timaeus, however, lived in Athens for fifty years, and certainly could have seen the monument. Plutarch himself could not have seen it, since it will have been torn down during the destruction of Corinth in 146 B.C.

Szabó has suggested that two fourth-century Celtic rings found near the shrine of Poseidon at Corinth may have formed part of the booty sent home by Timoleon after the battle of the R. Crimisus. Certainly Celtic mercenaries fought in the Punic army, according to Diodorus (73.3).[4]

[1] *REG* 77 (1964), Bulletin Epigraphique No. 175, p. 162. See also *SEG* 22 (1967), No. 218.

[2] H. Berve, *Gnomon* 25 (1953), 529 (review of Westlake, *Tyrants*).

[3] J. and L. Robert, *REG* 66 (1953), 136.

[4] M. Szabó, 'Zur Frage des Keltischen Fundes von Isthmia', *Acta Antiqua* 16 (1968), 173–7.

CHAPTER 5

Punic policy in Sicily in the age of Timoleon

Punic policy in Sicily in the age of Timoleon, as in every other age, is made difficult to determine by the fact that all our extant historical sources are Greek; in his narrative of Timoleon's career Diodorus once considers Punic feelings for more than a line or two (81.2–3), but this is very unusual. Most references to Punic policy are brief. Any estimation of Punic policy through Greek eyes is further hindered by the prejudice which Greek writers display against the Carthaginians (see especially Plut. 17.2–3).[1]

Carthage had made peace with Dionysius II (D.S. 16.5.2), and had tacitly supported the expedition of Dion in 357 (D.S. 16.9.4; Plut. *Dion* 25.11–14), probably because she considered that the enterprise would weaken Syracuse.

We know of no Punic action in Sicily, however, until shortly before Timoleon's arrival in the island (Plut. 2.1; D.S. 16.67: the exact interval between these operations and the arrival of Timoleon is not known). It seems likely that Carthage was making an unhurried attempt to gain power in the island by allying herself with the mercenary commanders who had seized power in many of the cities. In particular she negotiated with Hicetas, the most powerful of these mercenary commanders, and seems to have concluded some treaty of friendship with him.[2] Carthage was apparently willing to help Hicetas in his attempt to gain all Syracuse, but the extent of her help does not seem to

[1] The only useful modern discussion of affairs in Sicily during Timoleon's time from a Carthaginian viewpoint is that of B. H. Warmington, *Carthage* (London 1964), pp. 119–25. S. Luria takes the same viewpoint, but has little to add to Warmington's treatment ('Zum Problem der griechisch-karthagischen Beziehungen', *Acta Antiqua* 12 (1964), 53–75).

[2] According to Plutarch (2.3) Hicetas approached the Carthaginians in the first instance, but in Diodorus' version (67.1–2) the Carthaginians approach Hicetas.

have been great at this stage (Plut. 7.4). Some Punic ships blockaded the harbour at Syracuse (Plut. 11.5; 13.4). Others attempted to prevent Timoleon reaching Sicily with his mercenary force, probably because Carthage feared that Timoleon might have some influence on the situation in Sicily, and might disrupt the plans which had been made with Hicetas (Plut. 7.6; 9.4–10.5; 11.1–3; D.S. 68.4–7).

But Timoleon was able to reach Sicily by a trick, and so disrupted the plans of Hicetas that the latter summoned Punic aid to Syracuse on a large scale. In Diodorus' narrative (69.3) Hicetas called in the Carthaginians because he despaired of taking all Syracuse by himself, after Timoleon had beaten his best mercenaries at the battle of Adranum, and had then occupied the outlying parts of Syracuse; Dionysius remained in control of Ortygia. According to Plutarch (17.1), Hicetas called in the Carthaginians because after Timoleon's victory at Adranum the Corinthians took over Ortygia from Dionysius. Whichever version of events is correct, it is clear that a huge Punic force did occupy the area around the Great Harbour (D.S. 69.3; Plut. 17.2–3). This force probably arrived at the opening of the sailing season in 343, some months after Timoleon's victory at Adranum.[1]

But the force departed mysteriously, probably in the same year that it had come, and thereby enabled Timoleon to take Syracuse, after facing Hicetas alone (D.S. 69.5–6; Plut. 20.10–21). Plutarch's narrative supplies some motives for the extraordinary decision of the Punic commander, Mago, to depart without having usefully helped Hicetas at all.[2] Despite a Punic blockade small craft were still able to take supplies into Ortygia (18.1), while an attempt by Mago and Hicetas to capture Timoleon's camp at Catania ended in disaster: so negligent a guard was left in Syracuse that one of Timoleon's lieutenants, Neon, was able to break out of Ortygia and capture Achradina (18.2–7). Then news came that Timoleon's reinforcements from Corinth had evaded a Punic blockading squadron in the straits of Messana and had landed in Sicily (19.6). Meanwhile the siege of Ortygia

[1] See p. 48.
[2] On Mago, see also p. 10.

by Hicetas and Mago proceeded at a very slow pace, and the mercenaries of Timoleon seem to have taken advantage of the many truces to make contact with Hicetas' Greek mercenaries, and to induce them to desert (20.2–9). When Mago heard rumours that Hicetas' Greek mercenaries might desert, he finally made up his mind to abandon the siege. Plutarch describes him as χρῄҘοντι πάλαι προφάσεως (20.10), and says that he departed κατ' οὐδένα λογισμὸν ἀνθρώπινον (20.11). Diodorus gives no details of why the Carthaginians departed, but merely says that οἱ δὲ Καρχηδόνιοι φοβηθέντες ἀπέπλευσαν ἐκ τοῦ λιμένος ἀλόγως καὶ μετὰ πάσης τῆς δυνάμεως (69.5).

Holm[1] considered that Plutarch's reasons for Mago's mysterious departure are inadequate, and he tried to connect this strange episode with Hanno's attempt to seize power in Carthage at about this period. This is a reasonable suggestion, which has been favoured by more recent writers:[2] Mago felt that Hanno's threat to the internal stability of Carthage was of greater importance than the siege of Syracuse, which in any case had not been going well, and therefore he sailed away. The difficulty with the suggestion is that our main account of Hanno's attempt to seize power, that of Justin (21.4.1–8), gives no date for the attempt, which really might have occurred at any time in the mid fourth century. In his account Orosius says that 'haec temporibus Philippi gesta sunt' (4.6.20), that is between 359 and 336.[3]

Then the suggestion that Mago sailed away to intervene at home fits well with Plutarch's narrative, but it hardly fits with Diodorus' version of events. Plutarch (20.11) says that Mago returned to Libya with his force, and this is consistent with his narrative of the opening of the Crimisus campaign, where there seem to be no troops left in the Punic zone (cf. 25.3). Diodorus specifically states that the Carthaginians sailed from Syracuse εἰς τὴν ἰδίαν ἐπικράτειαν (69.5): this, too, is consistent with his later narrative of the Crimisus campaign, where he says that there were already Punic troops in Sicily before the arrival of the invading force (77.4).

---

[1] A. Holm, *Geschichte Siciliens im Alterthum* (Leipzig 1874), Vol. 2, p. 203.

[2] For example, by Berve, *Die Tyrannis*, Vol. 2, p. 664.

[3] Hanno's revolutionary attempt is also alluded to by Aristotle, *Politics* 1307a.5.

So if Plutarch's testimony on Mago's destination is followed, it is possible that Mago did return home because of Hanno's revolutionary attempt. But the difficulty with following Plutarch's narrative further is that the narrative itself then destroys the idea that Mago went home to intervene over Hanno. For Plutarch says that Mago committed suicide (22.8), hardly the action expected of a general who had mysteriously abandoned a siege to intervene in political affairs at home.

It would seem sensible to reject the suggestion that Mago sailed away from Carthage to intervene in Hanno's revolutionary attempt, and to abandon the presumption that Mago's reasons for leaving Syracuse were logical. Instead it might be better to follow the narrative of Diodorus and Plutarch, both of whom emphasize the illogicality of Mago's decision to leave. Plutarch provides some reasons for Mago's decision, but they may not seem decisive. Yet Mago does seem to have been a weak commander. His relations with Hicetas were strained, and certainly they would have become more so if Syracuse fell to their combined force: then each commander would want to hold the city for himself. Mago may have been unduly frightened by rumours of the possible desertion of Greek mercenaries from Hicetas; he may have been further frightened by Timoleon's propaganda, or by something not mentioned in our sources.[1] We cannot know. Mago committed suicide because he realized that he would be punished for his indefensible withdrawal.

The Carthaginians will have felt a great loss of prestige after Mago's ignominious departure, and will certainly have been disturbed by Timoleon's successful capture of all Syracuse. Plundering expeditions sent into Punic territory will only have increased their fear of Timoleon's growing power (Plut. 24.4; D.S. 73.1–2). Both Plutarch (22.8; 25.1–2) and Diodorus (73.3; 77.4) describe how Carthage made lengthy preparations for a war in Sicily, and they suggest that the invading force was intended to be unusually formidable because a levy was made from Carthaginian citizens: according to Plutarch (28.11; cf. 30.5) Carthage rarely sent her own citizens on campaigns.[2]

[1] For the hidden pressures behind Punic commanders, see D.S. 20.10.3–4.
[2] This is certainly borne out in Diodorus' narrative of Agathocles invasion of Africa in 310: see D.S. 20.3.3; 8.6; 9.4.

Diodorus does not state the aim of this Punic invading force, but Plutarch describes it as

ὡς οὐκ ἔτι ποιησόμενοι κατὰ μέρος τὸν πόλεμον, ἀλλ᾽ ὁμοῦ πάσης Σικελίας ἐξελάσοντες τοὺς Ἕλληνας· ἦν γὰρ ἡ δύναμις ἐξαρκοῦσα καὶ μὴ νοσοῦντας μηδὲ διεφθαρμένους ὑπ᾽ ἀλλήλων συλλαβέσθαι Σικελιώτας (25.1–2).

This statement of the invaders' aim may have been exaggerated by Greek prejudice: it is possible that the Carthaginians wished to do no more than re-establish their hold on the Punic zone of the island. But Plutarch is certainly right in believing that this Punic force might have conquered the island. Most of the organized Greek forces – those of Timoleon, Hicetas and the other Sicilian allies, together with mercenaries – seem to have been reconciled with each other in the face of the extreme danger, and they resisted the Carthaginians in a united body under Timoleon's leadership. The Carthaginians nevertheless outnumbered the Greeks, and would have met with little other serious resistance in Sicily if they had smashed Timoleon's army at the battle of the R. Crimisus.

So Timoleon's victory at the R. Crimisus enabled the Greek zone of Sicily to remain independent, quite apart from the fact that it drove the remnants of the invading force out of the island altogether, and seriously depleted the Carthaginian citizen body.[1]

Despite the crippling blow that she had suffered in the battle, Carthage still seems to have been willing to help those Sicilian tyrants who had allied themselves against Timoleon. Her aim in sending a force to Sicily at this juncture is not fully known, but presumably it will have been twofold: to drive Timoleon's forces from the Punic zone, and to take advantage of any success scored against Timoleon by the tyrants. According to Plutarch the Carthaginians were told to send a general εἰ μὴ παντάπασι βούλονται Σικελίας ἐκπεσεῖν (30.4). But Greek mercenaries were now hired, so that Carthaginian citizens should not have to risk

[1] See D.S. 80.4; 81.2; Plut. 28.10–11. Plutarch says that Carthage had never before lost so many citizens in a single battle. Nepos makes his one reference to the Carthaginians in his *Timoleon* when he mentions the battle of the R. Crimisus. His statement that the Carthaginians retained only Africa after being driven from Sicily is an exaggeration (2.4).

their lives again (D.S. 81.4; Plut. 30.5),[1] and a force was dispatched under Gisco with seventy ships (D.S. 81.3–4; Plut. 30.4–5).

Relations between the tyrants and the Carthaginians may not have been wholly satisfactory. Hicetas and the Carthaginians can hardly have trusted each other, after Mago had deserted Hicetas, and Hicetas' men had fought the Carthaginians at the battle of the R. Crimisus. But the alliance seems to have been successful enough to destroy a force of 400 of Timoleon's men in the territory of Messana, and to wipe out an unknown number of mercenaries under Euthymus near Hierae in the Punic zone (Plut. 30.6; 31.1; Timoleon's mercenaries had been left in the Punic zone after the battle of the R. Crimisus – Plut. 30.1).

Although Diodorus does not mention these operations, while Plutarch gives few details of Timoleon's defeats, it may be that Gisco campaigned more successfully than either author suggests. For the terms of the peace treaty made between Carthage and Timoleon do suggest that Gisco had managed to reconquer the Punic zone (Plut. 34.2; D.S. 82.3). Both Plutarch and Diodorus are biased in favour of Timoleon, and represent his peace with Carthage as a kindness on his part (D.S. 81.4 and 82.3), rather than as an agreement perhaps thankfully concluded by him to limit Punic recovery, and to allow himself a free hand against his tyrant opponents. That Gisco had been successful is certainly suggested by Polyaenus (5.11). However, after the battle of the R. Abolus both Gisco and Timoleon were ready to make peace. Much of Gisco's force had perished in the battle (Plut. 34.1), while Timoleon had still not been able to crush Mamercus and Hippon. Now that it could reasonably request to keep the Punic zone, the Carthaginian government may not have wanted to go to the trouble and expense of assembling another force to fight in Sicily.[2]

Under the terms of the peace treaty the boundary between the Punic and Greek zones in the island was fixed at the R. Halycus,[3]

[1] See p. 64.
[2] According to Diodorus (82.4), Hicetas and other minor tyrants were only crushed after the peace with Carthage, but this order is probably incorrect.
[3] Diodorus (82.3) and Plutarch (34.2) both set the boundary between the Punic and Syracusan zones at a river Λύκος. This is probably a mistake

and all Punic aid to Greek tyrants was forbidden. Emigration from the Punic zone to Syracuse was to be permitted.[1] The meaning of the clause recorded only by Diodorus, that τὰς μὲν Ἑλληνίδας πόλεις ἁπάσας ἐλευθέρας εἶναι is not clear. The clause may refer either to the Greek cities in the Greek zone, or to the Greek cities in the Punic zone. In the first instance it may have been inserted at the request of Carthage, because she did not want to see Syracusan domination of the Greek zone. In the second instance it may have been insisted upon by Timoleon, who wished that cities in the Punic zone occupied by his forces (for example, Entella, D.S. 73.2) should retain some form of autonomy despite Punic overlordship. Alternatively the clause could refer to the cities of both zones.[2]

I think that the evidence available is too meagre for us to be able to draw any firm conclusions. Mazzarino[3] thinks that the clause refers only to the Greek cities in the Greek zone. He argues (pp. 161–2) that it would be absurd for the clause to include the Greek cities in the Punic zone as well, because if these cities were free, there would be no need to permit emigration from the Punic zone to Syracuse. But this is unconvincing: even if the Greek cities in the Punic zone were free, the emigra-

for the river Ἁλυκός (cf. D.S. 15.17.5), the modern R. Platani, which enters the sea just west of Heraclea Minoa. G. Navarra has argued that the ancient Λύκος is the modern R. Platani, while the ancient Ἁλυκός is the modern R. Salso, which enters the sea at Licata (*Città sicane, sicule e greche nella zona di Gela* (Palermo 1964), pp. 70–5; for an assessment of this work, see A. G. Woodhead in *JHS* 87 (1967), pp. 188–9). This is not the place to discuss the many arguments which Navarra puts forward in support of his main idea that ancient Gela was situated at modern Licata; but he is almost certainly wrong in suggesting that the Halycus of 374 (Dionysius I's treaty with the Carthaginians) and the Lycus of 339 (Timoleon's treaty) cannot be the same river for the reason that the victory at the battle of the R. Crimisus will have enabled Timoleon to push the Carthaginians back from the R. Salso to the R. Platani (p. 84). This argument ignores the success achieved by Gisco against Timoleon in the campaign after the battle of the R. Crimisus. Navarra also lays great stress on the fact that Plutarch and Diodorus represent the Carthaginians as begging for peace (p. 83): but little weight should be attached to these statements when both authors are biased in favour of Timoleon.

[1] Cf. D.S. 19.2.7–8.

[2] As Navarra argues: *Città sicane, sicule e greche*, p. 83 n. 19.

[3] S. Mazzarino, *Introduzione alle guerre puniche. Saggi e Ricerche* XIII (Catania 1947), pp. 49–50.

tion clause would still be useful in that it would allow people living in the Punic zone, but not in a Greek city there, to emigrate to Syracuse.

Mazzarino also argues (pp. 161–2) that if the Greek cities in the Punic zone were free under the terms of Timoleon's treaty, then the clause in the treaty of 313, whereby Heraclea, Selinus and Himera were to be subject to Carthage καθὰ καὶ προϋπῆρχον (D.S. 19.71.7), becomes unintelligible. He would be correct if we could be certain that the vague expression καθὰ καὶ προϋπῆρχον does refer to Timoleon's treaty. Unfortunately the expression means no more than 'as they used to be', instead of 'as they used to be under Timoleon's treaty', which is required by Mazzarino's interpretation.

Those who think that the Greek cities in the Punic zone remained independent under Timoleon's treaty might argue that it seems strange for the three cities to be mentioned as coming under Punic control in 313, if they were already under that control at the time; yet it is quite natural for them to be mentioned if they were independent before the treaty of 313. In this case καθὰ καὶ προϋπῆρχον would refer to the years before Timoleon's expedition.[1]

Considering the seriousness of her defeat at the battle of the R. Crimisus, Carthage exacted generous terms in her treaty with Timoleon. It seems that once her attempt to dominate all Sicily through tyrants had clearly failed, she was willing to retain only her own zone, as before. We hear of no more attempts at

[1] By comparing Diodorus 16.82 with 19.71.7 Manni reaches the strange conclusion that under the terms of Timoleon's treaty all the Greek cities in Sicily were to recognize Syracusan hegemony, except for Heraclea, Selinus and Himera, which were to be under Punic control ('Agatocle e la politica estera di Siracusa', *Kokalos* 12 (1966), 152 and note 32).

R. van Compernolle seems to suggest that argument over this clause in Timoleon's treaty is quite unnecessary, because the only Greek cities remaining in Sicily at this time were all in the Greek zone. According to him, not one city in the Punic zone was thought of as Greek any longer, with the result that τὰς μὲν Ἑλληνίδας πόλεις ἁπάσας can refer only to the cities of the Greek zone. This is an ingenious argument, but I doubt whether Selinus, for example, had ceased to be considered a Greek city in c. 340 ('La clause territoriale du traité de 306/5 conclu entre Agathokles de Syracuse et Carthage', *Revue Belge de Philologie et d'Histoire* 32 (1954), 403–6 and 409).

aggrandizement during Timoleon's lifetime. As long as the cities of the Greek zone were not strong, united and hostile, but remained autonomous and peaceful, Carthage was content. She had no burning desire to acquire an empire by force.

Her failures in Sicily during Timoleon's lifetime seem to have been the fault of her commanders. Certainly Carthage did not fail to achieve her objectives because of lack of resources: all her expeditions were large and lavishly equipped. But her commanders did not serve her so well. The Punic squadron at Rhegium failed to prevent Timoleon's force landing in Sicily, while later Hanno failed to prevent the landing of Timoleon's reinforcements. Mago seems to have been a weak commander: his failure to take any action at Syracuse and his mysterious withdrawal were inexcusable blunders. Hasdrubal and Hamilcar were the victims of Timoleon's speed and surprise tactics at the R. Crimisus.[1] Only Gisco seems to have fought Timoleon successfully: he upheld his fine reputation (D.S. 81.3).

[1] I know of no evidence for Warmington's statement (*Carthage*, p. 123) that Hasdrubal was executed for his failure at the battle of the R. Crimisus. Finley also states this (*Ancient Sicily*, p. 97).

CHAPTER 6

Timoleon and the Sicilian tyrants

The policies of Hicetas

Hicetas appears as the villain in Plutarch's *Timoleon*, playing the same kind of role as Heracleides in *Dion*. His vices are continually contrasted with the virtues of Timoleon.[1] Even so, the black portrait of him which emerges from the Life as a whole is probably accurate in many respects. Diodorus' portrait of him seems less biased.

Hicetas was a Syracusan who had been a friend of Dion. We first hear of him in *Dion* (58.8–10), where Plutarch describes how after the fall of Callippus Hicetas was persuaded by Dion's enemies to put Andromache, Arete and Dion's baby son on a ship bound for the Peloponnese, and to give orders that they should be murdered during the voyage. Westlake[2] has sensibly suggested that this order may have been invented later by Timoleon to discredit Hicetas. In *Timoleon* Plutarch tells how Hicetas was put to death in revenge for these murders (33.3–4). But Hicetas would only have been needlessly discrediting himself by ordering the murders. Dion's sister and widow would not have been able to hinder him in Sicily, while Dion's son was only a baby. Once all three were in Greece they would not affect events in Sicily. Then Hicetas is hardly likely to have been chosen as leader by the Syracusan aristocrats, if he was known to have given orders for the murder of Dion's relations. But it is easy to see that Timoleon, or some other person wishing to discredit Hicetas, could have spread the story of Hicetas as the murderer of Dion's relations without difficulty. Hicetas did put the two women and the baby on board ship, but for some reason – perhaps pirates, or a storm – these three relations of Dion were never heard of again. There would be no evidence either to confirm or refute the charge made by Hicetas' opponents.

---

[1] See pp. 5–10.
[2] *Tyrants*, pp. 11–12. Compare H. A. Holden, *Plutarch's Life of Timoleon* (Cambridge 1898), p. 135.

At some time between the fall of Callippus and the arrival of
Timoleon in Sicily Hicetas seized power at Leontini, and seems
to have acquired a powerful mercenary force.[1] After he had
seized power at Leontini, he received an appeal from οἱ βέλτιστοι
καὶ γνωριμώτατοι of the Syracusan exiles, and was chosen by
them as their leader against Dionysius (Plut. 1.6). At about the
same time Hicetas concluded an agreement with the Carthaginians (Plut. 2.3; D.S. 67.1), and laid siege to Syracuse. Since
his supplies seem to have been inadequate to sustain a long siege,
he found himself compelled to retreat to Leontini. But as he did
this, Dionysius sallied out from Ortygia and attacked him.
Hicetas not only withstood Dionysius' attack, but also routed
the tyrant's mercenaries and then made a dash for Syracuse,
where he was able to occupy the whole city except Ortygia
(D.S. 68.1–3; cf. Plut. 9.3).

As Plutarch says (2.3), Hicetas' aim in besieging Syracuse
seems to have been to capture the city for himself, rather than to
hand it over to the Syracusan exiles. At the outset his difficulties
were twofold. He needed to convince the Syracusans that he
wished to become their liberator rather than their tyrant; and
he was keen to acquire all possible aid, without incurring too
many obligations in return. Thus he was keen to ally with the
Carthaginians, because he thought that the threat of Punic
intervention would discourage Corinth from sending help to the

---

[1] Westlake (*Tyrants*, pp. 12–13) suggested that Hicetas was not acknowledged tyrant of Leontini when Timoleon arrived in Sicily, because he is
described by Plutarch as τὸν δυναστεύοντα τῶν Λεοντίνων (1.6), rather than
as τύραννος. Berve believed this to be an unsatisfactory view (*Gnomon*
25 (1953), 528). Certainly Plutarch does not distinguish finely between
τύραννος and δυνάστης, although the former term carries with it more
unpleasant undertones (cf. Plut. 4.5; 6.6; 7.2; 34.4). Then Sicily was in so
disordered a state at the time of Timoleon's arrival there that it is hard to
see how Hicetas could have been anything other than a tyrant. The tone of
Plut. 1.5–6 implies that the opponents of Dionysius II were acutely em-
barrassed at being forced to call to their aid another tyrant, Hicetas, but that
only a tyrant could provide effective help.

In the list of Thearodokoi at Epidaurus there is a reference to Λεοντίνοις·
Ἱκέτας Νικάνορος. The relevant part of this inscription (*IG* iv², 1.95) is
discussed by G. de Sanctis, 'I Thearodokoi d'Epidauro', *Atti della Accad.
Sc. di Torino* 47 (1911–12), 442–50. This article has been reprinted in G. de
Sanctis, *Scritti Minori*, Vol. 1, pp. 171–9 (*Storia e Letteratura* 99, Rome
1966).

Syracusan exiles, and because he wanted the help of Punic ships. But he did not request Punic help at Syracuse itself at first, because he wanted to keep the city after its capture. He strongly opposed Timoleon's expedition, because it might disrupt his plan of gaining all Syracuse for himself (cf. Plut. 7.4–6).

As it turned out, Timoleon's expedition did indeed disrupt Hicetas' plans. At Rhegium Timoleon refused to be drawn by Hicetas' suspicious offer that he should send his troops back to Corinth, and should himself σύμβουλον ἥκειν παρ' Ἱκέτην καὶ κοινωνὸν εὖ διαπεπραγμένων ἁπάντων (Plut. 9.6). Timoleon then slipped through the Punic blockade to land at Tauromenium. His first encounter with Hicetas, at the battle of Adranum, will have been a severe shock to the latter. Timoleon unexpectedly put to flight a superior force composed of Hicetas' best mercenaries (D.S. 68.9–10; Plut. 12).

Westlake suggests that Timoleon was able to surprise Hicetas' army so successfully because Hicetas never expected to be attacked by Timoleon, and because he did not regard Timoleon as his rival for the possession of Syracuse.[1] Originally it may have been the intention of the Corinthian government that Timoleon should co-operate with Hicetas in freeing Syracuse. And Hicetas may have expected that Timoleon would co-operate in this action, with the result that he would not be prepared for an attack at Adranum. But this suggestion can only be right if Hicetas knew that Timoleon had been invited to intervene in the dispute of the people of Adranum. If Plutarch's account (12.1–2) is followed, it would seem reasonable to assume that Hicetas did know of possible intervention by Timoleon. However, Diodorus' brief narrative (68.9) differs considerably from that of Plutarch, in that Diodorus represents Hicetas as attacking Adranum because it was a city hostile to him. In these circumstances Hicetas might not know that the citizens of Adranum had appealed to Timoleon for help. We cannot tell which of the two narratives is the more accurate.

Westlake's suggestion seems uncertain for a further reason, in that it assumes that Hicetas will have expected Timoleon to co-operate with him. I doubt whether Hicetas will have expected

[1] *Tyrants*, pp. 15–16.

co-operation. Since he had received news of Timoleon's departure from Corinth (Plut. 9.4), Hicetas is also likely to have heard
of the Corinthians' hostility towards him (Plut. 7.7). If this news
was not sufficient to show him that Timoleon had no intention
of joining him, Timoleon's rejection of all overtures at Rhegium
must have made his attitude clear: both the Corinthians and
Timoleon recognized Hicetas' selfish policy (Plut. 9.5–6).[1] Then
Hicetas would hardly have been so keen to prevent Timoleon
crossing to Sicily, if he thought that Timoleon would be an
ally; nor would he have even tried to expel Timoleon once the
Corinthian force had reached Tauromenium (Plut. 11.2–3).
Altogether, therefore, it would seem sensible to reject the suggestion that he was not ready for battle at Adranum because he
did not expect to be attacked by Timoleon.

After the battle of Adranum, whether the narrative of Plutarch
is followed (that Timoleon took over Ortygia from Dionysius),
or whether the narrative of Diodorus is followed (that Timoleon
very soon captured the outlying parts of Syracuse), Hicetas
realized that it would not be possible for him to capture all
Syracuse without considerable help, having failed in his attempt
to have Timoleon assassinated (Plut. 16.5–9). The arrival of
Mago with a huge fleet in the Great Harbour (Plut. 17.2; D.S.
69.3) was an important turning-point in Hicetas' career. No
longer was it possible for him to pose to the Syracusan populace
as a liberator; his aim of gaining Syracuse for himself was now
fully exposed (cf. Nep. *Tim.* 2.3). On the other hand, it was no
longer possible for him to envisage keeping Syracuse to himself

---

[1] From the historical point of view the reading of the Budé text at Plut.
9.8 seems unlikely: ἐδόκει δ' ἀμήχανον ὑπερβαλέσθαι καὶ τὰς αὐτόθι τῶν
βαρβάρων ναῦς διπλασίας ἐφορμούσας καὶ τὴν ἐκεῖ μεθ' Ἱκέτου δύναμιν,
ᾗ συστρατεύσοντες ἥκοιεν. This is translated as: 'Et il leur semblait impossible de vaincre les navires des barbares, qui se trouvaient devant eux en
nombre double des leurs, et là-bas l'armée d'Hicétas, à laquelle ils étaient
venus se joindre pour combattre à côté d'elle!' As I have shown, Timoleon
had made it quite clear that he had no intention of becoming an ally of
Hicetas. This point is made by A. J. Kronenberg, 'Ad Plutarchi Vitas',
Mnemosyne 5 (1937), 306.

The Teubner text reads . . . καὶ τὴν ἐκεῖ μεθ' Ἱκέτου δύναμιν ᾗ ⟨συ⟩στρα-
τεύσοντες ἥκοιεν. The manuscripts read στρατηγήσαντες, where the Budé
and Teubner texts read συστρατεύσοντες and ⟨συ⟩στρατεύσοντες respectively.

once the whole city had been captured. His obligations to the Carthaginians, previously limited to some naval help, were now too great for the Carthaginian government to be content to grant him all Syracuse.

It was probably the weakness of Mago, combined with the conflicting interests of Mago and Hicetas, which led to the failure of the coalition between the two commanders. Each commander wished to keep Syracuse for himself after the fall of the city, and therefore distrusted the other. This distrust was not helped by a number of setbacks which began to occur after Mago's arrival. Light craft still seem to have supplied Ortygia despite the Punic blockade (Plut. 18.1). A combined expedition led by Mago and Hicetas set out to attack Timoleon's camp at Catania, but it had to return even before reaching Catania, because Timoleon's men had sallied out of Ortygia and had taken Achradina (Plut. 18.2–7). Then a Punic squadron under Hanno failed to prevent Timoleon's reinforcements from Corinth landing in Sicily (Plut. 19.2–6; cf. D.S. 69.4). Finally Mago was disturbed by rumours that Hicetas' Greek mercenaries might desert, and he may have feared that Hicetas would conclude some agreement with Timoleon.

Whatever the truth of the matter, Mago mysteriously disappeared with his whole force, leaving Hicetas to continue the siege alone (Plut. 20.11; D.S. 69.5). The next stage of the siege is also mysterious. Plutarch describes how Hicetas was quite prepared to resist any attack by Timoleon, and how he clung to those parts of the city still in his possession (21.2). He then goes on to describe how Timoleon attacked Hicetas' men from three directions (21.2–3). The men put up little resistance, and Timoleon captured all Syracuse, without the loss of a single man killed or wounded (21.4–5). This account is strangely inconsistent: it is impossible that on the one hand Hicetas should be keen to retain his position in the city, but that nevertheless Timoleon should capture the position without any losses.

There is certainly no reason why Hicetas should not have resisted Timoleon. The morale of his army may have been low after Mago's departure, but the total force will still have been large.[1]

---

[1] See pp. 62–3 and 103.

It is unlikely that many mercenaries did desert to Timoleon, since Hicetas later retreated to Leontini μετὰ δυνάμεως ἀξιολόγου, and successfully resisted an attack by Timoleon (D.S. 72.2).

Westlake's solution of the difficulty may be right.[1] He suggests that the details of the attack made on Hicetas' position by Timoleon, according to Plutarch, may be correct, but that Hicetas and Timoleon had agreed that no more than a show of resistance should be made by Hicetas' men. The speech of Timoleon's mercenary in Plutarch (20.7–9) shows that Timoleon may have been willing to negotiate; and this possibility is strengthened by the fact that Timoleon cannot have been certain of defeating Hicetas' large army in a pitched battle. Hicetas sensed that the morale of his army was low, and realized that his chances of gaining all Syracuse were thin now that he had been deserted by his Punic allies. All the same his position at Leontini was still open; he may have felt that it would be better to secure that position, abandoning the siege of Syracuse. Both he and Timoleon will have preferred to stage token fighting rather than to make a formal agreement. Hicetas will have wanted his reputation to suffer as little as possible. Likewise Timoleon would have preferred to conceal the fact that he had come to an agreement with his tyrant opponent. Then he would not have wanted to bind himself by a treaty, because he would be keen to eliminate Hicetas as quickly as possible after he had set Syracusan affairs in order.

Certainly this is what seems to have happened. In whatever way Hicetas did contrive his retreat from Syracuse to Leontini, it is clear that his army remained both sizeable and loyal. Yet Timoleon realized that Sicily could never be quiet until Hicetas had been eliminated: not only was Hicetas still powerful, but he would also join any opponents of Timoleon. Syracuse was not yet strong enough to be certain of withstanding the tyrant's forces in pitched battle. But Diodorus and Plutarch differ on the action taken by Timoleon. According to Diodorus he attacked Leontini, but was repulsed, and so broke off the siege (D.S. 72.2). While he then turned aside to attack Engyum (72.3), Hicetas led out his large force and attempted to besiege Syracuse. He then retreated swiftly to Leontini again, πολλοὺς δὲ τῶν

---

[1] *Tyrants*, pp. 33–5.

στρατιωτῶν ἀποβαλών (72.4). We do not know how these losses were caused. But according to Plutarch, Timoleon marched to Leontini and Ἱκέτην μὲν ἠνάγκασεν ἀποστάντα Καρχηδονίων ὁμολογῆσαι τὰς ἀκροπόλεις κατασκάψειν καὶ βιοτεύσειν ἰδιώτην ἐν Λεοντίνοις (24.1).

This narrative of Plutarch seems impossible to reconcile with Diodorus' next reference to Hicetas. According to him, before the Crimisus campaign Timoleon ἔχων δὲ πόλεμον πρὸς Ἱκέταν διελύσατο πρὸς αὐτὸν καὶ προσλαβόμενος τοὺς μετὰ τούτου στρατιώτας οὐ μετρίως ηὔξησε τὴν ἰδίαν δύναμιν (77.5). It is possible that neither author has told the full story of the relations of Timoleon and Hicetas between Timoleon's capture of all Syracuse and the battle of the R. Crimisus, with the result that the two narratives may not be contradictory. It is quite understandable that Diodorus should not have mentioned the agreement between Timoleon and Hicetas recorded by Plutarch, because it is clear that the terms were never carried out. Hicetas contributed a large body of troops to the Crimisus campaign, and had a large army after the battle of the R. Crimisus too. He despised Timoleon for having only a few soldiers at Calauria (Plut. 31.2), and suffered the loss of 1,000 men at the R. Lamyrias (Plut. 31.8). Then excavations do not suggest that any fortifications were pulled down at Leontini in the mid fourth century.[1]

It would be rash to argue that the agreement between Timoleon and Hicetas is a fabrication.[2] There seems no good reason why Plutarch or his source should have made up the story of the agreement. Rather it would be better to consider the occasions on which Timoleon could have imposed terms on Hicetas. The first of these is before Hicetas' retreat from Syracuse. Sordi has put forward the view that the agreement in Plutarch is in fact the agreement made on this occasion.[3] The second of the two occasions is after Hicetas has been compelled to retreat swiftly to Leontini again with the loss of many men (D.S. 72.4). It is

[1] G. Rizza, 'Leontini: Campagne di Scavi 1950–1951 e 1951–1952: La necropoli della Valle S. Mauro; le fortificazioni meridionali della città e la porta di Siracusa', *NSc* 9 (1955), 375.

[2] As Westlake argues in *Tyrants*, pp. 36–7.

[3] Sordi, pp. 41–6. Her idea is approved of by H. Berve, *Gnomon* 35 (1963), 380.

hard to see how Hicetas could have lost many men except in a battle with Timoleon's forces.[1]

In my view it seems more likely that Plutarch is recording an agreement made on the second occasion, rather than one made on the first occasion. Probably there was no formal agreement made between Hicetas and Timoleon when the former first retreated from Syracuse. And if there was an agreement, it is unlikely that Timoleon was then able to impose on Hicetas such harsh terms as Plutarch records. Hicetas may have given up his intention to capture Syracuse, but there is no evidence to suggest that he was then so weak as to agree that he should be stripped of all power. But Timoleon would be in a position to impose harsh terms after Hicetas had unsuccessfully besieged Syracuse again, and had apparently been defeated in battle. The assignment of an agreement recorded by Plutarch to this occasion has the further advantage that it confirms his arrangement of events. Those who follow Sordi in thinking that the agreement was made on the occasion of Hicetas' first retreat from Syracuse, must explain why Plutarch narrates the event out of order.

The agreement recorded by Plutarch cannot be assigned with certainty, but it is not of great importance in any event, because its terms were never carried out. Hicetas still had a large army at the time of the Crimisus campaign. There seems no reason to doubt Diodorus' statement that Hicetas did hand over this force to Timoleon (77.5). No such statement appears in Plutarch, but that is understandable when Plutarch implies that the terms of the agreement were actually carried out (with the result that Hicetas was only an ἰδιώτης), and when he ignores the whole contribution of the Sicilian allies to the victory at the R. Crimisus, except in one passing reference (27.7). In fact Timoleon's force was so outnumbered by the Punic army that the contribution of the allies – therefore of Hicetas, who provided many troops for the allied contingent – will have been of considerable importance.

[1] If there was a battle at this stage it seems strange that the tradition favourable to Timoleon has not taken the opportunity of recording the victory more fully. Yet I would guess that the sources' silence is understandable if the victory was won by Timoleon's lieutenants, not by Timoleon himself. The arrangement of D.S. 72.3–5 could suggest that Timoleon was at Engyum at the time of Hicetas' sudden attack on Syracuse.

We do not know Hicetas' reasons for ending his war with Timoleon and lending him troops to repel the Carthaginians. Certainly the action was not characteristic of a tyrant who showed that he was willing to use Punic help in order to gain his own ends, both before and after the battle of the R. Crimisus. It is possible that he wished to revenge himself on the Carthaginians for deserting him before the capture of Syracuse. But it is perhaps a little more likely that he both appreciated the seriousness of the Punic invasion, and realized that if Timoleon did not repel the invasion, there would be no force left in Sicily to prevent the Carthaginians sweeping across the island and eliminating all other rulers. Thus he may have seen that his only chance of survival lay in the repulse of the Carthaginians by Timoleon. Hicetas cannot have viewed the Punic threat lightly. If he had regarded the Carthaginians as no more than a band of raiders, who would easily be routed by Timoleon, then he would have kept his whole army at Leontini, and would have taken advantage of Timoleon's absence in the west of the island to attack Syracuse. Sensibly, however, he did not do this.[1]

Plutarch says that after the battle of the R. Crimisus Mamercus, Hicetas and the Carthaginians formed an alliance against Timoleon (30.4). It seems that after the defeat of the Carthaginians Hicetas and Timoleon both considered that they might revert to the policies which they had pursued before the Crimisus campaign. With Syracuse now much more secure than before, and with conditions in Sicily now favourable for the introduction of colonists to strengthen the citizen body, Timoleon made it plain that he intended to crush the remaining tyrannies. Hicetas, on the other hand, realized the advantages which Timoleon had been afforded by his victory, and set himself to defeat this implacable enemy of tyrants.

Plutarch is the only author who gives us any information on

[1] N. E. Cappellano (*Sulla venuta di Timoleonte in Sicilia* (Catania 1903), pp. 55–6) suggests that the agreement recorded at Plut. 24.1 relates to the occasion when Hicetas handed over his forces to Timoleon before the Crimisus campaign. This is an ingenious idea, but it seems difficult to reconcile with Plutarch's statement that Timoleon had actually compelled Hicetas to give up his alliance with the Carthaginians. If Cappellano's suggestion were correct, no such compulsion would be needed.

the campaign of Hicetas, Mamercus and the Carthaginians against Timoleon. Gisco, who led the Punic forces, seems to have been an efficient commander,[1] and two victories over Timoleon's men are mentioned by Plutarch (30.6). We do not hear of any Punic aid being given to Hicetas specifically. This may have been because the alliance was unsatisfactory. The three different members will have had different aims, while Hicetas and the Carthaginians will probably have distrusted each other, after Mago had deserted Hicetas, and Hicetas' men had fought the Carthaginians at the battle of the R. Crimisus.

With a force of only cavalry and light-armed troops Timoleon later defeated Hicetas at the R. Lamyrias, killing 1,000 of his men. He attacked Hicetas on this occasion in retaliation for a profitable raid which the latter had made on Syracusan territory (Plut. 31.2–8). Soon after the battle he marched to Leontini and captured alive Hicetas, his son, and his ἱππάρχης Euthymus. All three were handed over to Timoleon by Hicetas' own men (Plut. 32.1). So in all probability Hicetas was finally defeated because of the disloyalty of his own mercenaries. These men will have decided that Hicetas' cause was lost, that they had no chance of further employment from him, and that they would do best to transfer their allegiance to Timoleon. The booty which they had gained in Syracusan territory (31.2) will have been lost in the rout at the R. Lamyrias (31.8). They will have served under Timoleon in the Crimisus campaign, and will have been able to appreciate his qualities as a general and as a commander of mercenaries.

Timoleon put to death Hicetas and his son ὡς τύραννοι καὶ προδόται. Euthymus and the wives and daughters of Hicetas and his friends were also executed (Plut. 32.2; 33; Dion 58.10).[2] In killing Hicetas and his principal followers Timoleon wanted to show his determination to rid Sicily of tyranny. He may have executed Hicetas' son as a precaution against a later revival of tyranny. Hicetas died because his aims differed completely from those of Timoleon. He wished to retain power for himself, while

[1] See Polyaenus 5.11. Unfortunately he gives no details of Gisco's achievements.
[2] See also pp. 113–14.

Timoleon wished to restore ἐλευθερία and αὐτονομία to the cities of Sicily. Timoleon rightly realized that his aims could never be secured until Hicetas fell.[1]

The fall of Dionysius II

The period from the battle of Adranum to the capture of all Syracuse is the most vexed period of Timoleon's career, because the sources treating it display a direct conflict of evidence. There is little that the modern scholar can reasonably do with such material, beyond discussing the versions of our two main sources and reviewing some of the explanations put forward for the contradictory narratives.

Strangely, Diodorus (68.9–10) and Plutarch (12) agree substantially on the events of the battle of Adranum, but their narratives then disagree completely. In Diodorus' version Timoleon takes advantage of his unexpected victory over Hicetas to make a forced march to Syracuse, where he occupies the outskirts of the city (68.11). Ortygia is still held by Dionysius, and Achradina and Neapolis are still held by Hicetas' men (69.3).[2]

[1] Diodorus makes only a single reference to Hicetas in the period after the battle of the R. Crimisus, where he says that Timoleon τὸν μὲν Ἱκέταν καταπολεμήσας ἐθανάτωσε (82.4). He differs from Plutarch in placing the defeat and death of Hicetas after Timoleon's peace with the Carthaginians, rather than before it. Plutarch's order is perhaps the correct one, since in his narrative Punic troops fight for Mamercus at the battle of the R. Abolus after Hicetas' death (34.1).

According to Diodorus the population of Leontini was later removed to Syracuse (82.7), and from this Sordi feels able to argue that the hostile sources' portrait of Hicetas as a tyrant is incorrect (*Diodori Liber XVI*, p. 144). The city would seem to have been occupied again only a few years later (cf. Justin 22.2.2). T. Lenschau also takes a fairly generous view of Hicetas (*RE* 8 (1913) *s.v.* 'Hiketas', cols. 1594–6).

In reviewing M. Sordi, *Timoleonte*, Berve rightly rejects her idea that Hicetas opposed Timoleon because he pursued a policy of 'Sicily for the Sicilians' (see especially Sordi, p. 32). This idea ignores Hicetas' use of Punic aid, and fails to appreciate his selfish aims (H. Berve, *Gnomon* 35 (1963), 380).

[2] On the topography of Syracuse, see most recently H.-P. Drögemüller, *Syrakus: Zur Topographie und Geschichte einer griechischen Stadt* (Heidelberg 1969 – *Gymnasium* Beihefte, Heft 6), esp. p. 106. This work has little to say on fourth-century Syracuse, and not all of what it does say is satisfactory. Yet no other work seems available. Figure 20 (p. 101) *Syrakus seit Dionysios*

According to Diodorus, this situation, which came about in 345/4, became worse in 344/3, when a huge Punic force occupied the Great Harbour (69.3). But the Carthaginians mysteriously departed in the same year that they had come (69.5); Hicetas was then left isolated, and so withdrew, to enable Timoleon to take all Syracuse except Ortygia (69.6). Finally, in 343/2, Timoleon frightened Dionysius into giving up Ortygia, and sent him to Corinth (70.1–3).

In Plutarch's longer version, Dionysius gave up Ortygia to Timoleon shortly after the battle of Adranum (13.3). Timoleon therefore infiltrated 400 men into the besieged fortress (13.4); these took over the fortress with all its equipment (13.5–6), and joined up with Dionysius' mercenary force (13.7). Meanwhile Dionysius slipped through Hicetas' blockade to Timoleon's camp. From there he departed to Corinth (13.7–8). Hicetas continued his blockade (16.5), but with such small chance of eventual success that he called in a huge Punic force under Mago (17.1–3). Although the defenders of Ortygia were continually harassed (17.4), they were able to hold out, and were supplied by small craft which came from Catania and slipped through the blockade (18.1). Hicetas and Mago therefore decided to capture Catania, and sailed from Syracuse with a sizeable force (18.2). So negligent a force remained that Timoleon's men successfully sallied out of Ortygia and captured Achradina (18.3–5). This loss led Hicetas and Mago to abandon their attack on Catania (18.6–7). Then they were discouraged again by the news that Timoleon's reinforcements had evaded a Punic blockade and had landed in Sicily (19). Timoleon began to advance to Syracuse from Messana (20.1). By this time Mago had become so disheartened by adverse news, and by suspected disloyalty on the part of Hicetas' mercenaries (20.2–10), that he mysteriously departed from Syracuse with all his forces (20.11), the day before Timoleon reached the city (21.1). Timoleon attacked Hicetas from three sides (21.2–3), and dislodged the enemy forces without the loss of any of his own men (21.4–5), with the result that he gained all Syracuse.

I and Figure 21 (p. 107) *Bereich der Neapolis* are of some use. Good plans of Syracuse are to be found in the T.C.I. *Guida d'Italia: Sicilia* (Milan 1968).

Nepos agrees with Plutarch in placing Dionysius' departure to Corinth before Timoleon's major conflict with Hicetas over Syracuse (2.1–3).

Faced with such contradictory narratives it would be most convenient to eliminate one version by showing that it could never have happened, and must therefore be a fabrication. Westlake pursues this line of argument, attempting to show the impossible nature of Diodorus' narrative, but in my view he has dismissed this version of events too swiftly. He rightly considers it likely that Timoleon's force, having already covered 340 stadia (Plut. 12.5) from Tauromenium to Adranum in about one and a half days' marching (Plut. 12.5; D.S. 68.10), would not be able to continue the further 85 km or so to Syracuse at full speed immediately after the battle (D.S. 68.11). He therefore considers that Diodorus' account is almost incredible, even if it is assumed that Hicetas stopped for some days at Leontini after his defeat, and did not warn his troops in Syracuse that Timoleon was marching towards the city.[1]

However it seems possible to argue that Diodorus' account is plausible. Westlake's objections to the account are reasonable, but they do not decisively demonstrate the falsehood of the narrative. The manoeuvres which Diodorus describes are very characteristic of Timoleon, since the latter was a master of unconventional, surprise tactics. He employed such tactics at Rhegium (Plut. 10.3–6; D.S. 68.5–7) and at the battle of Adranum, and was to employ them again at the battle of the R. Crimisus (Plut. 27.6; D.S. 79.5). It would be quite reasonable to expect him to make a dash for Syracuse after routing Hicetas' force.

[1] H. D. Westlake, *Tyrants*, p. 18.

The account of Plutarch (12.5) would suggest that Timoleon marched from Tauromenium to Adranum by way of Randazzo and Bronte. The fact that he traversed χαλεπὰ χωρία is mentioned, while he may have attacked Hicetas from an unexpected quarter (see Westlake, *Tyrants*, p. 15 and note 2; cf. D.S. 68.10). By going west of Etna Timoleon would also avoid any contact with Mamercus.

On distances see p. 71. Tauromenium to Adranum is 79 km by road via Francavilla di Sicilia, Moio Alcantara, Randazzo and Bronte (Foglio 26). Adranum to Syracuse is 88 km by road via Paternò, Stazione di Motta S. Anastasia, Strada 192, and then Strada 114 along the coast to Syracuse (Fogli 26, 27).

If there was such a dash, it need not have been the incredible display of physical endurance which Westlake supposes. Diodorus writes that Timoleon moved on to Syracuse παραχρῆμα, but his account is abbreviated, and such an expression could cover the events of a number of days. There is certainly no need (as Westlake seems to imagine) to take παραχρῆμα as evidence that Timoleon marched from Adranum to Syracuse as soon as the battle ended.[1] Adranum is about 85 km distant from Syracuse by road today; if Timoleon covered this distance at full speed – δρομαῖος τὴν ὁδὸν διανύσας, as Diodorus says – he might have taken two full days' marching over the journey. (We know that he covered the 80 km or so from Tauromenium to Adranum in a day and a half.) Thus even if he had rested his men for the night of the battle, and for the following day and night, and had then marched on Syracuse, he would have reached the city late on the third day after the battle was fought.

Such a programme would indeed require physical endurance, but it would not be impossible. We know that later Timoleon led an army composed of his professional mercenaries, allies and of Syracusan citizens (who would perhaps not have been very fit) to the territory of Akragas in eight days (Plut. 25.5), and that after quelling a mutiny of part of the army, he took the remainder an unspecified distance to the R. Crimisus (25.6), where the Punic army was immediately attacked and beaten. Despite the many uncertain factors which prevent our calculating how far this army would have marched each day, it seems reasonable to suggest that it must have marched a little under 30 km each day to go from Syracuse along the coastal route to the territory of Akragas in eight days.[2]

---

[1] In an abbreviated account of earlier events by Plutarch we are told that Dion drove out Dionysius and was then assassinated εὐθύς. In fact the events covered by this εὐθύς are about three years apart (*Tim.* 1.2). Then Plutarch's remark at 26.4 that crowns of pine were introduced at the Isthmian Games οὐ πάλαι would only agree with Broneer's conclusion (p. 263) that such crowns were introduced during the second century B.C., if οὐ πάλαι is taken to cover about two centuries or more! But it may be that Plutarch has made a slip. Cf. *Mor.* 676D and see O. Broneer, 'The Isthmian victory crown', *AJA* 66 (1962), 259–63; strangely this article does not take into account the remark at Plut. *Tim.* 26.4.

[2] For a discussion of this march, see p. 74.

Two other examples of an army's physical endurance in Sicily may be mentioned briefly. First, Diodorus tells how in 396 Himilco took his men from Messana to Tauromenium along the coast (about 50 km) swiftly enough to keep pace with his ships, which sailed alongside (14.59.3). Having arrived at Tauromenium, Himilco found the direct route to Catania blocked by lava, and so led his men swiftly διὰ τῆς μεσογείου to reach Catania in only two days (14.61.4). Presumably Himilco went around Etna by way of Randazzo, Bronte and Adrano; if so, he would have covered over 110 km in two days' march, immediately after he had advanced from Messana to Tauromenium.[1] Secondly, it seems well authenticated that Landi's troops, having been defeated by Garibaldi at the battle of Calatafimi in 1860, retreated during the night after the battle and covered the 35 miles (that is, about 55 km) from Calatafimi to Palermo in just over 24 hours.[2]

So an advance on Syracuse from Adranum a few days after the victory would have required endurance on the part of Timoleon's men, but it would not have been impossible.

Westlake implies that Hicetas might have taken some steps either to prevent Timoleon's advance, or to warn his troops at Syracuse that Timoleon was about to attack the city. But both these ideas assume that Hicetas expected Timoleon's advance, and that he was in a position to stop it. Yet it would be a mistake to imagine that the troops who had fought under Hicetas at Adranum were ready for action again at once. They had been forced to fight immediately after their day's march, and were then put to flight at night. By morning they would probably have been dispersed over the neighbouring countryside. Their camp was lost, their equipment gone, and nearly a fifth of their number were killed or captured. They were about 85 km from Syracuse and about 65 km from Leontini: it would have taken a fit man, rested and fed, at least a day and a half to reach Leontini

[1] Messana to Tauromenium is 51.6 km by road along the coast (Foglio 26). Tauromenium to Catania is 114.8 km by road via Francavilla di Sicilia, Moio Alcantara, Randazzo, Bronte, Adrano, Paternò and Misterbianco (Foglio 26).

[2] G. M. Trevelyan, *Garibaldi and the Thousand* (London 1965; first edition 1909), pp. 238–9.

by a forced march; a hungry, demoralized fugitive who had lost his way in the dark would have taken much longer.

I do not believe that it would have been possible for Hicetas to re-assemble, rest and re-equip these men in a very short time. It would have been possible for Timoleon to advance a day or two after the battle, and for his forces to reach Syracuse before those of Hicetas, as Diodorus says. Once there Timoleon could certainly have taken Hicetas' garrison by surprise, in the same way that Neon later surprised the garrison of Achradina (Plut. 18.3–5). Nobody would have expected Timoleon's small force to advance on Syracuse immediately. If Diodorus is to be believed (68.9), Hicetas' inferior troops had been left to continue the siege of the city; these men can only have been discouraged by the news of the amazing defeat of their leader's best forces at Adranum, and they are unlikely to have put up stiff resistance when attacked by a completely unexpected enemy from the rear, a completely unexpected quarter. Their attention would have been concentrated on Ortygia, not on the outlying parts of the city.

Westlake suggests that the passage in the *Rhetorica ad Alexandrum* (Aristotle 8.1429b), where the author describes how the Carthaginians held τὴν δὲ πόλιν ἅπασαν πλὴν τῆς ἀκροπόλεως, is further evidence for the falsehood of Diodorus' version of events, because the author could not have written these words if part of the city were already in Corinthian hands.[1] This is a reasonable point, but again not a decisive one, because it ignores the character of the passage in the *Rhetorica ad Alexandrum*. Its character is vague and rhetorical rather than precise and historical. As a glance at the context will show, the passage is merely one of a number of examples which an orator might use to prove that superior numbers do not necessarily bring victory: some victories are won contrary to probability. A reader presented with this passage alone, and no further evidence, would reasonably infer that the nine Corinthian ships actually fought and conquered the 150 Punic ships, and that the Carthaginians alone held the whole city except the acropolis. Neither inference is exactly correct. The nine Corinthian ships never actually engaged

---

[1] *Tyrants*, p. 18; cf. H. D. Westlake, *AJP* 70 (1949), 66.

the Punic fleet, while at no time during the siege was Syracuse excluding the acropolis held only by the Carthaginians. Hicetas' forces were also present. Thus it might be best to ignore the evidence of this rhetorical passage because of its vagueness, and particularly because it does not inform us whether it was Dionysius or Timoleon who controlled the acropolis. The author of the work omits this information because he was interested only in the fact that a tiny force unexpectedly beat a large force.

Westlake's view that Timoleon's small force is unlikely to have been able to stand up to the massed armies of Hicetas and the Carthaginians later is an entirely valid one.[1] Yet it should be stressed that Timoleon may not have needed to fight against huge odds in order to capture the outlying parts of the city after the battle of Adranum. Hicetas' 5,000 best men were away; we do not know how many men were left to continue the siege. But it might be reasonable to assume a total of between 2,000 and 4,000.[2] Even if it were 4,000 (we cannot know for certain), Timoleon's capture of the outlying parts of the city still does not appear impossible. With about 1,000 men he will have appeared unexpectedly, and will have attacked from the rear. The cramped fighting conditions inside the city will have prevented the numerical superiority of Hicetas' force being used to full advantage, while some men will have been forced to continue watching Ortygia for any signs of activity from that quarter. Then Hicetas' dispirited men will have been defending themselves against an army elated by victory. In such conditions it seems by no means impossible that Timoleon should have succeeded in capturing the outlying parts of Syracuse by surprise.

It certainly does seem unbelievable that Timoleon's small force should still have held the positions which it had captured, even after the arrival of Hicetas' Punic reinforcements. Yet the difficulty about dismissing Diodorus' story of the capture of Syracuse as ridiculous at this point is that Diodorus does stress how the situation in Syracuse was indeed unbelievable. He describes how there was great confusion in the city, and how Timoleon's men were dismayed at the odds massed against them after the arrival of the Carthaginians (69.3). It is clear that at this

---

[1] *Tyrants*, p. 18.   [2] Compare *Tyrants*, p. 32.

stage Timoleon's men expected to be attacked and wiped out at any time. But for some unknown reason they were not attacked, and ἄλογός τις καὶ παράδοξος ἐγένετο μεταβολή (69.3). Once again Diodorus makes no attempt to conceal the incredible nature of the events. Mamercus came over to Timoleon's side with δύναμις ἀξιόλογος, to join the allies who had already contributed στρατιώτας οὐκ ὀλίγους (69.3), then πολλὰ τῶν φρουρίων joined Timoleon, and finally reinforcements were dispatched from Corinth (69.4). After all this, according to Diodorus, Τιμολέων μὲν ἐθάρρησεν (69.5): his position in Syracuse was much stronger than before.

No comment need be made here about the reasons for the mysterious withdrawal of the Carthaginians, or about Hicetas' departure from Syracuse. Both events are most strange, but both are attested by Diodorus and Plutarch.[1]

With the Carthaginians and Hicetas gone, according to Diodorus, Timoleon was able to persuade Dionysius to surrender Ortygia and to depart to Corinth (70.1–3). Thereby he gained all Syracuse in 343/2.

Westlake considers that serious difficulties are involved in believing that the agreement between Dionysius and Timoleon was negotiated only after the Carthaginians and Hicetas had withdrawn from Syracuse. He rightly says that the Corinthians did not possess equipment with which to reduce Ortygia by storm; that there was no reason why Dionysius should not have sailed off and established himself with his large force elsewhere (in South Italy perhaps); and that Timoleon would not have had the resources with which to bribe Dionysius' mercenaries to desert to him.[2] But the fact remains undisputed that at some stage during the siege Dionysius did negotiate with Timoleon, and did sail off to Corinth. And in my opinion, whatever *in fact* happened, it seems more *plausible* that Dionysius should make his agreement with Timoleon after the departure of the Carthaginians and Hicetas, rather than immediately after the battle of Adranum.

The difficulty with Plutarch's account is that he does not

[1] For discussion of these matters, see pp. 79–81 and pp. 91–2.
[2] *Tyrants*, p. 20.

suggest a plausible reason for Dionysius' surrender to Timoleon so soon after the battle of Adranum, when neither Timoleon nor any of his troops were near Syracuse. (This is to assume that Dionysius did have plausible reasons for his surrender.) Plutarch describes Dionysius at this point as ἀπειρηκὼς ἤδη ταῖς ἐλπίσι καὶ μικρὸν ἀπολείπων ἐκπολιορκεῖσθαι, and as so contemptuous of Hicetas after his defeat at Adranum that he decided to surrender to Timoleon, whom he admired (13.3; cf. Comp. 1.3). This description can hardly be borne out by the facts of the case. In the same chapter Plutarch describes how Dionysius had 2,000 soldiers in Ortygia, together with money (13.7), horses, machines, weapons and armour for as many as 70,000 men (13.6). That he felt contempt for Hicetas is improbable: only a few months before Hicetas had decisively defeated Dionysius in a pitched battle which enabled him to occupy all Syracuse except Ortygia (D.S. 68.2–3). Now Hicetas' defeat at Adranum would encourage Dionysius to keep hold of Ortygia rather than to leave it.[1]

It is certainly valid to argue that Dionysius would probably save his life by surrendering to Timoleon, whereas Hicetas would execute him, but Dionysius' surrender to Timoleon so soon after the battle of Adranum still remains strange. Timoleon had won no more than one victory, and had not advanced on Syracuse. Communications between blockaded Ortygia and Timoleon must have been difficult, while there was no certainty that Timoleon would be able to guarantee Dionysius' safety, even if the latter were able to reach Timoleon's camp unscathed. Dionysius had never met Timoleon and knew nothing of his ability or of his intentions. Even if Timoleon were prepared to grant him his life (not an assumption to be made lightly after Timoleon's treatment of his own brother, a tyrant like Dionysius), Dionysius could not have been certain that he would escape lynching by bitter Syracusan exiles or other Sicilians. The only reliable protection he had was a few friends (Plut. 13.7). All in all he was taking a far greater risk in leaving Ortygia and surrendering to Timoleon at this stage, than he would have been taking if he had remained secure in Ortygia to observe the course of events.

[1] *Tyrants*, p. 21.

As Westlake says,[1] it would have been quite uncharacteristic of Dionysius to surrender to Timoleon after the battle of Adranum. The circumstances of his earlier life do not show him to have been a coward, whatever hostile sources may say of him. He had abandoned Ortygia in 356/5 and had sailed off to Locri (D.S. 16.17.1–2; Plut. *Dion* 37.4), but he had taken the trouble to dispatch Nypsius with a mercenary force to hold Ortygia (D.S. 16.18; Plut. *Dion* 41.1), and had finally returned to Syracuse himself (Plut. *Tim.* 1.4–5; 13.9). These episodes show him as keen to retain his power in Syracuse. There is no reason known to us why he should have been keen to abandon his position in 344. It is possible that news of the murder of his wife and children at Locri discouraged him from seeking to uphold his power, and led him to lose his nerve, but it is not quite clear when the Locrian rising occurred. It may have occurred some considerable time before the battle of Adranum.[2]

Another possibility is that Dionysius was induced to surrender Ortygia because of a shortage of food. With his convenient base at Locri gone, he would find it more difficult to procure supplies. But he still possessed ships which could bring food through a blockade that was perhaps not strict until the Punic fleet arrived in force.[3] Plutarch has Dionysius himself slip through the blockade before the Punic ships come. In any case there does not seem to have been an acute shortage of food on Ortygia until the year after the battle of Adranum (Plut. 17.4–18.1; cf. 16.5). Then the shortage would have been brought about earlier than originally anticipated, by the addition of 400 of Timoleon's mercenaries to the garrison (Plut. 13.4). Thus it will almost certainly not have been lack of supplies which prompted Dionysius to leave Ortygia after the battle of Adranum.

Westlake's attempt to reconcile the accounts of Timoleon's

[1] *Tyrants*, p. 23.

[2] See Plut. *Tim.* 13.10; Strabo 6.1.8; Clearchus, at Athenaeus 12.541C–E; Aelian *VH* 6.12; Plut. *Mor.* 821D. Also Westlake, *Tyrants*, p. 20 n. 3. Strabo certainly represents Dionysius as very distressed at the capture of his family. For a discussion of the evidence on Dionysius' time at Locri, see P. Meloni, 'Il soggiorno di Dionisio II a Locri', *Studi Italiani di Filologia Classica* 25 (1951), 149–68.

[3] Dionysius must have returned to Syracuse from Locri by ship. See Westlake, *Tyrants*, p. 20 n. 2.

capture of Syracuse by Diodorus and Plutarch seems hazardous.[1] His attempt proceeds from the assumption, never specifically defended by him, that it is both possible and valid to reconcile the two contradictory accounts. Westlake finds some faults with both accounts,[2] but nevertheless feels himself able on the one hand to make use of evidence which he believes, and on the other hand able to reject evidence which he does not trust. Thus he is able to reject as almost incredible Diodorus' story that Timoleon successfully occupied the outlying parts of Syracuse very shortly after the battle of Adranum.[3] But although he suspects Plutarch's remark (16.2) that Timoleon gained Ortygia fifty days after he had landed in Sicily as a piece of exaggerated propaganda,[4] his suspicion does not prevent him from employing this dubious piece of propaganda in his argument. Rather he is able to make the assumption that the meaning of this piece of propaganda is that Dionysius made contact with Timoleon within fifty days of the latter's arrival in Sicily. Even though this assumption is not based on any firm evidence, Westlake concludes that it must be correct, and proceeds to build up his reconstruction of the capture of Syracuse on this shaky foundation.

To summarize Westlake's views briefly, he wishes to preserve Diodorus' chronology, by which Timoleon began his siege of Syracuse in 345/4, but only captured the whole city in 343/2,[5] yet to follow the general pattern of events described by Plutarch. Thus he suggests that although Dionysius effectively handed over the defence of Ortygia to Timoleon in 345/4, it was only in 343/2, after the Carthaginians had come and gone, and after Hicetas had retreated, that Dionysius actually abdicated and left for Corinth. Between 345/4 and 343/2 Dionysius stayed at Timoleon's camp, where he continued negotiations, even though he was little more than Timoleon's prisoner.

Westlake finds confirmation for his view that Dionysius did not renounce his claim to Ortygia until 343/2 in a sentence of Plutarch where Timoleon is described as γενόμενος δὲ τῆς ἄκρας κύριος (22.1) after the liberation of the whole city. He considers

---

[1] *Tyrants*, pp. 24–8. [2] *Tyrants*, p. 21.
[3] *Tyrants*, p. 18. [4] *Tyrants*, p. 24.
[5] Cf. *Ox. Pap.* 1.12.2; Westlake, *Tyrants*, p. 19.

that Plutarch would not have used this expression if Timoleon had gained undisputed possession of Ortygia in 345/4.[1] But, as Sordi has stressed,[2] his argument lays too great a weight on an imprecise phrase of Plutarch. The phrase need not imply that Timoleon only gained legal possession of Ortygia after his capture of all Syracuse. Rather the phrase is quite appropriate in its context, because in Plutarch's narrative Timoleon never goes to Ortygia (that is, becomes literally τῆς ἄκρας κύριος) until he has captured all Syracuse.

Quite apart from the sources' lack of support, there are other objections to Westlake's view. As he recognizes,[3] Timoleon's Sicilian allies will have been most suspicious of any negotiations with Dionysius. If Timoleon had wanted to retain any support at all in Sicily he would probably have removed Dionysius from his camp as soon as possible. That the two men negotiated for a year at Catania is unbelievable. Would Dionysius have been so incautious as to come almost unattended to the camp of a commander whose character and intentions were unknown, on the strength of a paper agreement, which could be repudiated at any time? It would have been safest for Dionysius, who wanted to keep his life, to depart for Corinth at once; this solution would also have been best for Timoleon, who wished to keep his allies. In Westlake's view Timoleon would then have been breaking his agreement with Dionysius,[4] but Timoleon never seems to have been worried by legal niceties at other times during his career. There would have been no advantage in keeping Dionysius at Catania, where his presence would only have caused the utmost resentment among the Sicilians, and where bad feeling would have hampered Timoleon's efforts to take Syracuse.[5]

It would be unwise to say that either Diodorus or Plutarch has copied his source wrongly. Even if one of them copied his main source wrongly at the outset, he would find that he had made a mistake from the other sources which he consulted. Then Plutarch's arrangement of events, whereby Dionysius

---

[1] *Tyrants*, p. 25 and note 3.　　[2] Sordi, p. 99.
[3] *Tyrants*, p. 26.　　[4] *Tyrants*, pp. 25–6.
[5] Cf. Sordi, p. 99.

departs before Hicetas, is confirmed in Nepos' brief summary. These two authors almost certainly had one source in common.[1]

While it is most unlikely that Diodorus and Plutarch copied their sources wrongly, it seems unlikely, too, that these main sources would have been misinformed about the events of the siege of Syracuse. Diodorus had a special interest in Sicilian affairs, and made some use of Theopompus, who seems not only to have been concerned more with the Dionysii than with Timoleon, but also to have devoted particular attention to Dionysius II.[2] Theopompus' narrative, whereby Dionysius only surrenders after Timoleon has captured all Syracuse, is unlikely to be a fabrication when it reflects so well on Dionysius himself. As Westlake says,[3] Theopompus was exceedingly hostile to Dionysius. But his view that Dionysius was a coward is not really borne out by his narrative, in which the tyrant withstood a siege from 345/4 to 343/2. It is the version of Plutarch, who was perhaps following Timaeus,[4] which best displays Dionysius as a coward. Timaeus, like Theopompus, took a harsh view of the Dionysii;[5] he also took an uncritically generous view of Timoleon, with the result that he might possibly have altered the sequence of events to reflect well on Timoleon in expelling Dionysius within fifty days of his arrival in Sicily, and to reflect badly on Dionysius as a weak coward.

But it would be very rash to think that a major historian would have deliberately falsified the order of events which were important and well known.[6] The narrative of Plutarch (and of Timaeus?) also seems much too detailed for a fabrication. On the other hand it would be unreasonable to accept the narrative of Plutarch in preference to the narrative of Diodorus, merely because the former happens to supply detail which the latter lacks.

Such an acceptance would be unreasonable, too, in this case where the detailed narrative is not always above suspicion.

---

[1] See pp. 23–5.
[2] See H. D. Westlake, 'The Sicilian Books of Theopompus' *Philippica*', *Historia* 2 (1953/4), 294.
[3] *Tyrants*, p. 22, and *Historia* 2 (1953/4), 295–6.   [4] See p. 22.
[5] See T. S. Brown, *Timaeus of Tauromenium* (California 1958), pp. 80–2.
[6] Especially when Timaeus was proud of the careful attention which he paid to chronology (Polyb. 12.10.4; cf. D.S. 5.1.3).

Plutarch's whole description of the capture of Syracuse betrays a bias in favour of Timoleon (for example, 16.1). As mentioned above, his judgement of Dionysius as ἀπειρηκὼς ἤδη ταῖς ἐλπίσι καὶ μικρὸν ἀπολείπων ἐκπολιορκεῖσθαι (13.3; cf. Comp. 1.3) hardly seems to be confirmed by the details of the equipment in Ortygia (13.6–7). Then Plutarch has certainly made some mistake over the narrative of Timoleon's final capture of Syracuse from Hicetas. On the one hand he describes how Hicetas was determined to retain his position in the city (21.2), and how Timoleon attacked him from three sides (21.2–3). But on the other hand he maintains that Hicetas' troops were quickly put to flight, and that not one of Timoleon's men was either killed or wounded (21.4–5). It seems impossible that both sections of this narrative should be true.[1]

While I acknowledge that one of our two accounts of Timoleon's capture of all Syracuse must be wrong, I do not think that it is possible to make a definite choice between the two, rejecting one and accepting the other. Four of the most recent treatments of the subject have followed the narrative of Plutarch, and have rejected that of Diodorus.[2] I believe that both authors' accounts are possible. I think it unlikely that either these authors or their sources would have invented parts of their narrative. I do not think that it is valid or possible to reconcile the two accounts. Those who are unwilling to leave the matter unresolved, by declaring their uncertainty, must firmly follow one account or the other.

Mamercus

Of Mamercus little is known. Nepos, Diodorus and Polyaenus mention him once each; Plutarch alone devotes more attention to him.[3]

[1] See Westlake, *Tyrants*, pp. 33–4; and also pp. 91–2.

[2] N. di Fede, *Dionigi il Giovane* (Catanzaro 1949), pp. 132–43; Sordi, pp. 36–46 and 96–101; H. Berve, *Die Tyrannis*, Vol. 1, pp. 277–8, Vol. 2, p. 664; M. I Finley, *Ancient Sicily*, p. 96. For a discussion which favours Diodorus' narrative, see N. E. Cappellano, *Sulla venuta di Timoleonte in Sicilia* (Catania 1903), pp. 37–46.

[3] See p. 10. Ovid, *Ibis* 545–6, may refer to Mamercus, but the correct reading of the name is uncertain. For further discussion of the names Mamercus/Marcus, see Note E, p. 199.

Nepos' sole reference is of interest in that Mamercus is described as 'Italicum ducem, hominem bellicosum et potentem, qui tyrannos adiutum in Siciliam venerat' (2.4). From this we may reasonably conclude that Mamercus had come to Sicily as a mercenary, like many others from Italy, and that he had taken advantage of the confusion and disorder in the island to seize Catania for himself. It is as tyrant of Catania that he first appears in Plutarch's narrative (13.2; cf. D.S. 69.4). We do not know how he managed to gain this tyranny, or when he did so. Nothing is known of the history of the city between 353, when Callippus established himself there for a short period, and the period after the battle of Adranum (Plut. *Dion* 58.4; *Tim.* 13.2).

Both Plutarch (13.2) and Diodorus (69.4) represent Mamercus as offering himself to Timoleon as an ally in the course of the siege of Syracuse. Although Plutarch places this event between the battle of Adranum and the capitulation of Dionysius II, whereas Diodorus places it after the arrival of Hicetas' Punic reinforcements, both authors agree on the incident. Both also agree that Mamercus was a powerful tyrant.

We do not know why Mamercus joined Timoleon at a time when the Corinthians still had small chance of success in Sicily. But it seems likely that he was chiefly interested in increasing his own power, like the other mercenary commanders who had become tyrants in Sicily, and that it was for this reason that he offered to join Timoleon. An alliance with the Corinthians would also provide him with an opportunity to attack Hicetas, and perhaps eventually a chance to gain control of the plain of Leontini, the most fertile corn-producing area in Sicily.[1] Timoleon accepted Mamercus as an ally, despite the fact that the latter was a tyrant and almost certainly not even a Greek; his reception in Sicily had been so cold (cf. Plut. 11.6) that he was prepared to accept any support offered at this stage.

Mamercus was a valuable ally because he had many resources (Plut. 13.2), and because his city of Catania provided a convenient base from which Timoleon could conduct the siege of Syracuse

---

[1] See Westlake, *Tyrants*, p. 45. For the fertility of the plain of Leontini see D.S. 5.2.4; 14.58.1; and T. J. Dunbabin, *The Western Greeks* (Oxford 1948), pp. 67–8 and 212–13.

and supply Ortygia (Plut. 18.1). Hicetas and Mago recognized
the importance of Catania as a base for Timoleon, and set out to
capture the city, but the attempt ended in disaster (Plut. 18.2–7).

Unfortunately we hear nothing further of the part played by
Mamercus in Sicilian affairs until after the battle of the R. Crimisus, when he allied with Hicetas and the Carthaginians against
Timoleon (Plut. 30.4). We do not know when he broke off his
alliance with Timoleon: it may have been before or after the battle
of the R. Crimisus. Presumably the break will have occurred
when he fully realized that Timoleon wished to stamp out all
the tyrannies in the island. Timoleon's victory at the R. Crimisus,
which greatly strengthened his prestige, will have shown Mamercus and Hicetas that they would need to attack him quickly,
before they were themselves attacked. In order to survive, both
tyrants were willing to take advantage of Punic help.

The alliance of Mamercus, Hicetas and the Carthaginians seems
to have been successful enough to inflict two defeats on Timoleon's men (Plut. 30.6). Mamercus composed an epigram about
the fine spoils captured from Timoleon's mercenaries, verses
which much annoyed the Syracusans (Plut. 31.1). But after the
defeat and execution of Hicetas, Timoleon turned his attention
to Mamercus, who was defeated at the R. Abolus, with the loss
of over 2,000 men, many of whom were Carthaginian mercenaries (Plut. 34.1).

Timoleon's peace with Carthage, which followed his victory
at the R. Abolus, was disastrous for Mamercus, in that it deprived
him of Punic support, and allowed Timoleon to devote all his
attention to the suppression of tyrants.[1] In despair Mamercus
set out to seek help from the Lucanians, but during the voyage
his men mutinied, turned back to Catania, and then handed
over the city to Timoleon (Plut. 34.3). Mamercus himself con-
trived to escape to Messana, where the tyrant Hippon was then
besieged on land and sea by Timoleon (Plut. 34.4; cf. 37.9).
The details of Mamercus' final surrender are not known, but
Plutarch says that he gave himself up to Timoleon (34.5).[2] At

[1] D.S. 82.3; Plut. 34.2. I have followed the order of events given by
Plutarch, rather than the order given by Diodorus.

[2] Nepos merely says that Timoleon captured Mamercus (2.4). On the
trial see also p. 113.

his trial before the people of Syracuse he tried to deliver a speech of defence which he had composed, but dashed his head on the stonework of the theatre when he was consistently shouted down by the crowd. He then underwent some further gruesome punishment before he died. Such is Plutarch's version of events (34.6–7). Polyaenus' version suggests that Timoleon deceived Mamercus into thinking that he would be tried, but in fact just had him executed at once (5.12.2).

Mamercus was attacked and executed like Hicetas because his aims were directly opposed to those of Timoleon, and because Timoleon realized that Sicily would never be safe until Mamercus' powerful tyranny fell.[1]

Timoleon's treatment of defeated tyrants

While it is clear that Timoleon was determined to carry through his aim of ridding Sicily of tyranny, it is not so clear why the various defeated tyrants were differently treated after their fall. Hicetas and Mamercus, who had both been allies as well as opponents of Timoleon at different times, seem to have been given some form of trial before their execution. Although a few details of this strange procedure are given in the case of Mamercus, it is not at all clear why he wished to go before a court, particularly after the unjust trial of Hicetas' family (see below). Certainly the citizens of Syracuse cannot have wanted any trial, since they would not listen to Mamercus' defence. The outcome of the proceedings seems to have been a foregone conclusion in their eyes.

We cannot be sure that a trial was held in the case of Hicetas, yet Plutarch's description of how he and his son ὡς τύραννοι καὶ προδόται κολασθέντες ἀπέθνῃσκον (32.2) might suggest that they were sentenced to death on a formal charge. Euthymus was probably tried, because we hear that an insult which he was accused of circulating prevented his being shown any mercy.[2]

---

[1] For discussion of scholars' suggestions about Mamercus, see Note F, pp. 200–1.

[2] Plut. 32.2. It is possible that κατηγορῶ is not used here in the technical sense of an accusation made in a law-court, but this seems unlikely in context.

The wives and daughters of Hicetas and his friends definitely were tried and sentenced by the Syracusan assembly (Plut. 33.1). As in the case of Mamercus, the outcome never seems to have been in doubt: Plutarch accuses Timoleon of having abandoned the women to the citizens' vengeful anger (33.2–3).

Hippon seems to have been tortured and executed without any trial. Unlike Hicetas and Mamercus, who were brought to Syracuse, he was put to death in Messana by the citizens he had ruled (Plut. 34.4).

Leptines was sent off to the Peloponnese. This could have been because he was an enemy less dangerous to Timoleon than the three tyrants mentioned above. But it seems possible that he kept his life as part of a bargain struck with Timoleon. In Diodorus' brief narrative Timoleon fails to take Leptines' city, Engyum, after frequent assaults, but then frightens the tyrant into surrender (72.3–5; cf. Plut. 24.2), a strange succession of events, from which I would suspect that Timoleon never did defeat Leptines properly. Possibly the latter realized that he would be unable to hold out indefinitely, and so decided to make terms with Timoleon before he was forced to capitulate unconditionally. Because of our lack of detailed knowledge this idea can only remain a guess, but it may show why Leptines alone of these four tyrants was able to follow Dionysius II into exile.

Andromachus

Little is known of Andromachus, who is mentioned briefly by Diodorus and at more length by Plutarch.[1] He had apparently gained Tauromenium in 358/7, when he had gathered together those who had survived Dionysius' destruction of Naxos (D.S. 16.7.1). Plutarch gives a very favourable picture of him because he almost certainly used Timaeus, Andromachus' son, as a main source. Thus Plutarch does not call Andromachus τύραννος, but carefully differentiates his position and conduct from those of the τύραννοι (10.7), while Diodorus refers to Andromachus as no more than ὁ δὲ τῆς πόλεως ταύτης ἡγούμενος (68.8). Westlake[2]

[1] For Plutarch's characterization of him, see p. 10.
[2] *Tyrants*, p. 12.

has been led by these favourable terms into thinking that Andromachus' position in Tauromenium was not actually that of a τύραννος. But it seems unrealistic to think that Andromachus would have been able to maintain his position without the use of force during the unstable period before Timoleon's arrival in Sicily. As Timmerman observes,[1] there is certainly no evidence which actually illustrates Andromachus' alleged opposition to tyranny before his invitation to Timoleon. Andromachus is not heard of providing his city as a refuge for enemies of tyranny, or as a rallying-point for opponents of Dionysius II, for example. Then his contribution of perhaps only 200 troops at the battle of Adranum[2] might suggest that he was neither very concerned at eliminating Hicetas, nor very strong.

In any event Plutarch's bias in favour of Andromachus leads to some strange inconsistencies. His description of Andromachus as πολὺ κράτιστος τῶν τότε δυναστευόντων ἐν Σικελίᾳ nearly contradicts his remark about Hicetas at 1.6, and it is hardly consistent with the later statement that Tauromenium was a mere πολίχνη (11.5). Yet in this latter passage Plutarch uses the diminutive form of πόλις to stress Timoleon's thin chance of success at the time when he landed in Sicily.

Andromachus' position did differ from that of the other tyrants in Sicily in that he was never overthrown by Timoleon (cf. Marcellinus, *Vit. Thuc.* 27). He escaped this fate because he invited Timoleon to Sicily, received him kindly at a time when the Corinthians had no other support in the island, and seems to have remained consistently loyal to him.[3] We do not know exactly why he invited Timoleon to Sicily.

[1] A. G. Timmerman, *De Dionis et Timoleontis Vitis Capita Quaedam* (Amsterdam dissertation published at Leiden, 1893), p. 103.

[2] See p. 57.

[3] Plut. 10.6–8; 11.2–3 and 5–6; D.S. 68.7–8. Plutarch (10.6) says that Andromachus had invited Timoleon to Tauromenium πάλαι: we do not know what length of time Plutarch means this word to cover.

CHAPTER 7

Constitutional studies

Timoleon and Plato

Amazingly diverse opinions have been held on the matter of Platonic influence on Timoleon. R. von Scheliha[1] was the first of recent writers to put forward the view that Timoleon carried out the recommendations for the salvation of Sicily made by Plato in the Seventh and Eighth Letters. This view was accepted in part by Stier,[2] but it was strongly attacked by Berve[3] on the grounds that Timoleon's constitution bore no resemblance to that recommended by Plato. Sordi has decided to resurrect the idea that Plato influenced Timoleon, partly because her interpretation of Timoleon's constitution differs from that of Berve. Her opinion of Platonic influence on Timoleon seems to be shared by C. Mossé.[4] I give a fairly detailed outline of Sordi's opinion of Platonic influences on Timoleon because her treatment of the subject is the most recent, the most dangerous, and the most extreme. She has pushed the idea of Platonic influence on Timoleon to its limit.

She devotes pages 22 and 25 of her *Timoleonte* to a demonstration of her view that Timoleon not only knew the Seventh and Eighth Letters of Plato, but also employed the Eighth Letter for propaganda purposes. In her opinion Timoleon faithfully put into practice the three main points recommended by Plato, a war against the Carthaginians, colonization of Sicily (with settlers from Sicily itself and from mainland Greece), and legislation.

---

[1] R. von Scheliha, *Dion: die platonische Staatsgründung in Sizilien* (*Das Erbe der Alten* 25, Leipzig 1934); see especially pp. 96–7, with notes on pp. 158–9.

[2] *RE* VIA. *s.v.* 'Timoleon', col. 1290.

[3] H. Berve, *Dion, Akad. der Wiss. in Mainz, Abh. der Geistes- und Sozialwiss. Kl.* Nr. 10 (Wiesbaden 1956), 137–8 = (877–8).

[4] C. Mossé, *La fin de la démocratie athénienne* (Paris 1962) pp. 344–5. See also P. Lévêque, *Kokalos* 14–15 (1968/9), 137, and C. Mossé, *ibidem*, pp. 151–2; and A. Momigliano, *The Development of Greek Biography* (Harvard 1971), p. 61.

As evidence for her view that Timoleon employed the Eighth Letter for propaganda purposes, Sordi points to the similarity between the passages in the Letter where Plato maintains that Sicily is in such danger of 'barbarization' that the foreigners in the island should be driven out (353A–E; 357A–B), and Plutarch's version of the Syracusans' reaction when Mago arrived in the Great Harbour with a large force: ὥστε πάντας οἴεσθαι τὴν πάλαι λεγομένην καὶ προσδοκωμένην ἐκβαρβάρωσιν ἥκειν ἐπὶ τὴν Σικελίαν (Plut. 17.2). This likeness is not accidental, and indicates Timoleon's knowledge of the Eighth Letter. As evidence for her contention that Timoleon actually carried out Plato's plans for Sicily, Sordi points to the passages in the Seventh Letter where Plato recommends legislation, colonization and a war against the Carthaginians, all three of which were undertaken by Timoleon.[1]

She goes further in suggesting that Timoleon's constitution of 338 was inspired by Plato, in particular by the Seventh Letter. Timoleon's Council of Six Hundred was based on the legislative council recommended in the Seventh Letter (pp. 78–9).[2] Then the Amphipolia of Olympian Zeus was based on the βασιλεία suggested in the Eighth Letter (p. 117).[3] Next, she considers that Timoleon followed Platonic ideas on τύχη, with the result that she can maintain that: 'Da Platone Timoleonte trasse dunque, oltre al programma politico per la sua azione siciliana, anche il fondamento ideologico della sua propaganda e della sua stessa religiosità' (pp. 83–5; quotation from p. 85). Finally it should be noted that she does not consider Timoleon to have been a keen follower of Plato all his life. According to her: 'Nel primo periodo siciliano di Timoleonte l' influenza platonica appare limitata alle idee sulla colonizzazione e sulla lotta contro i barbari' (p. 117 n. 8). It was only after the battle of the R. Crimisus that Timoleon abandoned his life-long democratic views (pp. 7 and 86) and promulgated an oligarchic constitution (p. 78). Presumably it must have been between the battle of the R. Crimisus and the making of the constitution in 338 that Timoleon undertook a profound study of Platonic works,

[1] 332E–333A; 335E–336A; 336D; 337B–C; 8.355Bff. is also mentioned.
[2] 337B–C.
[3] 355E; 356A–B and D–E.

covering *Meno*, *Republic* and *Laws*, with all of which Sordi expects him to be acquainted (see, for example, pp. 78 and 84).

Because Sordi never reviews all her diverse conjectures on Platonic influence together in one chapter, the individual conjectures do not possess that air of nonsense which only appears when all of them are gathered together, as above. The business of gathering them is not helped by the fact that the book has no index of any kind. Quite apart from the absurdity of Sordi's transformation of Timoleon from Plutarch's ἱερὸς ἀνήρ (16.12), or Finley's 'man of military action',[1] into a disciple of the Academy, the assumptions on which her views rest are of a most insecure nature.

She assumes first that the Seventh and Eighth Letters were both written by Plato himself, and that they both recommend the same policy (p. 22). Secondly she notes that those who take Theopompus to be the source of part of Diodorus' quite favourable narrative of Timoleon's career will not accept the view that Timoleon followed Plato, since Theopompus was such a strong opponent of the Academy. If Timoleon had followed Plato, Theopompus would have maligned him. But Sordi removes this difficulty by her assertion that Theopompus was not Diodorus' source.[2] However, both her assumption that the two Letters are genuine and consistent, and her rejection of Theopompus as a possible source of Diodorus,[3] are bound to make her view that Timoleon followed Plato seem very dubious. Furthermore there is no evidence to support her contention that Timoleon was a democrat for most of his life, while her opinion that the foundation of the Council of Six Hundred was inspired by Plato rests on the insecure assumptions that Timoleon did found a Council and that its membership was aristocratic. Then her view that the Amphipolia was inspired by Plato's βασιλεία rests on the assumption, for which there is no support in the evidence, that the office was set up after the battle of the R. Crimisus rather than before it, as Diodorus states. Finally Sordi cites no significant evidence to show that the ideas of Plato and Timoleon on τύχη were connected. The fact that both men appear to have held views on

[1] *Ancient Sicily*, p. 93. [2] P. 23, with nn. 7 to 9.
[3] See Sordi, pp. 93-5 and *Diodori Liber XVI*, pp. xli–xliv.

τύχη which were current in the fourth century is not sufficient proof of specifically Platonic influence on Timoleon in this sphere.

Despite Sordi's contention that 'il sogno di Platone era stato attuato alla lettera' (p. 86), I find it disappointing that she never explains why Timoleon did not carry out Plato's plans more faithfully, if he was such a very keen admirer of Plato's work. For example, the Seventh Letter recommends that a legislative council of, say, fifty men be established to frame laws (337B–C): why, then, did Timoleon call in two Corinthian legislators, Cephalus and Dionysius, instead of adopting Plato's procedure? It seems very weak to maintain that Timoleon was a keen disciple of Plato who followed the barest outlines of Plato's main recommendations, but ignored all his more detailed ideas.

Confidence in Sordi's view of Platonic influence on Timoleon is hardly strengthened by the fact that there is not a shred of evidence in all our sources to suggest either that Timoleon admired Plato (we know only that he admired Epaminondas: Plut. 36.1), or that he read the Letters in Greece; rather, Plutarch stresses that Timoleon completely withdrew from the world for the twenty years after the murder of Timophanes (3.2; 5.4; Comp. 2.11). Further, Plutarch knew the Letters well, as he used them for his *Dion*,[1] but never once does he suggest in *Timoleon* that Timoleon carried out the advice of Plato.[2]

There does remain a noticeable similarity between the outlines, if not the details, of Plato's three main recommendations and the three cardinal features of Timoleon's programme for the revival of Sicily. Conclusions completely opposite to those of M. Sordi have been drawn by L. Edelstein on the basis of this similarity.[3] I deal with his views in some detail, as he is the most recent author who not only rejects the idea that Plato influenced Timoleon, but also suggests an explanation for the apparent similarity between the recommendations of Plato and the programme of Timoleon.

---

[1] See Berve, *Dion*, p. 14 (= p. 754), n. 1.

[2] Sordi's whole view of Platonic influence on Timoleon has rightly been rejected by Berve, *Gnomon* 35 (1963), 379, 381, 383.

[3] L. Edelstein, *Plato's Seventh Letter* (*Philosophia Antiqua* 14, Leiden 1966).

Edelstein starts his work with the assumption that the Seventh Letter is genuinely by Plato (p. 4), but he finds himself compelled to acknowledge during the course of his investigation that the Letter is not genuine (p. 56). He suggests that the Seventh Letter was written some time after both Plato and Timoleon had died (pp. 62 and 167–8), and that its purpose was not only to describe Plato's share in the Sicilian enterprise, but also to show why Plato failed over so long a period, where Timoleon was brilliantly successful in such a short time (pp. 61–2). In Edelstein's view the advice given in the Seventh Letter has little relevance to the time at which it claims to have been written (pp. 31–4).[1] He considers that the plans put forward for the salvation of Sicily in the Letter are really no more than a *vaticinium ex eventu*, a re-interpretation of Plato's intentions in the light of what was actually achieved later by Timoleon (pp. 37–8). He suggests that the agreement between the intentions of Plato and the programme of Timoleon (an agreement apparently unnoticed either by Timoleon himself or by Plutarch) is hardly likely to be 'providential' (pp. 36–7).

Although Edelstein's argument up to this point seems sensible, he goes too far in suggesting that Timoleon is perhaps the model for the Plato of the Seventh Letter (pp. 55–6). He is led to put forward this view because he considers the contrast drawn between Plato, whose plans were destroyed by τύχη, and Timoleon, whose success was brought about by the same power, to be very striking. Edelstein rightly notes that Timoleon ascribed all his successes to τύχη (Plut. 36.5), but the idea that his personal success is contrasted with Plato's failure seems far-fetched when there is not even one passage in the Letter which might be interpreted as a reference to Timoleon himself, as opposed to the main points of his programme.

[1] The review of Edelstein's book by F. Solmsen (*Gnomon* 41 (1969), 29–34) is mainly concerned with the philosophical side of the work, but Solmsen rightly disagrees with Edelstein's contention (pp. 32–3) that there was no need for colonization in Sicily in 353. As Solmsen says (pp. 32–3), the disorders of the previous fifty years would have led to a decline in the population of Sicily. While I recognize that a consideration of the philosophical ideas put forward in the Seventh Letter is a most important part of any complete discussion of the Letter's authenticity, it seems inappropriate to discuss those ideas here.

Edelstein considers that the writer of the Eighth Letter was acquainted with the Seventh Letter, but that he was not the same person as the writer of the Seventh Letter (p. 154). He believes that the advice given in the Eighth Letter is in no way consistent with that of the Seventh Letter, but that the two Letters disagree sharply (pp. 151–2).

The above paragraphs, outlining the extreme views of Sordi and Edelstein, illustrate the amazingly diverse opinions that are held on the content of the Seventh and Eighth Letters. The views of both these authors, however, are not particularly helpful when the problem of the authenticity of the Letters remains unresolved. Sordi's views lean heavily on the supposition that the Letters are genuine, while Edelstein's views depend on the contention that the Letters were written after the deaths of both Plato and Timoleon. The historian of Timoleon's career may only state with certainty that Timoleon's programme for the revival of Sicily owes nothing to Plato. There is not a single piece of ancient evidence to suggest that Plato influenced Timoleon in any way whatsoever. For the historian of Timoleon's career further discussion is unnecessary when it is accepted that Timoleon was not a disciple of Plato. There remains the similarity – on which Sordi and Edelstein base so much – between the three main recommendations of Plato and the three main points of Timoleon's programme. Those who consider the two Letters to be the work of Platonic apologists may perhaps regard the similarity as the adaptation of the intentions of Plato to the achievements of Timoleon. Those who regard the two Letters as genuine may regard the similarity as an interesting coincidence, which possibly demonstrates Plato's prophetic insight into the needs of Sicily. I would argue that there is nothing especially striking about the general similarity between the recommendations of Plato and the programme of Timoleon. Sicily's population would have declined badly in the disorders of the half-century before 353, the year in which the Seventh Letter is set, so that new settlers would certainly be needed to restore prosperity. Then legislation and the expulsion of the Carthaginians from Greek Sicily would both be essential before peace and order could be fully restored in the area. In my view these measures would have been suggested by any perceptive observer in 353 or in 343.

Timoleon's offices

Evidence on Syracusan constitutional matters during Timoleon's time is scanty, mainly because our two principal sources, Plutarch and Diodorus, show little interest in constitutional details, and are indifferent to official titles.

Because of these circumstances we can gain no exact idea of Timoleon's official position from the sources. According to Plutarch the Syracusan exiles first ask Corinth for nothing more explicit than βοήθεια (2.1); then οἱ Κορίνθιοι vote to help, and search for a στρατηγός (3.1–2; cf. 7.5). Very much the same story of a request for a στρατηγός is given by Diodorus, although in his version a more explicit request is made by the exiles than a plain call for βοήθεια (65.1–2 and 7; 66.1; cf. Nep. *Tim.* 2.1). We hear nothing of the orders given to Timoleon; the fact that, according to Diodorus, the Syracusan exiles asked for στρατηγὸν τὸν ἐπιμελησόμενον τῆς πόλεως καὶ καταλύσοντα τὴν τῶν τυραννεῖν ἐπιβαλομένων πλεονεξίαν (65.1) is no guarantee that such orders were given to Timoleon when he was actually appointed. For the Syracusan exiles in no sense represented the government of their city, and had no official authority. Whatever the exact phrasing of their request, they really seem to have been asking Corinth to aid them in an attempt to overthrow the established government of Syracuse. Dionysius' regime may indeed have been distasteful and somewhat insecure, but at the time of the exiles' appeal it was nevertheless the established government of Syracuse. Further, Corinth had never yet granted official support to any attacks on Dionysius II or his father, and Plutarch has no real foundation for praising the city's active hatred of tyranny (2.2). So it is understandable that while Dionysius still retained power, Corinth may have been reluctant to grant Timoleon official authority, or to support him too ostentatiously, since a response to the exiles' appeal would amount to direct interference in the domestic affairs of Syracuse on the side of rebels. Until Dionysius had actually fallen and Syracuse had been captured, Timoleon can have had no legally justifiable position in Sicily; yet the confusion and disorder which prevailed in the island naturally made a legal justification of his presence quite unnecessary.[1]

There are noticeable differences in the phrasing of the maxim spoken to Timoleon before he set out from Corinth. Plutarch (7.2) makes it the remark of one of the foremost citizens of Corinth, Teleclides, and refers to Timoleon's future activities by the vague verb ἀγωνίζομαι (Ἄν μὲν γὰρ νῦν καλῶς ἀγωνίσῃ ...). But Diodorus (65.8) makes it part of the proposal of the γερουσία of Corinth, and refers to Timoleon's future activities by the more definite verb ἄρχομαι (ἐὰν μὲν καλῶς ἄρξῃ τῶν Συρακοσίων...). From this it might be inferred that Timoleon was given a mandate by the Corinthians to be ἄρχων of Syracuse, but – quite apart from the fact that we cannot be sure exactly what the Corinthians would mean by ἄρχων – it would not be wise to lay any weight on Diodorus' words here. The fact that the anecdote appears in different circumstances in Plutarch and Diodorus must indicate that its context is uncertain, while ἄρχομαι in this passage of Diodorus is probably to be thought of as no more exact a term than the English verb 'rule'.

In my view Corinth merely helped Timoleon to recruit mercenaries and provided him with ships (Plut. 7.3 and 5; 8.1–2 and 4). She must also have provided him with some kind of vague official blessing, but there is no evidence that she went so far as to make him στρατηγός or στρατηγὸς αὐτοκράτωρ of Corinth.

Kahrstedt[2] takes the view that Timoleon was made *strategos autocrator* of Corinth before he set out for Sicily, and that he retained this office for an unknown length of time in Sicily. His reasons for this view are that Timoleon may have been no more than an ordinary Corinthian office-holder who was sent over to Syracuse, and that his enterprise is described definitely as 'Corinthian' in many passages (pp. 366–7). But Plutarch's narrative (3.2) makes it clear that Timoleon was not an ordinary Corinthian

---

[1] The unofficial nature of the Syracusan exiles' appeal to Corinth is stressed by J. Seibert, *Metropolis und Apoikie: Historische Beiträge zur Geschichte ihrer gegenseitigen Beziehungen* (Würzburg 1963), p. 117.

[2] U. Kahrstedt, *Griechisches Staatsrecht*, Vol. 1, *Sparta und seine Symmachie* (Göttingen 1922), pp. 365–8.

office-holder, while the fact that his enterprise is described as 'Corinthian' – a term used indiscriminately by Plutarch in *Timoleon*[1] – is not conclusive evidence that he was an official Corinthian general.

Although it was perhaps hypothetically possible for Corinth to appoint a general with authority in her colony Syracuse, it seems most unlikely; no case is recorded. The decree of the Syracusan assembly mentioned at Plut. 38.4 lays down that Syracuse should request a Corinthian *strategos* in the event of a war πρὸς ἀλλοφύλους, not that Corinth should impose a *strategos* on Syracuse.[2] And indeed Acestoridas, who was sent out at some time after Timoleon's death, was elected *strategos* in Syracuse, not in Corinth (D.S. 19.5.1). What little evidence we possess on contacts between Syracuse and Corinth in the fourth century does not suggest that Corinth had any control over Syracuse. Corinth had been unhelpful to Syracuse in this century, as well as in the fifth century. Those who wish to argue that Corinth did have the power to appoint a *strategos* with authority in Syracuse in the fourth century must explain how she gained this power, when she had not possessed it in the fifth century.[3]

As further evidence for his belief that Timoleon was a Corinthian general Kahrstedt lays weight on Plutarch's statement in Comp. 2.7: Τιμολέων αἰτησαμένοις καὶ δεηθεῖσιν αὐτοκράτωρ πεμφθεὶς Συρακουσίοις; but, as Westlake has sensibly suggested, Plutarch would be even less exact in his use of terminology in a Comparison, where he was writing without a source, than in a Life, where he was often following a source. Westlake's suggestion that Plutarch's choice of αὐτοκράτωρ is influenced by the use of the word in his own time as a translation of the Latin *imperator* seems a good one.[4]

---

[1] See pp. 31–2 above.

[2] The last sentence of the speech which Diodorus puts in the mouth of Theodoros at the Syracusan assembly (under 396) might suggest that the decree mentioned by Plutarch at 38.4 merely involved the amendment of an old law. For Theodoros says of the leadership of the Syracusans: τὴν δὲ ἡγεμονίαν δοτέον κατὰ τοὺς νόμους πολίταις ἢ τοῖς κατὰ τὴν μητρόπολιν οἰκοῦσι Κορινθίοις ἢ τοῖς ἀφηγουμένοις τῆς Ἑλλάδος Σπαρτιάταις (D.S. 14.69.5). No other reference to such a law is known. For discussion of the expression πρὸς ἀλλοφύλους see Note G, p. 201.

[3] See pp. 52–4 above.   [4] H. D. Westlake, *CHJ* 7 (1942), 74.

Unfortunately the idea that Timoleon was a *strategos* of Corinth has been put forward by other scholars, writing after Kahrstedt. Hüttl[1] and Berve[2] both reproduce it, and give as one main reason the passage of Diodorus which narrates how Timoleon retired in 337/6, στρατηγήσας ἔτη ὀκτώ (90.1). But to maintain that this passage shows that Timoleon remained a *strategos* of Corinth throughout his career in Sicily is to imply that Diodorus was obsessed with constitutional detail. A far more likely and more natural meaning of στρατηγήσας here is something no more technical than 'having commanded troops'; that it should mean 'having been a *strategos* of Corinth' is rather far-fetched.

The same kind of argument applies to the passage in Plutarch, where Timoleon ὡς δ' ἐπανῆλθεν εἰς Συρακούσας εὐθὺς ἀποθέσθαι τὴν μοναρχίαν (37.10): μοναρχία in this context should be considered as no more technical a term than the English 'sole command'. On the other two occasions when the words μοναρχία (3.6) and μόναρχος (11.6) are used by Plutarch in *Timoleon*, they have unpleasant connotations, and refer to tyranny and tyrants.[3] To make μοναρχία at 37.10 mean 'the position of *strategos autocrator* at Corinth' is quite ridiculous. Westlake regards Plutarch's use of μοναρχία here as striking because it occurs in a quotation from Athanis, a contemporary of Timoleon.[4] But it might be rash to assume that Athanis would reproduce official terminology accurately. And even if Athanis did so, it is possible that Plutarch would not reproduce the terminology with similar accuracy; further, Westlake is optimistic in his view that Plutarch would reproduce the original text of Athanis unaltered, after it had been handled, as he thinks, both by Timaeus and by a Hellenistic biographer.

In my opinion the relationship between Corinth and Timoleon is left vague by the sources because it was indeed a vague one. When the appeal came from the Syracusan exiles, Corinth strangely decided to respond, but deliberately did not risk one of her regular *strategoi* on a venture which amounted to an un-

---

[1] W. Hüttl, *Verfassungsgeschichte von Syrakus* (Prague 1929), p. 127.
[2] H. Berve, *Die Tyrannis*, Vol. 2, p. 666.
[3] Compare the use of μοναρχία at Comp. 2.3.
[4] *CHJ* 7 (1942), 74 and n. 7.

provoked attack on the established government of Syracuse, and which in any case had small chance of success. Instead she sent Timoleon, who was elderly, had taken no part in public life for the previous twenty years, and had had no experience in Sicily, as far as we know. In these circumstances it would have been amazing if Corinth had given Timoleon an office, like the *strategia*, which could be exercised in Corinth itself. Rather the city provided a little money for mercenaries,[1] a few ships, and her blessing; she gave Timoleon no precise instructions, although I suspect that she made it clear that in the unlikely event of success, he should recompense Corinth for her investment in the venture.[2] This suspicion is aroused by the fact that as soon as Corinth realized that Timoleon was likely to achieve success, she dispatched reinforcements greater than the original force (Plut. 16.3; D.S. 69.4). Then when Timoleon did win his major victory over the Carthaginians at the battle of the R. Crimisus, booty was sent to Corinth (Plut. 29.5–6; D.S. 80.6). That Corinth and Timoleon should be on friendly terms was important to both parties. Timoleon above all wanted an 'agent' in Greece. Corinth was the city where he might send defeated tyrants,[3] the city which would send him skilled legislators, experts who could not be found in Sicily (Plut. 24.3; D.S. 82.7). Finally he wished to keep on good terms with Corinth because she had some control over the sea route between Greece and Sicily, and so would be in a position to hamper trade between the two countries. Corinth, on the other hand, was keen to reap a reward for her investment in Timoleon's expedition, both in the form of booty and in the more lasting form of trade. The latter must be one of the reasons why she was willing to convey colonists to Sicily at her own expense (Plut. 23.3). Colonists, as indeed it turned out, would revive the agriculture of the island and would boost trade.

None of this evidence suggests that Timoleon held a Corinthian

[1] But I do not think that these mercenaries were properly paid: see pp. 56–7 above.

[2] For discussion of the views of H. D. Westlake, 'The Purpose of Timoleon's Mission', *AJP* 70 (1949), 65–75, see Note H, pp. 201–2.

[3] Dionysius II: Plut. 14.1; D.S. 70.2; Nep. 2.2. Leptines: Plut. 24.2; D.S. 72.5.

office for all his career in Sicily, or even during part of it. It merely shows that the links between Corinth and Timoleon were informal and were based on mutual advantage rather than on formal agreements. So far as we know, the political links between Corinth and Syracuse remained as loose both during and after Timoleon's time as they had been before his expedition.

Although Timoleon did not hold a Corinthian office, it does seem highly likely that he held an office at Syracuse for part of his career. No such statement is given to us by any source. But Plutarch's statement about Demaenetus πολλὰ κατηγορή-σαντος ἐν ἐκκλησίᾳ τῆς στρατηγίας (37.3; cf. Nep. 5.3) would imply that Timoleon held a Syracusan office; while at 36.7, in the reference to στρατηγίας ἀριστεῖον, στρατηγία could refer to an official Syracusan office, but the reference is ambiguous. That Timoleon did hold a Syracusan office seems the only reasonable way of explaining how he effected a number of somewhat autocratic measures. We hear of him enlarging the citizen body and bringing in colonists, dividing land, organizing a sale of all the houses in Syracuse,[1] transplanting the population of Leontini to Syracuse (D.S. 82.7), and dismissing mercenaries from Sicily (Plut. 30.2–3; D.S. 82.1–2). These are measures effected by a man who must have been invested with greater authority than a plain military command. If Timoleon had merely led the troops of Syracuse in war, there would have been no need for him to have held a Syracusan office; he could have led the troops of Syracuse in the same way as the Spartiate Cleandridas led the forces of Thurii in the fifth century,[2] or as Cleandridas' son, Gylippus, conducted military operations at Syracuse.[3] But

[1] These measures are referred to by Plut. 22.4–23; D.S. 82.5; 19.2.8; Nep. 3.1–2. On the division of land, see further D. Asheri, *Distribuzioni di terre nell'antica Grecia, Memoria dell'Accademia delle Scienze di Torino, Classe di Scienze morali, storiche e filologiche*, Serie 4a, No. 10 (1966), 29–30 and 91–3.

[2] We are not told that Cleandridas held an office at Thurii, and indeed none would be necessary if he did no more than command troops. See Strabo 6.1.14 (p. 264), where Cleandridas is termed *strategos* by Antiochus. At Polyaenus 2.10.1 he is described as ἄγων τὴν στρατιάν. He did become a citizen of Thurii at some stage (Thuc. 6.104.2).

[3] Gylippus is described by Thucydides as ἄρχοντα τοῖς Συρακοσίοις (6.93.2, cf. 6.91.4 and 7.2.1), although Plutarch refers vaguely to the *strategia* of Gylippus at Comp. 2.4.

Timoleon's sweeping civil measures can only have been carried out with official Syracusan authority.

So it would seem that Timoleon must have become *strategos autocrator* of Syracuse, the only office in the state which possessed supreme military and civil authority. The most likely time at which he would have been appointed to this office is after his capture of all Syracuse. It would appear that a *strategos autocrator* might only be elected by the whole citizen body,[1] with the result that no legally valid election could have taken place before Timoleon's capture of the whole city, while it is unlikely that the Syracusans, who had suffered under earlier commanders (Plut. 11.6), would have wished to elect Timoleon to such a position before they had complete trust in him.

The exact nature of the office of *strategos autocrator* held by Timoleon is not clear. As Westlake's investigation shows,[2] examination of earlier and later instances when the office was held is not particularly helpful, because an appointment was only made after a crisis had occurred, with the result that normal government had to be suspended. Thus the powers of a *strategos autocrator* were extremely wide – so much so that the holder entered into a kind of partnership with the Syracusan state[3] – although he was expected to lay down the office when the crisis had passed. It was because Timoleon did lay down the office 'cum primum potuit' (Nep. 3.4; cf. Plut. 37.10), unlike Dionysius I, for example, that he earned the unbounded gratitude of the Syracusans. We do not know whether Timoleon was elected first for a year, and then re-elected annually, or whether he was elected for an undefined period.[4]

[1] See D.S. 19.9.4; Polyaenus 5.3.7.

[2] *CHJ* 7 (1942), 77–9.

[3] Note the way in which Plutarch writes at 22.7: ἔδοξε τῷ Τιμολέοντι καὶ τοῖς Συρακοσίοις γράψαι πρὸς τοὺς Κορινθίους.

[4] Both Kahrstedt (*Griechisches Staatsrecht*, Vol. 1, pp. 367–8) and Hüttl (*Verfassungsgeschichte*, p. 127) would agree that Timoleon was *strategos autocrator* at Syracuse for a period, but Berve (*Die Tyrannis*, Vol. 2, p. 666) states that the only authority which Timoleon ever possessed was his Corinthian generalship, held by him throughout his career in Sicily. Unfortunately Berve does not give reasons for his unusual view. Finley, although he says that 'for all this activity Timoleon had no legitimate Sicilian authority' (p. 97), would seem to agree that Timoleon held some

The fact that Timoleon kept his Corinthian citizenship all his life (Plut. 39.5; D.S. 90.1) does nothing to help either the argument that in Sicily he was a Corinthian *strategos* or any other argument. Westlake speculates that Timoleon kept Corinthian citizenship in order to maintain ties between Syracuse and Corinth,[1] but this can be no more than a conjecture. Certainly from some time after he had captured all Syracuse Timoleon must have been regarded as a Syracusan citizen *de facto*, if not *de jure*. To be an office-holder he must have been a citizen. Then not only did he attend the assembly (Plut. 38.5–7; Nep. 4.2) and speak in it (Plut. 36.5, δημηγορῶν πρὸς τοὺς Συρακουσίους),[2] but he was also attacked in the assembly for his conduct of a *strategia* (Plut. 37.1–3; Nep. 5.3). That he actually became a Syracusan citizen might also be inferred from Nepos' statement 'nullus honos huic defuit' (3.5; cf. Plut. 38.4). That he is called Κορίνθιος in the funeral decree need not be particularly significant. Even if he had become a citizen of Syracuse, he would still be thought of by all as Κορίνθιος rather than as Συρακούσιος. Corinth was where he was born, and where he had spent the greater part of his life. The assumption that if he remained a citizen of Corinth, he cannot possibly have become a citizen of Syracuse also, is unreasonable because it implies a far greater preoccupation with legalistic niceties than Timoleon ever exhibited in any other sphere of his activities. In any event there were many prominent men who were citizens of more than one city. Dionysius I, for example, was a citizen of Syracuse and Athens; Dion was a citizen of Syracuse and Sparta (Plut. *Dion* 17.8). Hicetas may have been a citizen of Syracuse and Leontini. Whether Timoleon was a citizen of Syracuse is really a quibble: if he held an office in Syracuse, he must have been a citizen.

office at Syracuse (p. 95). Scheele doubts whether Timoleon was *strategos autocrator* at Syracuse: M. Scheele, ΣΤΡΑΤΗΓΟΣ ΑΥΤΟΚΡΑΤΩΡ: *Staatsrechtliche Studien zur griechischen Geschichte des 5. und 4. Jahrhunderts* (Leipzig 1932), pp. 47–9.

[1] *CHJ* 7 (1942), 75.

[2] It is true that it was not necessary to be a citizen to attend the assembly, or even to speak there: non-citizens might attend and speak by invitation, as Timoleon did at Rhegium (Plut. 10.4; D.S. 68.5–6). But non-citizens would not come to the assembly regularly.

Timoleon's constitution

Our knowledge of Timoleon's constitution is limited, but it should be remembered that, whatever we think of it, the ancient authors considered it a δημοκρατία. Plutarch and Diodorus, both writers biased in favour of Timoleon to a certain extent, make this point clear.[1] There are frequent references to the activity of the assembly, to which it would appear that any Syracusan citizen might come: Diodorus says that Timoleon proclaimed in Greece that Συρακόσιοι διδόασι χώραν καὶ οἰκίας τοῖς βουλομένοις μετέχειν τῆς ἐν Συρακούσσαις πολιτείας (82.5). Plutarch tells how statues were auctioned off after a vote of condemnation had been passed against each one (23.7), and how the Syracusans punished the wives and daughters of Hicetas and his friends, ἐν ἐκκλησίᾳ καταστήσαντες εἰς κρίσιν ἀπέκτειναν (33.1). We hear of Mamercus, too, ἀχθεὶς δ᾽ εἰς τὰς Συρακούσας καὶ παρελθὼν εἰς τὸν δῆμον (34.6; cf. Polyaenus 5.12.2). Then the assembly vótes that Syracuse should always employ a Corinthian general in certain circumstances (Plut. 38.4), and it adopts Timoleon's opinion on more important matters (Plut. 38.5–7; Nep. 3.5–6 and 4.2). Finally both Plutarch and Diodorus quote the decree passed by ὁ δῆμος ὁ Συρακουσίων on the occasion of Timoleon's funeral (Plut. 39.5; D.S. 90.1).

From Diodorus' narrative of Agathocles' rise to power we gather that the assembly appointed Agathocles chiliarch (19.3.4) and elected generals (19.5.5). Agathocles denounces his opponents in the assembly (19.3.5), and summons it after his seizure of power (19.9.1).

Yet the fact that the ancient authors consistently describe Timoleon's constitution as δημοκρατία, and give instances of decisions taken by the assembly, need not mean that the real power in the state was always held by the δῆμος.[2] As Finley says,[3]

[1] Plut. 22.3; 37.1. D.S. 70.5; cf. 19.4.3; 5.4–5.

[2] Indeed J. A. O. Larsen would argue that the term *demokratia* can be an especially vague one, denoting no more than rule by the people instead of by a king, so that it 'could be applied to any state with a republican form of government no matter how narrow or liberal' ('Demokratia', *Classical Philology* 68 (1973), 45–6).

[3] *Ancient Sicily*, p. 98. Cf. C. Mossé, *La Fin de la démocratie athénienne*, pp. 341–2.

popular assemblies have continued to meet even under tyrannies. Plutarch seems to refer to a meeting of the assembly at Leontini under Hicetas' tyranny (32.3), and he mentions how before Timoleon's capture of all Syracuse many people φρίκη καὶ μῖσος εἶχε πάντας ἀγορᾶς καὶ πολιτείας καὶ βήματος, ἐξ ὧν ἀνέφυσαν αὐτοῖς οἱ πλεῖστοι τῶν τυράννων (22.6).

Because of Plutarch's bias towards Timoleon his testimony that Timoleon's constitution was always a democratic one should be treated with caution. In general Plutarch appears to have been very distrustful of the δῆμος.[1] In *Dion* he notes that Corinth was an oligarchy: (Δίων) ὁρῶν καὶ τοὺς Κορινθίους ὀλιγαρχικώτερόν τε πολιτευομένους καὶ μὴ πολλὰ τῶν κοινῶν ἐν τῷ δήμῳ πράττοντας (53.4). And the oligarchic nature of the Corinthian government of the period is borne out by Diodorus' description of the choice of Timoleon to command the expedition to Sicily: the decision is taken by the γερουσία in the βουλευτήριον (65.6–9). But in *Timoleon* Plutarch first portrays the government of Corinth as a democracy (5.2), where Timoleon is nominated for the command by εἶς ἐκ τῶν πολλῶν (3.2), and later he portrays Timoleon putting power into the hands of the δῆμος after liberating Syracuse from tyranny. He wishes to create the impression that Timoleon was a popular choice for the mission of liberating Syracuse; and once Syracuse is liberated he wishes to stress Timoleon's insistence on δημοκρατία and ἐλευθερία, in contrast to the tyrannical oppression of Dionysius II and his predecessors. Plutarch's enthusiasm for Timoleon, combined with the latter's undoubted attempt to remove all signs of tyranny at Syracuse,[2] has created the misleading impression in the Life that Timoleon was a convinced democrat, and that he promoted a single constitution where the δῆμος continued to hold power; but it does not follow that a man who is μισοτύραννος (3.4) is necessarily a democrat. Closer examination of the accounts of Timoleon's constitution given by Diodorus and Plutarch is needed to see where the final control of the state lay.

Plutarch devotes no more than one vague passage to Timoleon's constitutional arrangements (24.3), which he places after the

---

[1] See, for example, *Theseus* 25; *Camillus* 36; *Marius* 28.
[2] Plut. 22.1–3; D.S. 70.4; Nep. 3.3.

capture of all Syracuse and before the battle of the R. Crimisus. According to him, Cephalus and Dionysius, simply termed νομοθέται, came from Corinth to help in the work. Diodorus, on the other hand, who gives us our most important evidence on Timoleon's constitution, places one set of reforms immediately after the capture of all Syracuse (under 343/2), and a further set of reforms at some time after the battle of the R. Crimisus (under 339/8) (70.5–6 and 82.6 respectively). He says that Cephalus was summoned from Corinth to arrange the second set of reforms, and that he bore the more precise title ἐπιστάτης καὶ διορθωτὴς τῆς νομοθεσίας (82.7).

Hammond[1] has argued that each of the two passages in Diodorus is a summary of Timoleon's legislation. But this view seems open to question. Certainly Diodorus' references to ἰδιωτικὰ συμβόλαια can only be thought consistent if the two passages are taken to refer to two separate occasions: in the first passage Diodorus says that Timoleon formulated precise laws concerning ἰδιωτικὰ συμβόλαια, and then in the second passage he specifically tells us that earlier legislation on these matters was left unaltered. Altogether it might be more reasonable to trust Diodorus' account of Timoleon's reforms, especially when that account may fit well with known events. In the first passage Diodorus tells how Timoleon set to work on a constitution immediately after he had expelled Dionysius II and had gained all Syracuse. Some form of fresh constitution must indeed have been urgently required to take the place of the tyranny which had prevailed in the preceding period. Yet Syracuse was still not secure against attack from the Carthaginians, or from other tyrants, with the result that the constitution hastily formulated now might be open to alteration later, when stability was eventually restored. At this early stage Timoleon may have felt it wise to respond to the citizens' joy at their liberation, by formulating the democratic constitution mentioned by Diodorus and Plutarch. This action, together with the immediate demolition of the tyrant's stronghold on Ortygia, will presumably have brought him an immense popular support, and will have served to remove any suspicion that he contemplated tyranny for himself. In taking

[1] CQ 32 (1938), 140–1; see also p. 33 above.

these steps he displayed a political astuteness and a flexibility which Dion had lacked (cf. Plut. 22.1–3). It is doubtful whether his own freedom of action was seriously hampered by the democratic constitution, since he seems to have been granted the extraordinary office of *strategos autocrator*.[1]

There is no evidence to suggest that Timoleon was a democrat by conviction. It is therefore not surprising that when an opportune moment arrived, he should have revised certain features of his earlier laws, in order to create a constitution which conformed more closely to his own views.[2] I believe that it is this revision which is recorded in Diodorus' second passage, under 339/8. Stability had now been restored and the work of reconstruction was beginning in earnest.

Although we have no explicit statement that Timoleon converted the Syracusan constitution into an oligarchy at this stage, the fact that he is known to have made substantial alterations to the democratic constitution could in itself suggest that he was instituting a less democratic form of government. In addition, Timoleon's own political preference is likely to have been for an oligarchy, since he was a member of a prominent family at Corinth, a city under oligarchic government. Similarly the legislators, whom he went to the trouble of summoning from Corinth, are likely to have been at least sympathetic to oligarchy. It is certainly possible that Timoleon summoned legislators to Syracuse from Corinth for no reason other than the historical link between the two cities. But it seems plausible to add the further reason, that legislators from Corinth would be sympathetic to oligarchy, and would therefore be in broad agreement with Timoleon's own constitutional views. It is perhaps worth remembering that Dion had deliberately summoned Corinthian counsellors because their views would be likely to correspond to his own (Plut. *Dion* 53.3).[3]

[1] See pp. 127–8 above.

[2] Cf. D.S. 82.6 πρὸς τὴν ἰδίαν ὑπόστασιν; for a similar use of ὑπόστασις as 'purpose', 'plan' or 'design' by Diodorus, see, for example, 1.3.2; 15.70.2; 16.32.3.

[3] Manni finds it impossible to regard Timoleon's revised constitution as oligarchic (p. 151). But he overemphasizes Corinthian influence at Syracuse (p. 147), and reaches his conclusion from an examination of the events in

Timoleon's reform of the constitution may have been generally acceptable to the original citizens of Syracuse, partly because they seem to have been given the opportunity to attain a strong position in the state (cf. Plut. 23.7), and partly because they must have seen that the city was about to be transformed by the influx of thousands of colonists. It is surely significant that Diodorus links the influx of colonists and Timoleon's revision of the constitution; and it is interesting that the variant reading of one manuscript of Diodorus 82.6 (ὡς τότ' ἐδόκει for ὡς ποτ' ἐδόκει) stresses the close link between the timing of the two events. In effect Timoleon was legislating for a new πόλις, where the incoming citizens would outnumber the original ones. Yet if the attacks of the δημαγωγοί Laphystius and Demaenetus are to be thought of as occurring after the second set of Timoleon's reforms, it would appear that not all opposition was silenced. It is possible that criticisms of Timoleon's *strategia* and an attempt to ensure his presence at a certain trial were the outward signs of a deeper disagreement with his various reforms (Plut. 37.1–3; Nep. 5.2–3).[1]

In the second of his two passages about Timoleon's constitutional reforms (82.6) Diodorus says that Timoleon revised τοὺς προϋπάρχοντας νόμους, which had been drawn up by Diocles; but in his first reference to these matters (70.5) he says that Timoleon himself formulated a democratic constitution, not that he delegated the work to a Diocles, or merely re-enacted the older laws of a Diocles. It is true that a Diocles is said to have

Sicily and Greece in the period before Agathocles' seizure of power in 317, rather than from a close examination of the evidence directly relating to Timoleon's constitution. E. Manni, 'Agatocle e la politica estera di Siracusa', *Kokalos* 12 (1966), 144–62.

[1] Westlake briefly suggests that Diodorus is correct in saying that Timoleon legislated twice (*CHJ* 7 (1942), 92), and this view is argued more fully by Sordi (pp. 47–8 and 102–4). However there is no evidence for her opinion that Timoleon was a convinced democrat until the time of the second set of legislation (cf. pp. 7 and 77–80), or for her strange conjecture that the foundation of the Amphipolia of Olympian Zeus is more likely to belong to the second set of legislation – inspired by Plato's oligarchic views – rather than to the first set (pp. 79–80 and 116–18). Diodorus places the foundation of the Amphipolia firmly in the first set of legislation, and suspected 'Platonic inspiration' cannot be adequate grounds for transferring it to the second set.

introduced a democratic constitution at Syracuse in 412 (D.S. 13.34.6–35.1; cf. 13.19.4), and this might possibly have been re-enacted by Timoleon. But Diodorus does not actually suggest such an idea.

Diodorus' statement at 82.6 might be reconciled with that at 70.5, if he is thought to mean that in promulgating a democratic constitution Timoleon drew largely on laws composed by the fifth-century democrat Diocles. This conjecture might be supported by a further reference in Diodorus (13.35.3), which would suggest that the Syracusans were using the laws of Diocles at the time when Cephalus was asked to make constitutional reforms:

οἱ δ' οὖν Συρακόσιοι κατὰ τοὺς νεωτέρους χρόνους κατὰ μὲν Τιμολέοντα νομοθετήσαντος αὐτοῖς Κεφάλου, κατὰ δὲ τὸν Ἱέρωνα τὸν βασιλέα Πολυδώρου, οὐδέτερον αὐτῶν ὠνόμασαν νομοθέτην, ἀλλ' ἢ ἐξηγητὴν τοῦ νομοθέτου, διὰ τὸ τοὺς νόμους γεγραμμένους ἀρχαίᾳ διαλέκτῳ δοκεῖν εἶναι δυσκατανοήτους.

But in other ways this statement seems extraordinary. If Diodorus is referring to the fifth-century Diocles here, it is unbelievable that Syracusans of the mid fourth century should have first re-introduced his laws, only to 'revise' them after a few years' use, because their archaic style had proved difficult to understand. It would certainly have been possible for the fifth-century Diocles to wrap his laws in archaic language, but as he was a democratic leader, he is hardly likely to have done so. Then if his law code did present substantial difficulties of comprehension for the Syracusans, it would never have been re-introduced at all in the mid fourth century. Furthermore, Diodorus' statement that many Sicilian cities continued to use the laws of Diocles into Roman times (13.35.3) could imply that these cities at least did not suffer from the difficulties of comprehension which the Syracusans apparently faced.

While some scholars have upheld the view that Diodorus does refer to the laws of the fifth-century Diocles,[1] others have conjectured that he may have confused the fifth-century democrat with an archaic Syracusan lawgiver, otherwise unknown, whose

[1] For example, E. Pais, 'A proposito della legislazione di Diocle siracusano', *Studi Italiani di Filologia Classica* 7 (1899), 75–98.

laws might well have been written in a language which was difficult to interpret in the mid fourth century.[1] The democrat might even have revised some laws of the archaic lawgiver. If such a conjecture is admitted, it may be that in Syracuse and in other Sicilian cities the 'laws of Diocles' came to be a traditional name for what were commonly represented to be the ancient laws of the state, in the same way that the Spartans claimed to adhere to the original 'laws of Lycurgus'. It is conceivable that a core of archaic laws did remain intact, beside later additions and alterations, and that for this reason the whole code continued to be ascribed to an archaic Diocles.[2] According to Diodorus, the Syracusans in the time of Hieron II seem to have regarded their laws as essentially those of Diocles, even after the adjustments made by Cephalus in Timoleon's time.

It would seem foolish to believe that in the mid fourth century the Syracusans did actually revive archaic laws unaltered, and that therefore the Corinthian Cephalus was summoned in 339/8 merely to elucidate passages which had proved difficult to understand. It is more reasonable to guess that, while Cephalus was summoned to make definite reforms, Timoleon tactfully minimized the scope of his assignment, and therefore had him termed ἐξηγητὴς τοῦ νομοθέτου, rather than νομοθέτης (cf. 16.82.7, where Cephalus is called ἐπιστάτης καὶ διορθωτὴς τῆς νομοθεσίας). Such tact on Timoleon's part could have contributed to Syracusan acceptance of a Corinthian legislator on this occasion in contrast to the hostility shown towards Corinthian counsellors in Dion's time (Plut. *Dion* 53.2–3).

Under Timoleon's first constitution the most exalted office was the Amphipolia of Olympian Zeus (D.S. 70.6). From the surviving sources which mention the Amphipolia it is not clear whether Timoleon elevated an office which was already in

---

[1] For example, G. de Sanctis, 'Diocle di Siracusa', *Studi Italiani di Filologia Classica* 11 (1903), 433–55 = *Scritti Minori*, Vol. 1, pp. 31–42 (*Storia e Letteratura* 99, Rome 1966); and V. Costanzi, 'Dioclea', *ASSO* 16–17 (1919/20), 1–7.

[2] The suggestion that the fifth-century Diocles may have deliberately taken over the language of older laws in some passages is made, for example, by J. de Crozals, 'Timoléon et la constitution de Syracuse au IVe siècle', *Annales de l'enseignement supérieur de Grenoble* 1 (1889), 400–1.

existence, or whether he created a completely new office.[1] But there is no doubt that even if the office did exist before Timoleon's reforms, as seems likely, he radically transformed it. From Diodorus' account it would appear that tenure of the office was limited to a year, and that the Syracusan year was now dated by the name of the Amphipolos. The office survived into Roman times, and indeed it is Cicero who describes the method of election:

Syracusis lex est de religione, quae in annos singulos Iovis sacerdotem sortito capi iubeat: quod apud illos amplissimum sacerdotium putatur. Quum suffragiis tres ex tribus generibus creati sunt, res revocatur ad sortem.[2]

The meaning of *genera* is not certain ('families'? 'classes'?), but it is clear from Cicero's account that election to the office was restricted to a limited number of citizens who were qualified by birth.

Timoleon's reasons for the foundation of the Amphipolia are not known. He may have wished to honour Zeus Eleutherios for his preservation of the city in a time of danger (cf. D.S. 10.28.1–2; 11.72.2). Although we know little about the office and its character, it is probable that it was not a political office in any narrow sense. It cannot have been an entirely meaningless office, however: Timoleon is not likely to have been so foolish as to set up a meaningless office, while those qualified to hold it would hardly have bothered to accept it. It seems more likely that the office carried with it some vague guardianship of the laws, the kind of function performed by the Areopagus at Athens.

Because selection was by lot, the best candidate would not always gain the office. We do not know even so much as the names of the men who held it before Roman times, except for Callimenes, the first holder (D.S. 70.6).[3] We do not hear of Timoleon himself occupying it. If the holders had taken part in political affairs, it seems strange that their participation should

---

[1] This point is discussed by W. Hüttl, *Verfassungsgeschichte*, pp. 121–2.

[2] *In Verrem Actio Secunda* 2.51.126–7; cf. 4.61.137, where Heraclius is described as 'homo nobilis, qui sacerdos Iovis fuisset'.

[3] A complete survey of known holders is given by Hüttl, *Verfassungsgeschichte*, pp. 122–3.

never be mentioned in any extant source, and that the office should have survived unscathed into Roman times. Hüttl (p. 123) suggested that Timoleon invested this most exalted office in the state with a religious sanctity in order to prevent any attempt to overthrow the constitution, yet this seems doubtful. Timoleon was surely not so naive as to imagine that a priest who held no power would be sufficient to stop revolutionaries. Certainly we hear of no attempt by an Amphipolos to curb the many disorders which filled Syracuse after Timoleon's time. The sanctity of the office might be sufficient to save the priest from murder by revolutionaries, and perhaps to stop him becoming tyrant himself; but he only held office for a year. Rather it would seem that Timoleon intended the Amphipolos to be little more than a figurehead, a nominal head of state, who should take no part in day-to-day affairs. It might even be that he intended this office to conceal where the real power in the state lay.[1]

Of the other office-holders in the state we know next to nothing:[2] Plutarch is not interested in any figure at Syracuse except Timoleon, while Diodorus' narrative for the whole period from the battle of the R. Crimisus to Agathocles' seizure of power in 317 is extremely brief. But it seems reasonable to infer that when Timoleon resigned from the position of *strategos autocrator*, he was replaced by a board of *strategoi*, who probably held office for a year. According to Diodorus, Damas was elected *strategos* against Acragas (19.3.1), while Antandrus was one of a number of *strategoi* who led an expedition to help Croton (19.3.3). That there was a board of *strategoi* is borne out by Agathocles' refusal to have other *strategoi* rule with him in 317 (19.9.3–4). Presumably the powers of the board were limited to the extent that for a war πρὸς ἀλλοφύλους a *strategos* had to be summoned from Corinth, in accordance with a decree of the

---

[1] If this was Timoleon's intention, he has apparently succeeded in pulling the wool over the eyes of Hüttl, who gives an inordinately long discussion of the Amphipolia (*Verfassungsgeschichte*, pp. 121–4). For a better discussion, see H. D. Westlake, *CHJ* 7 (1942), 90–1. Stier (*RE* VIA *s.v.* 'Timoleon', col. 1288) sees the Amphipolia as a political innovation. The discussion by H. Wentker, *Sizilien und Athen* (Heidelberg 1956), pp. 16–17, is unreliable.

[2] Cf. Hüttl, *Verfassungsgeschichte*, pp. 124–5; Westlake, *CHJ* 7 (1942), 91–2.

Syracusan assembly passed during Timoleon's lifetime (Plut. 38.4).[1] This decree was perhaps an attempt to prevent a victorious Syracusan *strategos* setting himself up as tyrant, in the way that Dionysius I had done. Certainly it is noticeable that in 314 the people of Acragas were prepared to trust a foreigner as *strategos* when they would not trust their οἰκεῖοι πολιτικοί, who might aim at tyranny (D.S. 19.70.2–4). We know of only one occasion when the Syracusan decree was put into effect, and Acestoridas was sent out from Corinth. Diodorus says that he was elected *strategos* in Syracuse (19.5.1).

We now come to consideration of whether Timoleon established a council at some stage. In my opinion his revised constitution at least will have included some form of council, with a limited membership. It is clear that he never gave control of the state to the Amphipolos, and it seems unbelievable that under the revised constitution he would have given such control to the popular assembly alone. This assembly would probably have been an unwieldy body. Its theoretical membership will have been huge, as it will have included all the established citizens of Syracuse, all the immigrants who settled in Syracuse itself, the people of Leontini who had been transferred to Syracuse (D.S. 82.7), the citizens of Centuripe and Agyrium (D.S. 82.4), and all the immigrants who settled on Syracusan territory (D.S. 19.2.8; cf. Justin 22.1.6). There is no doubt that this Syracusan territory was extensive and that it was colonized by a great number of immigrants, even if we cannot be certain of the total figure (D.S. 82.5). Most of those who belonged to the assembly in theory will have lived too far away to be able to attend meetings except on the rarest occasions. Plutarch makes the significant remark that when Timoleon died the Syracusans delayed the funeral for a few days, so that the περίοικοι καὶ ξένοι might come (39.2). Although there is no reason to suppose that any of the immigrants were περίοικοι in the technical, Spartan sense of men who were less than full citizens, it is certainly true that distance will have prevented many of those who lived in the outlying parts of Syracusan territory from exercising their right to attend

---

[1] For a discussion of the meaning of the phrase πρὸς ἀλλοφύλους, see Note G, p. 201.

the assembly.¹ So the assembly will have been an unrepresentative body, dominated by those who lived in Syracuse itself.

It is not likely that Timoleon and his legislators, all from oligarchic Corinth, would be willing to grant supreme power in the state to the assembly alone. Rather Timoleon would be keen to see that the city's prosperity should be revived as quickly as possible: a council, composed of οἱ βέλτιστοι καὶ γνωριμώτατοι (Plut. 1.6), would bring this about far more effectively than a popular assembly. Then there is no other Greek city known to us which did not have a council of some kind. Diodorus alludes to the existence of a council during this period at Agyrium, a far smaller city than Syracuse (83.3). Without a council of some kind efficient government of Syracuse would have been impossible.

To put forward this view, however, is to raise one of the most vexed points in Timoleon's career, mainly because there is no evidence in our sources for the existence of a council at Syracuse in his time. The only good evidence for the existence of a council at Syracuse comes from Diodorus' garbled account of Agathocles' rise to power. This council he describes most fully at 19.5.6. It would be dangerous to assume from this section anything more than that this συνέδριον ruled Syracuse during the time of the oligarchy (that is, presumably, after the return of the Syracusan forces sent to help Croton: see D.S. 19.3.5 and 4.3); and that it was composed of the principal wealthy citizens. It cannot be justly inferred from this passage alone either that the *synedrion* had a legal mandate to rule Syracuse, or that the *synedrion* was a council set up by Timoleon.

From two further passages it must be inferred that the *synedrion* did not have a legal mandate to rule Syracuse, and that it was not a council set up by Timoleon. First, at 19.4.3 Diodorus states:

ἔπειτα τῆς ἐν Συρακούσσαις δυναστείας καταλυθείσης καὶ τῶν περὶ τὸν Σώστρατον φυγόντων κατῆλθεν εἰς τὴν πατρίδα ['Αγαθοκλῆς]. συνεκπεσόντων δὲ τοῖς δυνάσταις πολλῶν ἐνδόξων ἀνδρῶν, ὡς ἂν τῆς ὀλιγαρχίας κεκοινωνηκότων τῆς τῶν ἑξακοσίων τῶν ἐπιφανεστάτων, ἐνέστη πόλεμος τοῖς φυγάσι πρὸς τοὺς ἀντεχομένους τῆς δημοκρατίας.

¹ According to Diodorus (5.2.2), Syracusan territory stretched southwards as far as Cape Pachynus.

Secondly, at 19.6.4, Diodorus describes Agathocles as αὐτὸς δὲ μεταπεμπόμενος τοὺς περὶ Πείσαρχον καὶ Διοκλέα, τοὺς δοκοῦντας προεστάναι τῆς τῶν ἑξακοσίων ἑταιρίας ... The first passage shows that the Six Hundred cannot have held power legally in Syracuse, while the second passage, in describing the Six Hundred as ἑταιρία (that is, a political party),[1] rather than as *synedrion*, demonstrates the same point. The possibility that the Six Hundred was a party rather than a legally constituted council would seem to be increased by the fact that it had no official leaders: in the second passage Agathocles calls for the followers of those who appear to be the leaders.

To maintain that τὸ τῶν ἑξακοσίων συνέδριον was the council set up by Timoleon, it is necessary to regard that body as being the legal *synedrion*, which degenerated at some stage into a political party (*hetairia*). Members of the *synedrion* would presumably have served for longer than one year when the Six Hundred controlled Syracuse by itself, although it is likely that membership of any council under Timoleon would have changed annually. Westlake suggests that it would be easier for the legal *synedrion* to change itself into an oppressive *hetairia* without undue disturbance than it would be for a revolutionary group of Six Hundred to seize control of the state: he considers that, although Diodorus' record of the period is cursory, there would at least be some mention of a violent seizure of power, if it had happened.[2] But this plea is a speculative one. As Westlake recognizes, there may be pieces of narrative of this period missing from the extant text of Diodorus.[3] Then to draw conclusions from what we might expect Diodorus to tell us is perilous, especially in cases where his extant narrative of a period is garbled. Westlake considers that a council of some kind was the effective ruler of Syracuse under Timoleon's constitution, so that we might reasonably expect Diodorus to mention this council, in a section where his narrative is comparatively clear. But he does not do so.

[1] ἑταιρία in this context should not be translated as 'club', 'conspiracy' or 'clique': these three terms imply that the body was small and informal. In fact the body was large and to some extent organized.

[2] *CHJ* 7 (1942), 89.

[3] See D.S. 19.3.3 and 10.3, where he refers to passages in the previous book which have not come down to us.

How much more dangerous is it to draw a conclusion from the fact that he does not mention an event in a garbled section.[1] Finally, Westlake does not stress sufficiently the point that the opening chapters of Diodorus' Book 19 are not intended to be a brief history of Syracuse from the death of Timoleon to 317; they are just a treatment of how Agathocles rose to power.[2] Thus any event which does not involve Agathocles in some way is liable to have been omitted.

We must recognize that we cannot resolve the problem of whether the Six Hundred was a legally constituted council or whether it was a political party, because our surviving evidence is so scanty. Lack of evidence also prevents us from telling whether Timoleon founded a council which survived in the period after his death. But in my opinion it does not matter which of the three alternative opinions is taken: that Timoleon founded a council, which continued in existence after his death and degenerated into a dominant political party; that he did not found a council, but some time after his death a revolutionary council seized power; that he did found a council, but for some reason it was disbanded, and then later a revolutionary council seized power.

I still believe that Timoleon did incorporate a council in his revised constitution at least. I repeat that there is no evidence to support this belief, or the belief that this constitution incorporated no council. The testimony of Diodorus' Book 19 on what happened after Timoleon's death is merely confusing. All we can say is that there is nothing in Book 19 to prove that Timoleon did not establish a council, and that the Book shows that a council was an institution familiar to the Syracusans. Instead, for want of evidence, we are unfortunately thrown back on judging solely from what Timoleon is *likely* to have established. In my view he is likely to have set up a council.[3]

---

[1] To take another example, we might reasonably expect Thucydides to tell us of the Athenian βουλή and the Spartan γερουσία: but he hardly ever mentions the former, and never refers to the latter by name.

[2] See D.S. 19.2.1: ἕνεκα δὲ τοῦ σαφεστέρας γενέσθαι τὰς κατὰ μέρος πράξεις βραχέα προαναληψόμεθα περὶ τοῦ προειρημένου δυνάστου.

[3] Justin's account (22.2.10–11) of Agathocles' rise to power does not resolve the problem of whether the Six Hundred was a legally constituted

We have no exact knowledge of how Timoleon might have divided power between office holders, council and popular assembly.

Timoleon's alliance

Our evidence on the relations of Syracuse with the other cities in the Greek zone of the island would suggest that Timoleon aimed to create a federation headed by Syracuse, in which each city remained independent. According to Plutarch (24.1; cf. 11.6) and Diodorus (72.5; 73.1; 82.4), Timoleon freed the cities of the island in order to restore their ἐλευθερία and αὐτονομία (cf. Nep. 1.1; 3.2). Diodorus' text of the funeral decree mentions that Timoleon αἴτιος ἐγενήθη τᾶς ἐλευθερίας τοῖς Σικελιώταις (90.1). It would seem that he began to link the cities of the Greek zone in a συμμαχία in the period between his capture of all Syracuse and the Carthaginian invasion (D.S. 73.2; cf. 77.5). Probably the nucleus of the alliance will have been formed by those cities which joined him for the express purpose of over-throwing Dionysius.[1] At first the alliance would presumably

council or a political party. He uses the term *senatus* (22.2.11: 'senatum trucidat'), but we cannot be sure either of the Greek word that he is trans-lating (*synedrion?*), or of whether he is actually referring to the Six Hundred by this term.

There is little value in giving an exhaustive bibliography on the problem of the Six Hundred. There are sensible discussions of the matter in H. J. W. Tillyard, *Agathocles* (Cambridge 1908), pp. 92–3, and in *CHJ* 7 (1942), 88–90, by H. D. Westlake. Hüttl, *Verfassungsgeschichte*, pp. 124–5, treats the problem. Of more recent writers H. Berve has taken the view that there is no evidence for the Six Hundred being a constitutional assembly; instead it was only a kind of *hetairia* (*Gnomon* 35 (1963), 381). Berve's views are also put forward in pp. 23–4 n. 17 of *Die Herrschaft von Agathokles*, which contains a list of some previous considerations of the problem (*Sitzungs-berichte der Bayerischen Akademie der Wissenschaften* 1952, Heft 5). Sordi (p. 79) believes that Timoleon instituted a council of Six Hundred, and Mossé, *La fin de la démocratie athénienne*, pp. 340 and 344, also leans towards this view. Ghinati considers the Six Hundred to have been an oligarchic council set up by Timoleon, and he cites evidence to demonstrate his unusual view that this council survived fundamentally unchanged into Roman times (p. 135 and notes 69 to 72): F. Ghinati, 'Synkletoi Italiote e Siceliote', *Kokalos* 5 (1959), 119–44.

[1] See Plut. 10.6 and D.S. 68.9 for Tauromenium; Plut. 12.9 for Adranum; D.S. 69.3 for Tyndaris; Plut. 13.2 and D.S. 69.4 for Catania. For discussion of Morgantina's alleged links with Timoleon, see Note J, pp. 202–3.

have been an offensive one, although it may well not have remained so after the battle of the R. Crimisus, which was won with the help of a number of allied contingents (Plut. 27.7; D.S. 78.2; 80.6).

It is certain that the συμμαχία remained in some form after the victory, as Diodorus says that Timoleon τὰς πόλεις ἐλευθερώσας εἰς τὴν συμμαχίαν προσεδέξατο (82.4). Acragas, Gela (both at Plut. 35.2) and Camarina (D.S. 82.7) seem to have been independent under Timoleon, and certainly what little we know of their relations with Syracuse in the period after his death does not suggest that Syracuse dictated their foreign policies.[1] According to Diodorus the people of Acragas remembered Timoleon as a man who had not tried to abuse his position by attempting to become tyrant (19.70.2–4). As Berve shows,[2] there is no evidence to support Sordi's thesis[3] that Timoleon changed his συμμαχία into a Syracusan 'empire'. The fact that for some unknown reason Centuripe and Agyrium were granted Syracusan citizenship (D.S. 82.4) is not sufficient evidence for the view that all the cities of the Greek zone received this grant of citizenship; while the clause in Timoleon's peace treaty with Carthage that τὰς μὲν Ἑλληνίδας πόλεις ἁπάσας ἐλευθέρας εἶναι (D.S. 82.3; this clause is not mentioned by Plutarch), if it refers to the cities of the Greek zone, would suggest a Carthaginian demand that Syracuse should not be given the chance to unite and dominate the zone.[4] Finally Timoleon is described by Plutarch as τὴν Σικελίαν ... παραδοὺς τοῖς κατοικοῦσιν (37.6), while the thousands of περίοικοι καὶ ξένοι who attended Timoleon's funeral (Plut. 39.2–3) apparently came to mourn a liberator, not a tyrant.

We do not know the extent to which Syracuse interfered in the

---

[1] For Acragas see D.S. 19.3.1; Gela, D.S. 19.4.4–7; Camarina, D.S. 19.110.3. However, according to D.S. 19.6.3, Morgantina helped Agathocles against Syracuse because her citizens so detested having to obey Syracusan orders (cf. Justin 22.2.1).

[2] H. Berve, *Gnomon* 35 (1963), 382–3.

[3] Sordi, pp. 69–71.

[4] For a discussion of the meaning of this clause, see pp. 84–5 above. In Sordi's view the treaty displays Timoleon rejecting the alliance's former ideals of equality in favour of the imperialist policy of earlier Syracusan tyrants (*Diodori Liber XVI*, p. 142).

internal affairs of the other Greek cities in Timoleon's time, but there is no evidence of any Syracusan attempt at domination. To the end of his life Timoleon seems to have been called upon to give advice on legal and constitutional matters (Plut. 35.4; Nep. 3.2–3; 4.1). Plutarch's text of the funeral decree says that Timoleon ἀπέδωκε τοὺς νόμους τοῖς Σικελιώταις (39.5). There are a few traces of an Amphipolia on inscriptions found in Sicilian cities, but in these cases we cannot tell whether the office was introduced in Timoleon's time, or how closely it resembled the Amphipolia at Syracuse.[1]

Nothing is known of the constitutions adopted by those cities which Timoleon refounded or freed from tyranny. Diodorus makes a passing reference to the fact that a βουλευτήριον was built at Agyrium (83.3), but we do not know exactly when this was done. Since many of the cities liberated by Timoleon will not have been able to formulate their own constitutions unaided, it is reasonable to imagine that they took his advice on constitutional matters (Plut. 35.4).[2]

[1] These inscriptions are listed by W. Hüttl, *Verfassungsgeschichte*, p. 123.

In 1963 Tusa published two inscriptions found during excavations at Solunto: these relate to an Amphipolia of Olympian Zeus in this city, and are dated by Tusa to between the end of the third century and the middle of the second century B.C. He reviews the other inscriptions relating to Amphipoliai in Sicily, and comes to the reasonable conclusion that the Amphipolia of Solunto seems to be the one most closely related to the Syracusan Amphipolia founded by Timoleon. He conjectures that some Syracusans brought this institution from their own city to Solunto, but there is no firm evidence on this point (V. Tusa, 'L'Anfipolia a Solunto', *Kokalos* 9 (1963), 185–94).

[2] The fact that Timoleon is known to have given advice to some cities on constitutional matters might help to explain why many cities later claimed to use the same laws as Syracuse (D.S. 13.35.3).

F. Sartori sensibly rejects any idea that the office of πρόαγορος, which appears on Hellenistic and Roman inscriptions in some Sicilian cities, was instituted by Timoleon. No source mentions a πρόαγορος at Syracuse. ('Proagori in città Siceliote', *Kokalos* 7 (1961), 63–6). Although G. Manganaro does not discuss this particular point, he seems to agree with Sartori on the matter ('Tre tavole di bronzo con decreti di *proxenia* del Museo di Napoli e il problema dei proagori in Sicilia', *Kokalos* 9 (1963), 216). Finally T. Ardizzone has a discussion of some length in support of Sartori ('Proagori in città Siceliote', *Kokalos* 13 (1967), 155–60).

CHAPTER 8

Archaeological evidence for Timoleon's revival of the Greek zone of Sicily[1]

Excavations carried out in the Greek zone of Sicily since the Second World War have enabled us to view the Timoleontic period in a completely new light. The old idea that the Timoleontic revival was a brief and insignificant episode shamelessly over-praised by biased sources has now been superseded; and the wealth of evidence for the island's revival seems to present us with a strange case where the ancient authors' generous praise is perhaps not sufficiently lavish. Certainly our new knowledge gained from archaeology might make the highest figure for the total number of colonists introduced by Timoleon, 60,000, seem an under-estimate rather than an exaggeration.[2] Archaeology has now confirmed the view of the ancient sources that from 405 to c. 340 much of southern Sicily was ruined, undeveloped and under-populated. The destruction first wrought by the Carthaginians at the end of the fifth century was not repaired until Timoleon's day.[3]

The moment at which he first asked for colonists is not certain. Diodorus (82.4) and Nepos (3.1 – 'quibus rebus confectis') place the whole colonization programme after the battle of the R. Crimisus, but Plutarch has the programme start before the battle (22.7) and continue afterwards (35). While his version may be the more exact, the great majority of colonists will certainly only have come after fears of another Punic invasion had been dispelled by Timoleon's decisive victory.

[1] For the position of sites in the central part of southern Sicily, reference may be made to the map in *NSc* 12 (1958), 289.

[2] Athanis in Plut. 23.6; cf. D.S. 82.5. The reliability of these figures in Plutarch and Diodorus is discussed by H. Schaefer, 'Πόλις μυρίανδρος', *Historia* 10 (1961), 294–5.

[3] For literary references to the ruin of southern Sicily in the first half of the fourth century, see Plut. 1.3; 22.4–6; 35.1–2; D.S. 65.9; 83.1; Nep. 3.1–3.

My sections below, devoted to excavation sites which display the revival of the Greek zone under Timoleon, are unfortunately brief, and inevitably seem isolated when the literary evidence to which they might be related has perished. Only major developments are covered. Consideration of pottery and other finds is lacking.[1] Because Timoleon worked only in the Greek zone of Sicily I have not covered the Punic zone or Lipari: in fact both areas seem to have thrived during the second half of the fourth century. Further, two cities in the Greek zone receive no consideration despite their prominence in our sources for Timoleon's career. At Syracuse there seem to have been a few alterations to the Euryalus fortress during the third quarter of the fourth century,[2] but uninterrupted occupation of the city in ancient and modern times has prevented any widespread search for traces of Timoleontic Syracuse.[3] Then at Agyrium there seem to be no significant archaeological remains.[4]

The contrast between the desolation of southern Sicily in the first half of the fourth century and its rapid recovery of prosperity in the second half is certainly striking. But equally striking is the fact that the whole island remained prosperous during the Agathoclean period and beyond it (D.S. 16.83.2). Expansion continued at Megara Hyblaea and Morgantina, for example,

[1] For a full treatment of vases, see A. D. Trendall, *Red-figured vases of Lucania, Campania and Sicily: Book III, Sicilian* (Oxford 1967). Trendall considers that production of red figured vases flourished in Sicily during the second half of the fourth century, after a decline in the first half (see pp. 194; 210; 577). He believes that the 'Manfria painter' may have come from Campania to Sicily in the decade 340–330; indeed there was perhaps two-way traffic between these areas (pp. 448 and 582).

[2] F. E. Winter, 'The chronology of the Euryalos Fortress at Syracuse', *AJA* 67 (1963), 377.

[3] H.-P. Drögemüller, *Syrakus: Zur Topographie und Geschichte einer griechischen Stadt* (Heidelberg 1969 – *Gymnasium* Beihefte, Heft 6), p. 106, believes that Neapolis was built up in Timoleon's time: he refers to the excavations of G. V. Gentili, 'Scoperte nelle due nuove arterie stradali, la Via di Circonvallazione, ora Viale P. Orsi, e la Via Archeologica, ora Viale F. S. Cavallari', *NSc* 5 (1951), 261–334, esp. 332.

[4] This is the opinion of G. Agnello, 'Il castello di Agira', *Siculorum Gymnasium* 13 (1960), 226. Archaeology has not yet confirmed the conjecture of V. Casagrandi-Orsini that the area around modern Troina, to the north-east of Agyrium, was settled in Timoleon's day by colonists from Cilicia Trachea (*Catalecta di storia antica* (Catania 1898), pp. 167–73).

despite political disturbances. Coin evidence points to the same conclusion. Only at Gela and in its immediate hinterland do we find some developments curtailed after the fighting between Agathocles and the Carthaginians in that area during 311/10. Because there is no visible break which an archaeologist may detect between the 'age of Timoleon' and the 'age of Agathocles', the former is peculiarly difficult to define. I use the term with reference to the years *c.* 340 to 317, for although Timoleon himself had died in the 330s, his settlement of affairs lasted for the most part unchanged till 317. And 317, the year of Agathocles' seizure of power at Syracuse, only marked the end of Timoleon's political influence; the prosperity he set in motion continued to increase.

Tyndaris

Founded by Dionysius I in 396 as a colony to guard the north coast of Sicily (D.S. 14.78.5–6), Tyndaris is known to have allied with Timoleon after the battle of Adranum (D.S. 16.69.3). Excavations have been conducted here, but the difficulties of precise dating have made it hard to distinguish constructions erected in Timoleon's time from those erected either just before his time or just after it. For the city was occupied without interruption during the fourth century, so that there was no clear break between occupation of an earlier age and a Timoleontic revival (as there was at Megara Hyblaea or Gela, for example). Then later alterations made to the surviving monuments have sometimes destroyed evidence useful for dating purposes.

These difficulties have led to a somewhat acrimonious debate between archaeologists over the date of major alterations made to the original walls of the city. Barreca would place these alterations at some point in the fourth century, possibly before 317, whereas Lamboglia maintains that they were not carried out until the period between the death of Agathocles and the Mamertine conquest (289–278 B.C.).

The theatre may be dated more securely, although extensive re-modelling in Roman times has changed its appearance considerably. After a very detailed examination of the evidence

Bernabò Brea concludes that building began in the late fourth/ early third centuries B.C., that is, just after the Timoleontic period. Yet the start of such an ambitious and costly project at this time shows that Tyndaris must have flourished under Timoleon.

Megara Hyblaea

Excavations conducted since 1949 by Villard and Vallet have brought to light remains of the Hellenistic city, which is first heard of in Diodorus' narrative for 309 (20.32.3–4). The date of the city's re-foundation after its destruction by Gelon before 480 (Herod. 7.156.2–3) was previously not known, although the revival was definitely later than the Athenian siege of Syracuse, since Thucydides mentions that the site was deserted at that time (6.49.4).

Villard and Vallet have now shown convincingly that the north-east angle of the plateau was re-occupied in Timoleon's time along the lines of the old city. The flood of colonists into Syracusan territory (cf. D.S. 16.82.5) makes such re-occupation of the spot seem likely. The pottery and coins[1] found in the area point to the same conclusion, while a small necropolis on the edge has yielded vases datable to the second half of the fourth century; the siting of this necropolis shows that the first settlement was intended to be small.

A Doric temple came to light in 1959. Its date of construction has been cautiously placed between 320 and 310 by the French archaeologists, who believe that it was probably dedicated to Aphrodite, and that it was built by the colonists whom Timoleon invited from all over the Greek world.

It was not until the third century that the whole site of the ancient city was re-occupied, yet the initial impetus for its revival seems to have come from Timoleon.

Camarina

Like nearby Gela, Camarina was destroyed by the Carthaginians in 405 B.C. (D.S. 13.108.3 and 111.3–6; cf. 14.68.2). Diodorus' remark that Timoleon did no more than reinforce the population

---

[1] See Megara Hyblaea 1949 hoard, No. 16 in my list of Hoards.

of the city (16.82.7), instead of building it up from nothing, might suggest that the place was re-occupied before the middle of the fourth century (in 397 perhaps, after the defeat of the Carthaginians). Yet although there may have been some insignificant re-occupation, no work on fortifications was allowed (D.S. 13.114.1), and no real restoration of the city was undertaken before the second half of the fourth century, according to di Vita, who has conducted excavations there.[1]

In his opinion all the archaeological evidence points to a revival of the city in Timoleon's time. Little pottery attributable to the first half of the fourth century was found during his excavations, while coins of this period were completely lacking. Further, only a tiny proportion of the tombs in the city's main necropolis, at Passo Marinaro, can be assigned to this time. On the other hand, pottery, coins and burials datable to the second half of the fourth century are far more numerous.

Di Vita also places within this period the building of a wall to defend the acropolis, and the organization of the sacred area to the west of this part of the city. The private houses built at this time are large and wealthy, and display the careful workmanship of their construction. Probably the full extent of the fifth-century city was eventually re-occupied by the colonists (180 hectares). They certainly repaired the perimeter wall; in this connection di Vita has paid particular attention to an almost square tower built in the mid fifth century, destroyed at the end of that century, and then restored in Timoleon's time.

Camarina seems to have continued to thrive, at least until c. 280 when it was attacked by the Mamertines (D.S. 23.1.4).[2]

---

[1] From the historical point of view Καμάριναν is therefore implausible at Plut. 31.2: see Note K, pp. 203–4.

[2] A mid third-century inscription from the sanctuary of Asclepius on Cos suggests that colonists from the island took part in the revival of Camarina in Timoleon's time. Coans seem to have possessed συγγένεια, οἰκειότης and ἰσοπολιτεία in Camarina, and religious links were maintained between the two places. For the text of the inscription, see R. Herzog and G. Klaffenbach, *Asylieurkunden aus Kos, Abhandlungen der Deutschen Akademie der Wissenschaften zu Berlin* 1 (1952), 21–3. For a full discussion, with bibliography, see J. Seibert, *Metropolis und Apoikie: Historische Beiträge zur Geschichte ihrer gegenseitigen Beziehungen* (Würzburg 1963), pp. 129–32, and Note L, pp. 204–5 below.

Scornavacche

Situated at the confluence of the two branches of the R. Dirillo (one from near Vizzini, the other from near Chiaramonte), Scornavacche was founded in the first half of the sixth century as a station on the interior road from Syracuse to Gela, but it was destroyed at the end of the fifth century by the Punic force which swept over the territories of Gela and Camarina (D.S. 13.108.3).

Excavations by di Vita have shown that this centre was restored in Timoleon's time: as many as eighty per cent of the coins found there were issued in this period.[1] The dwelling area, with its little houses probably arranged along a few parallel roads, was small in size and was apparently not defended. This vulnerability left the place dangerously exposed to attack, and it was finally destroyed around 280, never to be re-occupied.

These circumstances have been of great significance for the archaeologists, since it has been possible to make a detailed examination of the centre's main activity, the manufacture of pottery from local clay, within a well-defined period (*c.* 340–*c.* 280). The finds of moulds, terracottas and kilns, and the large pottery deposits have not only enabled the archaeologists to reconstruct a whole potter's workshop, but they also furnish excellent evidence for the continuing prosperity brought about by the remarkable recovery made under Timoleon. The pottery manufactured at Scornavacche was sold to the local population and to travellers passing along the road from Syracuse to Gela.

Of some historical interest is the classicizing bent of the potters at Scornavacche, a bent also found in contemporary pottery of Gela. Di Vita shows that these men were certainly influenced by the new designs they saw, but that even at the time of the destruction of their centre, they were still following some designs used in the early Timoleontic period. Such designs were in their turn old-fashioned by Greek standards in the mid fourth century, but they were followed because development in pottery types was unknown in southern Sicily in the first half of the fourth century, when production had been at a standstill. Poverty and

---

[1] No detailed report on the coin finds has been published, but see *Archivio Storico Siracusano* 2 (1956), 38 n. 20, and *Bollettino d'Arte* 44 (1959), 362 n. 49.

disorder had isolated the area from the artistic currents of that period. Probably the old designs remained current into the third century because they were in demand, and were therefore profitable to manufacture.

Castiglione

Di Vita has also excavated a large centre at Castiglione, near Comiso. Its history seems similar to that of Scornavacche. It was founded in the sixth century, but was destroyed at the end of the fifth century. Revival under Timoleon followed in the mid fourth century. Then the place was probably destroyed again at the same time as Scornavacche; certainly it was deserted by 250 B.C.

Helorus

Little is known of this city in the fourth century, but excavations in 1958 and 1959 uncovered a perimeter wall, which seems to have been reconstructed in Timoleon's time. This dating is supported by the find of a Timoleontic coin in the foundation layer. In 1964 a sanctuary was discovered just outside the city. Dedicated to Demeter and Kore it was first erected in the sixth century, and was later reconstructed, probably in the Timoleontic period.[1]

Morgantina

Morgantina is not referred to in any of the sources for Timoleon's career. The excavations conducted there in recent years by Princeton University have shown that the city was prosperous in Timoleon's time, but that it flourished even more under Agathocles.

One of the most significant finds made by the American archaeologists is that of a sanctuary of Demeter and Kore (one of two in the city), which seems to have reached its most developed form in the third quarter of the fourth century B.C. Since remains of an earlier, more rudimentary sanctuary also came to light, it is possible to speculate that a permanent building was erected for the shrine during Timoleon's time because of the

[1] Cf. T.C.I. *Guida d'Italia: Sicilia*, p. 674.

favour enjoyed by Demeter and Kore after his success in the island. The two goddesses were said to have accompanied him on his expedition (Plut. 8.1–2 and 5–8; D.S. 66.3–5).

Further constructions have been dated to the Timoleontic period. Sjöqvist would place the erection of the city wall encircling the Serra Orlando ridge within the decade 340–330,[1] and he believes that Necropolis III, which extends along the city wall, was first used at the same time.[2]

Even more significant is his dating of the grid plan in Areas IV and V to Timoleon's time. Although the grid was not filled out immediately, it nevertheless dictated the siting of the great agora, which only began to be built in the Agathoclean period. Thus it seems to have been in Timoleon's time that an ambitious and lavish expansion of Morgantina was envisaged, even though the actual scheme was not put into effect until later.[3]

There was some simple form of theatre in the city in Timoleon's time, but nearly all traces of it were swept away by the Agathoclean theatre.

A burial plot, perhaps belonging to one or more rural villas, was found by the bank of the R. Gornalunga a few miles northeast of Morgantina: Ross Holloway's dating of the objects in the plot to c. 325 B.C. suggests that the peaceful conditions of this time prompted the re-settlement of the countryside around the city.[4] A similar pattern of re-settlement is seen in the hinterlands of Gela and Agrigento.

Gela

Excavations conducted by Orlandini and Adamesteanu at Gela have provided the most complete evidence for the revival of a Sicilian city under Timoleon. This brief section can hardly do full justice to their work.

[1] *AJA* 64 (1960), 127.   [2] *AJA* 64 (1960), 128.
[3] See *AJA* 64 (1960), 133; cf. *AJA* 66 (1962), 142 and *AJA* 71 (1967), 249.
[4] *AJA* 67 (1963), 289–91. Further evidence for the re-settlement of the Sicilian countryside in the second half of the fourth century is provided by J.-P. Morel, 'Recherches archéologiques et topographiques dans la région d'Assoro (Province d'Enna, Sicile)', *MEFR* 75 (1963), 263–301; and by V. Tusa, 'Libertinia, Rinvenimenti archeologici', *NSc* 13 (1959), 350–7.

After the city had been sacked by the Carthaginians in 405 (D.S. 13.111.2) there was some insignificant re-occupation, but no revival until Timoleon's time (Plut. 35.2; cf. Note L, pp. 204–5). The city then continued to be inhabited until *c*. 280 when it was attacked by the Mamertines (D.S. 23.1.4) and the people were removed by Phintias to a new city at Licata, which he named after himself (D.S. 22.2.2). There was then no important restoration until mediaeval times. The absence of later layers of occupation, such as are found at Syracuse or Agrigento, for example, has made it possible to study the remains of the period *c*. 340 to *c*. 280 in considerable detail. And this study has been further aided by the fact that there is a clean break in the city's history between 405 and *c*. 340.

The revival of Gela in Timoleon's time is an impressive achievement, of which only the main features may be mentioned here. A new city wall was built to enclose the whole hill of Gela, whereas the earlier city had been limited to the western section of the hill. The finest part of this wall to survive is at Capo Soprano. Even the bricks forming the upper part have been preserved intact by the sand which covered all the fortifications from ancient times until their discovery in 1948. It is thought that the Timoleontic wall extended to a height of approximately three metres; the sections of the wall higher than this were added later, most probably because sand immediately began to envelop the lower section.

Secure in the protection of their extended perimeter wall the Geloans laid out a new dwelling area on an orthogonal plan in the western part of the hill. Great pressure to expand must have come from the many new colonists, but the fact that expansion occurred in this particular direction seems remarkable, since it involved building over what had been the city's necropolis in the fifth century.

On the acropolis a former sacred area was turned into a sector for private houses laid out in terraces. This sector was destroyed by Agathocles in 311/10 (D.S. 19.107).

Various shrines were also restored.

By comparing material found at Gela with material found elsewhere, and by examining the strata and the finds made in them (especially coins), Orlandini has distinguished three phases in the material at Gela. It is the first of these, running from 339 to 320, which may be termed Timoleontic. The abundance of rich material dating from this period and the great expansion of the city both testify to the importance of Gela's fourth-century revival. Timoleon certainly deserved to be considered second founder of the city (Plut. 35.3; cf. Nepos 3.2).

Hinterlands of Agrigento and Gela

Extensive excavations carried out in this area have shown the close links between the lives of these two cities and their surrounding country. Almost all the centres of the hinterland seem to have been sacked by the Carthaginians in 405 (D.S. 13.108.3), and unstable conditions in the island did not allow much re-occupation before Timoleon's time. Then, along with Agrigento and Gela, the centres grew to enjoy a period of prosperity. The simultaneous revival of a large part of the Greek zone of Sicily is excellent evidence for the thoroughness of Timoleon's work. I note here only the main developments in each centre.

Excavations at *Butera* presented some difficulties because the modern town occupies the site of the ancient town, but Adamesteanu was able to examine the necropolis in the zone of *Piano della Fiera*. Here there were no burials between c. 580 B.C. and the mid fourth century. Those of the latter date resemble the pyramidal funerary monuments noted by Diodorus at Agyrium (16.83.3). The sanctuary of *Fontana Calda* was also excavated: the dedications made here from c. 340 onwards far outnumber those made prior to 405.

Monte Desusino, which Adamesteanu would identify with the ancient Phalarion, was an important centre, dominating the road from Gela to Licata. Here the town plan is probably to be attributed to Timoleon's time, as are perhaps some of the fortifications, although these may have been altered by Agathocles in 311/10 (cf. D.S. 19.108.2). He may have pulled down Timoleontic buildings in the course of this work.[1]

At *Monte Bubbonia*, a flourishing town destroyed in 405, life resumed in Timoleon's time, but for some unknown reason the

[1] *NSc* 12 (1958), 343-5.

place does not seem to have done well, and those who returned clustered round the higher of the two platforms enclosed by archaic fortifications. These fourth-century inhabitants built a far more modest wall to defend their settlement.

The position of *Monte Saraceno*, directly in the path of any invader moving from Agrigento to Gela, together with the absence of material from the first half of the fourth century, makes it likely that the town was sacked by the Carthaginians in 405. At the time of the Timoleontic revival the whole of the acropolis area seems to have been restored, fine houses were erected, and a sixth-century temple was rebuilt. The town plan, with its arrangement of houses in terraces, also dates from Timoleon's time.

It is not known how *Vassallaggi*, situated by the route from Agrigento to Enna, fared at the time of the Punic invasion of 405. Yet Adamesteanu's excavations have made it clear that there was a significant revival here in Timoleon's time. Houses were rebuilt and were laid out in terraces, and alterations were made to the town's defence works. In the necropolis the tombs, with their rich vases, also display Vassallaggi's wealth at this period.

Situated on the western bank of the R. Salso, *Gibil Gabib* does not seem to have been sacked by the Carthaginians, but it, too, experienced an upsurge of prosperity from *c.* 340 onwards. A town plan was created and important alterations were made to the fortifications: both these new developments are firmly dated by finds of Timoleontic coins and pottery. A local pottery workshop was also opened here.

Sabucina, to the north-east of Caltanissetta, was abandoned in the first half of the fourth century, but finds of coins, new houses and alterations to the defences all show that the place revived in Timoleon's day. The city at *Montagna di Marzo*, north-west of Piazza Armerina, seems to have flourished too.[1]

The lack of any objects which may be assigned a date after 310 at Vassallaggi, Gibil Gabib and Sabucina suggests that these three centres were deserted at that time.

Aerial photographs and preliminary investigations suggest that *Monte Lavanca Nera, Balate, Castellazzo, Cozzo Mususino* and *Terravecchia* (the last four in the Marianopoli area) may all have

[1] Montagna di Marzo is not marked on the map in *NSc* 12 (1958), 289.

been laid out with new town plans in Timoleon's time, but no definite conclusions may be formed before the places are excavated fully.

In addition to small towns and fortified posts, farms in the hinterland of Gela have been investigated. Nearly all of them were abandoned or destroyed at the time of the Punic invasion, and life only resumed under Timoleon.

One of the most important of these farms was at *Manfria*, near the coast west of Gela. There are weak traces of life here during the first half of the fourth century, but it was in Timoleon's time that buildings were erected and a workshop opened, as the rich pottery deposits indicate. The elegant vases produced by the 'Manfria painter' are of considerable significance in the history of vase painting in Sicily.[1] Both farm and workshop were destroyed in the course of the fighting between Agathocles and the Carthaginians in 311/10, and the site was not re-occupied in classical times.

Excavations at *Milingiana* and *Priorato* have uncovered farms built in the Timoleontic period, on the ruins of farms of the archaic period. Neither of these sites has yielded traces of occupation during the first half of the fourth century. In the area where the two farms are situated have been found the ruins of a number of other farms, so far unexcavated, which may well have histories similar to that of Milingiana and Priorato. It seems likely that the colonists invited to Sicily by Timoleon spread all over the fertile plains west of Gela.

Finds at *Feudo Nobile* and *Contrada Farello*, east of Gela, suggest that the settlements in these places were also revived during Timoleon's time.[2]

Timoleontic buildings and a necropolis have been found at *Monte Raffe*, but no detailed report on the excavations at this site is known to me.[3]

[1] See above, p. 147 n. 1, and D. Adamesteanu, 'Vasi figurati di Manfria', in *Istituto di Archeologia dell'Università di Catania: Scritti in onore di Guido Libertini* (Florence 1958), pp. 25–34.

[2] Contrada Farello is not marked on the map in *NSc* 12 (1958), 289.

[3] The excavations are mentioned most fully in *SIFET* 2–3 (1957), 81–4; *Rev. Arch.* 49 (1957), 175–7; P. Griffo, *Sulle Orme della Civiltà gelese* (Agrigento 1958), pp. 28–9; and *Fasti Archeologici* 12 (1959), No. 2853.

Agrigento

Although Agrigento was sacked by the Carthaginians in 406 (D.S. 13.90.1–5) and was revived by Timoleon (Plut. 35.2), it was inhabited throughout Hellenistic and Roman times, with the result that it is hard to isolate the Timoleontic phase of the city's development.

Before the Second World War Marconi's investigation of the fortifications of Agrigento led him to the view that the city was given a new defensive system in Timoleon's time, and this view was confirmed by the discovery of Timoleontic coins under the foundations of a square turret to the north of the temple of Juno.[1] Marconi's conclusions have also been supported by Griffo and Schmiedt, who have been able to increase our knowledge of the defences with the help of aerial photographs.

Aerial photography has made an even more significant contribution to our knowledge of Agrigento in showing that the city had an extensive urban plan, a point doubted until recent years. Photographic testimony was confirmed by the excavations of de Miro in the San Nicola quarter. He believes that this area had been unoccupied for about a century and a half before it was rebuilt in the second half of the fourth century. Since the urban plan of the area seems to have been conceived in conjunction with the defences, it might be possible to believe that it was laid out for the first time in Timoleon's day. But the plan is also closely linked with the temple of Olympian Zeus, while traces of earlier houses have been found under the Timoleontic buildings in the San Nicola quarter, so that the original layout must have been created much earlier than the mid fourth century. Yet the fact that this quarter, which had remained unoccupied for perhaps 150 years, was rebuilt under Timoleon is excellent evidence for the expansion of the city in his time.

Further excavations conducted by de Miro in 1958 between the temple of Olympian Zeus and the southern wall of the city have brought to light a group of buildings connected with a shrine,

---

[1] I am not sure whether a report on the excavation of this turret has been published. Its discovery is known to me only from brief references in *Kokalos* 4 (1958), 28 and in P. Mingazzini and L. Rocchetti, 'Agrigento', p. 150, in *Enciclopedia dell'Arte*, Vol. 1.

already investigated by Gabrici in 1922. De Miro shows that the whole complex was erected in the second half of the fourth century, and that it remained in use for thirty to forty years. On the basis of finds made he suggests that the buildings may have been used for a cult of Tyche, possibly linked with a form of chthonic cult. It is impossible to say whether this dedication is in its turn linked with Timoleon's interest in Tyche, or whether it reflected the religious interests of the new colonists from Elea (Plut. 35.2).[1]

Excavations have also been carried out in the Rock Sanctuary (of Demeter) near Gate I. The site has been much altered and damaged, but according to Zuntz, who has examined it closely, it was restored in Timoleon's time after long neglect, and was made into a Nymphaeum.

Heraclea Minoa

Situated on the eastern bank of the R. Halycus (modern R. Platani) Heraclea Minoa came into Punic hands under the terms of the treaty of 383 B.C. (D.S. 15.17.5), and it was still a Punic city when Dion landed there in 357 (D.S. 16.9.4; Plut. *Dion* 25.11). Then it reverted to the Greek zone after Timoleon's peace with the Carthaginians, when it was agreed that the R. Halycus should form the eastern boundary of Punic territory in Sicily (Plut. *Tim.* 34.2; D.S. 16.82.3). But in 313 the city was ceded to the Carthaginians once more (D.S. 19.71.7).

Excavations by de Miro have shown that there was considerable activity at Heraclea Minoa in the second half of the fourth century. He reasonably suggests that the revival of the city was made possible by the peace and prosperity which Timoleon won for the Greek zone of Sicily. Work has centred round the perimeter wall and the theatre. In de Miro's opinion the colonists who repopulated the city in Timoleon's time constructed a fine perimeter wall (probably in double technique), which incorporated the remains of an older, ruined wall. Particular attention was paid to the defence of the eastern side of the city, which lay exposed to attack. Towers and gates were placed

---

[1] On the colonists who came to Gela and Acragas mentioned at Plut. 35.2, see Note L, pp. 204–5.

at intervals along the fortification. In all the perimeter wall was about six kilometres long.

The construction of a large theatre seems good evidence for the ambitious outlook and prosperity of the citizens. No certain date can be given for the start of the work, but de Miro's opinion that building began in the last decades of the fourth century appears to be soundly based. He reaches this view after examining significant finds made during the excavation, after comparing the plan and construction of this theatre with those of others, and after considering the periods when the city might have had the wealth to undertake such a costly project. The building may not have been completed until the early third century.

Less attention has so far been paid to the city's dwelling area, which seems to have reached its greatest extent in the late fourth century.[1] Aerial photographs show that the city was laid out on an orthogonal plan, but the period at which this plan was put into effect is not yet known.[2] The colonists who restored and enlarged the city in the second half of the fourth century may have made the plan, but it is also possible that they built along the lines of an earlier plan.

For a bibliography of archaeological works, see pp. 219–29.

[1] For a brief report see *NSc* 12 (1958), 260–7.
[2] For the urban plan see G. Schmiedt, *Kokalos* 3 (1957), 25–7; and F. Castagnoli, 'Recenti ricerche sull'urbanistica Ippodamea', *Arch. Cl.* 15 (1963), 196.

CHAPTER 9

Corinthian silver coinage and the Sicilian economy, c.340 to c.290 B.C.

Detailed study of Sicilian coin hoards of the fourth and early third centuries B.C. has recently added to our knowledge of the revival of Sicilian prosperity begun by Timoleon. The extraordinary predominance of Corinthian coins during much of this period requires examination and discussion if we are to form as full a picture as possible of the Sicilian economy in the second half of the fourth century.[1]

In the second half of the fifth century the mints of the various Sicilian cities produced silver issues in sufficiently large quantities for there to be little use of foreign coinage in the island. Hoards of this period do contain a number of Athenian coins, but it is clear that Athenian issues did not circulate widely in Sicily.[2] A few Corinthian coins begin to appear in hoards of the early fourth century. Yet in the second half of the century the pattern changes totally: the coinage of Corinth and her Western dependencies becomes dominant in Sicily from about 340 onwards. Kraay has calculated that: 'Of thirty substantial hoards buried in Sicily between 340 and 290 in only two does the proportion of Corinthian coinage fall below seventy per cent.'[3] This dominance

---

[1] This chapter was first published in *NC* 11 (1971), 53–66, and is reproduced here with a few small additions by kind permission of the Royal Numismatic Society.

My discussion of silver coinage in Sicily during the fourth century owes much to the important treatment of the subject by C. M. Kraay, *Greek Coins and History: Some Current Problems* (London 1969), pp. 52–63. Of earlier work the most important publication is that of G. K. Jenkins, 'A Note on Corinthian coins in the West', *CPANS*, pp. 367–79. Sicilian coin hoards have received attention from K. Christ, 'Historische Probleme der griechisch-sizilischen Numismatik', *Historia* 3 (1954/5), 385–95. The domination of Pegasi in Sicily during the latter half of the fourth century has been discussed by L. Breglia, 'Prospetto unitario della Monetazione nella Sicilia antica', *AIIN* 9–11 (1962/4), 37–42.

[2] G. K. Jenkins, *CPANS*, p. 369.

[3] *Greek Coins and History*, p. 54.

ends by the end of Agathocles' reign in 289: hoards buried after that time contain few Corinthian coins.

In the course of the fourth century Corinthian coinage under-went certain changes, which seem to have been brought about because of a reform of the mint. Pegasi minted before the changes – that is, Pegasi of Ravel's Period IV[1] – carry symbols on the reverse, whereas those minted after the changes (in Ravel's Period V) carry symbols and letters.[2] Then in Period IV the dies can be distinguished and counted, whereas in Period V not only do the dies become difficult to tell apart, they also seem far too numerous to count.[3] The purpose of these changes was pre-sumably to produce a far greater number of coins: certainly the number produced in Period IV seems to have been quite modest, as Corinth's known poverty might lead us to expect, whereas in Period V it was huge.

The date at which Corinthian Pegasi began to reach Sicily has been suggested by Jenkins.[4] He made a particular examination of the Centuripe 1952 (No. 1 in my list below), the Licata 1926 (No. 2) and the Leonforte (Nissoria) 1952 (No. 3) hoards. From the fact that the Leonforte hoard contains one of the last coins of Ambracia, captured by Philip of Macedon in 338, he deduced that it will have been buried around 330. Then on the basis of the fact that this hoard (c. 330) contains Pegasi of Period IV and of Period V with two letters (E and N, presumably the first two letters), he deduced that the Centuripe hoard, containing Pegasi of Period IV and of Period V with one letter (E), must have been buried a little earlier. The Licata hoard must also have been buried about the same period as the Centuripe hoard, since all its Pegasi are of Period IV, except for a single one of Period V with letter E.[5]

Two important conclusions may be drawn from Jenkins' dating.

---

[1] O. E. Ravel, Les 'Poulains' de Corinthe, Vol. 2: de 414 à 300 av. J.-C. (London 1948).

[2] For the letters, which may represent officials in charge of the mint, see J. Warren, 'The trihemidrachms of Corinth', in Essays in Greek Coinage presented to Stanley Robinson, ed. C. M. Kraay and G. K. Jenkins (Oxford 1968), 138–40.   [3] See Ravel, Les 'Poulains' de Corinthe, pp. 5 and 26.

[4] G. K. Jenkins, CPANS, pp. 372–5.

[5] The assumption that the mint of Ambracia must have been closed in 338 on Philip's occupation of the city is discussed in Note M, p. 206.

First, it would seem that the changes made in Corinthian coinage were effected at almost exactly the same time as large numbers of Pegasi appeared in Sicily. Secondly it seems certain that this appearance of Pegasi is connected with Timoleon's successful expedition to the island.

Although no precise date may be fixed, it is probably reasonable to place the first significant appearance of Pegasi in the years after the battle of the R. Crimisus. That the flood of Pegasi should have begun before this battle is almost impossible to believe: Sicily was disorganized, no work of restoration had begun, and we know that there was a definite shortage of money. The literary sources show that Timoleon had acute difficulty in finding pay even for a moderate number of mercenaries. Indeed, according to Diodorus (78.5–6), 1,000 mercenaries deserted him just before the battle of the R. Crimisus because their pay was in arrears. But both Plutarch (29) and Diodorus (80.5–81.2) stress the huge amount of booty which the Greeks gained after this victory. Plutarch makes the remarkable statement that: ἐλάχιστος γὰρ ἦν χαλκῶν καὶ σιδηρῶν τοῖς σκυλεύουσι λόγος · οὕτως ἄφθονος μὲν ἦν ἄργυρος, ἄφθονος δὲ χρυσός (29.1); while Diodorus says that there were as many as 15,000 Carthaginians taken captive (80.5), most of whom will probably have been ransomed. Since we know that fine spoils from the battle were sent to Corinth,[1] it seems reasonable to connect this source of silver with Corinth's upsurge of minting. Certainly the connection which might be made between Corinth and the battle of the R. Crimisus seems very similar to that which Kraay himself makes between Syracuse and the battle of Himera (480). On the latter he writes:

A further happy result of the lower chronology [for Syracusan tetradrachms of the fifth century] is that on the one hand it does not attribute to Gelon a vast but unexplained output of coinage before 480, while on the other it permits very heavy issues to begin immediately after 480, when bullion was available from the 2,000 talents of war indemnity claimed from the Carthaginians.[2]

The silver gained as spoil at the battle of the R. Crimisus will not have been able to supply the mint of Corinth for anything

[1] D.S. 80.6; Plut. 29.5–6; see also pp. 76–7.
[2] *Greek Coins and History*, p. 30; cf. pp. 26 and 35.

more than a short period. We do not know the source of Corinth's silver for most of the years between *c.* 340 and 308, when Ptolemaic occupation curtailed the output of her mint (cf. D.S. 20.37.1–2). But the domination of Pegasi in Sicilian hoards of this time, to the virtual exclusion of other 'foreign' coins, suggests that Corinth may have acted as a *bureau de change* in mainland Greece. Greek merchants intending to trade in Sicily realized that Pegasi were the most acceptable coins there, and so exchanged the money of their own cities for Pegasi before leaving Greece. Corinth then re-minted the coins of the other cities as Pegasi.[1] This explanation of Corinth's source of silver, which can be no more than a guess, seems more sensible than any idea that the city suddenly found a profitable silver mine, for example, or that it re-minted old Pegasi. Even if all the Pegasi of Period IV had been re-minted, they would have formed only a moderate proportion of the Pegasi minted during Period V.

Since it suggests that the coins of other cities provided Corinth with much silver, my explanation has the advantage of supplying a plausible reason for the flow of Pegasi into Sicily. The profitable silver mine explanation, for example, remains inadequate not least because it fails to show why Corinth poured a vast quantity of her own money into Sicily for no apparent return. She would not want to import a huge amount of Sicily's main export, agricultural produce. And it seems ridiculous to suggest that she was replenishing the stocks of coin in Sicily out of simple kindness. Not only would such action have been unthinkable on her part, it would also have been little help to the Sicilians. Seed, tools, skilled craftsmen and colonists (who were sent by Corinth) would all have been more useful in the work of reconstruction. Then if Corinth did not melt down the coins of other cities trading with Sicily, we might expect more such coins to have been found in the island, as well as larger Syracusan issues of Pegasi, since Syracuse would probably have been the main recipient of 'foreign' coins.[2]

[1] Compare Xenophon, *De Vectigal.* 3.2.
[2] A suggestion by Prof. M. I Finley that the main centre for minting Pegasi might have been Syracuse, not Corinth, is discussed in Note N, pp. 206–7.

As I have suggested, the flow of Pegasi into Sicily must be the result of enormously increased exports from the island to mainland Greece and elsewhere. Agricultural produce will presumably have formed the bulk of these exports. Certainly Diodorus believed that it was the revival of agriculture which quickly restored Sicilian prosperity,[1] and we have no reason to doubt his testimony on the point.

Agricultural produce leaves no traces which the archaeologist may detect, but our meagre literary evidence does confirm Diodorus' belief.[2] Demosthenes' speech *Against Zenothemis* (No. 32), delivered about 330 B.C. perhaps,[3] is wholly devoted to the matter of corn shipments from Syracuse to Athens. Then in a speech in the Demosthenic corpus (No. 56, *Against Dionysodorus*), delivered at some unknown date after 323 B.C.,[4] the speaker refers to ὁ Σικελικὸς κατάπλους, which so lowered the price of corn at Athens that the news of its arrival induced one of the defendants in the case, Parmeniscus, to break the contract saying that he would bring the cornship to nowhere but Athens, and to sell the corn in Rhodes instead (sections 9–10). Since no explanation is given of the term ὁ Σικελικὸς κατάπλους, it was presumably familiar to the Athenian jury; and we might infer from this that the arrival of a corn convoy from Sicily was a regular annual event at this period.[5] Further, the fact that corn prices dropped significantly might well be a sign that the quantity of Sicilian corn being imported was considerable.[6] Finally a remark made by Theophrastus in his *Enquiry into Plants* (8.4.5) also implies that Sicilian wheat was being exported to Greece

[1] D.S. 83.1; cf. 83.3, ... διὰ τὴν προειρημένην ἐκ τῶν καρπῶν εὐπορίαν.

[2] Some incidental references in his own work show the importance of the corn harvests throughout the island: for example, 19.110.2 and 5; 20.29.3; 20.32.2.

[3] For the date see F. Blass, *Die Attische Beredsamkeit* (Leipzig 1893), Vol. 3, p. 492. A. C. Cosman would date the speech to the period 339–330 B.C., and within these limits he favours 332–330 (*Demosthenes' Rede tegen Zenothemis met Inleiding en Commentaar* (Leiden 1939), pp. 29–30).

[4] For the date, see F. Blass, *Die Attische Beredsamkeit*, Vol. 3, pp. 583–4.

[5] Athenian merchant ships certainly went to Sicily: we hear of two at Syracuse in 312 (D.S. 19.103.4).

[6] Another fall in the price of corn at Athens is referred to at Dem. 32.25–6, but no reason is given for it.

during this period.[1] Other products may have contributed to Sicily's revival, but we know of none which were exported. Sicily's economy depended on agriculture at this period, as it did throughout ancient times.

Even less is known of the buyers of Sicilian produce than of the produce itself. Athens alone of the cities in mainland Greece is known to have imported Sicilian corn. And although we have no clue to how much corn other cities imported, or how often they did so, it might still be reasonable to guess that Athens' size, position and wealth made her the largest consumer of Sicilian corn in mainland Greece. Athens apart, there seems to be no obvious place in Greece of sufficient size or wealth to import large amounts of corn at this period. Corinth's needs will have been small, while those of her Western dependencies will have been even more modest.[2]

It is perhaps possible to suggest why the Pegasi which reached Sicily in Timoleon's time were not melted down and re-minted. The extraordinary conditions prevailing in the island during the first half of the fourth century meant that the Corinthian coinage which appeared from c. 340 onwards found almost no rival coinage. Because of the destruction wrought by the Carthaginians and warfare between the various cities, Syracuse had remained the only Greek mint to issue silver coinage during the first half of the century. A number of Siculo-Punic issues minted by the Carthaginians were also in circulation.[3] The Corinthian

[1] For further discussion of Sicilian trade with Athens, see H. D. Westlake, *CHJ* 7 (1942), 97–8. On two fragmentary inscriptions which suggest that Athens imported Sicilian corn during this period, see G. Manganaro, 'Per la storia della circolazione della moneta attica nella Sicilia Orientale', in *La Circolazione della Moneta Ateniese in Sicilia e in Magna Grecia* (Istituto Italiano di Numismatica, Rome 1969), p. 156.

[2] It is conceivable that much Sicilian corn will have been exported to mainland Greece during the famine there in 330 to 326, but clearly these will have been years when there was exceptional demand for corn from abroad. On the famine, see M. N. Tod, *A Selection of Greek Historical Inscriptions*, Vol. 2 (Oxford 1948), No. 196, pp. 273–6. Amorós' view that there was significant Syracusan influence on Emporion in the fourth century B.C. is discussed in Note O, p. 207.

[3] Christ's table of all the coinages minted in Sicily shows the almost total lack of silver issues in the Greek zone during the first half of the fourth century (the issues attributed to Megara Hyblaea should be

coins were presumably not melted down and re-minted in Sicily because they entered a 'coinage vacuum', where no silver coin had been minted for some time: Plutarch tells of the lack of money at Syracuse in the period after Timoleon's capture of the whole city. Confidence in Corinthian Pegasi grew up in the Greek zone of the island in such a way that Pegasi became the accepted coin of the realm.[1]

Pegasi remained dominant in Sicily for as long as forty years. Probably Agathocles was content to allow these coins to remain the principal currency in the Greek zone since they proved so acceptable to the Sicilians. He issued his own coins to circulate beside the Pegasi from early in his reign,[2] and it was not until c. 295, when he abandoned the Corinthian standard, that he took any step against Pegasi. In fact by c. 295 the dominance of Pegasi must have been declining gradually, since no new issues will have come from Corinth after 308.[3]

Probably there will never have been any pressing need for Agathocles to withdraw Pegasi in order to obtain silver for his own issues. For the large amount of archaeological evidence which we now possess, together with a few literary references,[4] shows that Sicily continued prosperous long after the death of

ignored). K. Christ, 'Literaturüberblicke der griechischen Numismatik: Sizilien', *JNG* 5–6 (1954–5), 226–8.

On Siculo-Punic issues, see G. K. Jenkins, 'Coins of Punic Sicily', Part I, *Schweizerische Numismatische Rundschau* 50 (1971), 25–78.

[1] On Syracusan poverty, see Plut. 23.7; and compare Ps. Dio Chrysostom 37.20–1.

An Athenian inscription of 375/4, although not directly relevant to the matter of Corinthian coinage in the West, does seem to illustrate clearly difficulties which could arise over the acceptance of coin-types. Professor R. S. Stroud was kind enough to send me a copy of the text, publication of which is eagerly awaited.

[2] See Kraay, *Greek Coins and History*, pp. 61–2.

[3] The contents of the Scoglitti 1938 hoard of c. 289 (No. 34 in my list) may perhaps be thought to show how the predominance of Pegasi declined towards the end of Agathocles' reign. In this hoard 159 of the 191 silver coins are Pegasi, but the total number of coins is 255. This hoard is the only one of the 34 listed by me in which coins of a metal other than silver are known to make up more than a negligible proportion of the total contents.

[4] D.S. 19.72.1 (large revenues of Agathocles, under 314); 19.107.3 (prosperity of Gela); 20.4.5–8 (wealthy merchant community at Syracuse, under 310).

Timoleon himself. The political upheavals brought about by Agathocles and others do not seem to have seriously disrupted the booming economy. Indeed Diodorus appears to regard the period of prosperity begun by Timoleon as continuing unbroken into the reign of Hieron II. In his section on Timoleon he remarks that: διὰ τὴν ἐκ τούτων εὐπορίαν πολλὰ καὶ μεγάλα κατεσκευάσθη κατ᾽ ἐκείνους τοὺς χρόνους ἀναθήματα (83.2); but then he only describes monuments erected by Agathocles and Hieron, omitting any reference to monuments of Timoleon's time.

The Pegasi issued in the second half of the fourth century by cities in Western Greece, Italy and Sicily raise further problems. In the first half of this century Leucas and Ambracia were the only Corinthian dependencies with mints in operation.[1] In the second half of the century, however, Pegasi were issued by fifteen different mints among Corinth's Western dependencies alone, although it was not usual for thirteen of these places to mint any Corinthian-type coinage at all before this period. Some of the issues seem to be tiny, with no more than one type known, but Leucas, the principal mint of the dependencies, produced a considerable quantity of Pegasi over many years.[2]

Pegasi are also known to have been issued at this time by six cities in South Italy, and by three cities in Sicily. All these issues, except for those of Syracuse, seem to have been small.

There seems little support for Kraay's suggestion that the coinages produced at this time by Corinth's dependencies in the West were a federal issue, connected with the establishment of a 'League of Corinth' by Philip of Macedon in 337/6.[3] If the coinages were federal, we should possibly expect other states in the League to have issued similar types too. Then as Kraay himself recognizes, Corinth was no more than an ordinary member of the League (the name 'League of Corinth' being a modern invention based on the city where the delegates met), and

---

[1] Kraay, *Greek Coins and History*, p. 55.

[2] Less than a quarter of the number produced by Corinth according to Kraay (*Greek Coins and History*, p. 56), but this is still a large amount. There were 75 Leucadian Pegasi found in the Leonforte (Nissoria) 1952 hoard (No. 3 in my list); 44 in Sicily Uncertain 1912/13 (no. 6); 40 in Sicily Unknown (no date) (No. 14); 68 in Pachino 1957 (No. 23); 43 in Sicily Unknown *c.* 1837 (No. 26); and 43 in Megara Hyblaea 1967 (No. 27).

[3] Kraay, *Greek Coins and History*, p. 60.

she had no real control over her Western dependencies. Further it is most unlikely that she should have founded a 'Corinthian League' inside the 'League of the Greeks' set up by Philip.

There seems equally small support for Kraay's idea that the closure of Ambracia's mint may have prompted other places in the vicinity to issue coins.[1] Small places, like Stratus, which issued only one type of Pegasus at this time, having never minted any coins before, are hardly likely to have taken the trouble to make this issue unless they had good cause. If they had used the coins of Ambracia previously, then it would have been more convenient for them to use the coins of another nearby mint after Ambracia's fall (Leucas, for example), instead of beginning to mint themselves. In any event the cities which produced only one issue of Pegasi made no very serious attempt to have coins of their own permanently, and they must still have relied on the coins of a nearby mint for the most part. Finally I should add that neither of these suggested explanations for the issues made by the Western dependencies can offer any reason for the issues made by cities in South Italy or Sicily. These places were not members of the League of Corinth, nor will they have relied on the coinage of Ambracia.

The most likely explanation for the many Pegasus issues made at this time by places which had never minted such coins before is hinted at by Kraay.[2] For in my view all these places decided to take advantage of the new prosperity of trade between Sicily and Greece.[3] The coins issued by them are very similar to those of Corinth because it was in all probability Corinth which supplied the dies. Cities which had never issued Pegasi before would clearly ask Corinth for help and advice. It was important that all issues should be like the Pegasi of Corinth so that the coins

---

[1] Kraay, *Greek Coins and History*, p. 60.

[2] *Greek Coins and History*, p. 61; cf. C. M. Kraay and M. Hirmer, *Greek Coins* (London 1966), pp. 280–1.

[3] Corinth's Western dependencies were situated on the main sailing route between Sicily and Greece (cf. Xen. *Hell.* 6.2.9; and for Leucas, Plut. 15.2). Men from Leucas (Plut. 30.6), Corcyra (Plut. 8.4; D.S. 66.2) and Apollonia (*SEG* 22 (1967), No. 218 and H. Berve in *Gnomon* 25 (1953), 529) are known to have joined Timoleon. Of cities in South Italy Rhegium helped Timoleon (Plut. 9.7–10.5; D.S. 68.4–6). Colonists later came to Sicily from Italy (Plut. 23.6; 35.2).

would be accepted in Sicily without difficulty. Cities which only issued once or twice will just have been attempting to draw a quick profit from an unexpected trade boom. It seems likely that they never intended to issue coins permanently.

We do not know where any of these cities obtained their silver, although it might be sensible to guess that some of them melted down either raw silver or the coins of another city which had been exchanged for Pegasi. Leucas' issues were so large that she would have needed some source of silver on which she could rely over a period of years. Possibly merchants of non-Corinthian cities supplied this. Yet certainly Leucas produced far more Pegasi than she would ever have required for her own needs. This point, coupled with the fact that the huge majority of Leucadian Pegasi have been found in Sicily, not in mainland Greece, may well be seen as support for my view that these issues of Pegasi were made deliberately to gain a profit from trade with Sicily.

Sicilian coin hoards of c. 340 to c. 290 B.C.

There follows a list of 33 hoards which show the spread of Pegasi into Sicily during the fourth century B.C., together with one contemporary hoard from South Italy (No. 12). This list has been composed with the help of detailed notes which Dr C. M. Kraay most kindly put at my disposal. I have not given detailed information about the contents of each hoard: in nearly all cases where the contents of a hoard were recorded this may be obtained from the publications cited in the list, or from publications cited by Noe.[1] Rather my aim has been to show the proportion of Pegasi in each hoard.

Any work on the Pegasi found in Sicily has been hampered by the fact that until recent years the contents of hoards were often not recorded precisely. The very predominance of Pegasi meant that they received scant attention, and indeed Ravel could write in 1928:

Although hoards of Pegasi have been numerous in Sicily, it is greatly to be regretted that not a single detailed record has been made

[1] S. P. Noe, *A Bibliography of Greek Coin Hoards* (second edition), *Numismatic Notes and Monographs* No. 78 (1937).

of them. Even when the other coins found with them have been carefully described and published, the colts have been completely neglected. This is due to several reasons – a general contempt for them, the very erroneous idea that they are such common coins that it is not worth wasting time over them and the scarcity of books of reference dealing with them.[1]

Fourth-century Pegasi of Corinth have been fully covered by Ravel,[2] although his dating of Pegasi of Periods IV and V has now been shown to be incorrect.[3]

Ravel has also classified the Pegasi of Ambracia.[4] Unless otherwise stated below, the types of other mints may be found in *BMC Corinth*.

To prevent misunderstanding I have noted the cases where no coins of a mint have appeared in Sicilian hoards. This absence is not very significant in view of the poor record which has been kept of the hoards.

A question mark (?) indicates that the identity of the mint is probable, but not certain.

WESTERN DEPENDENCIES OF CORINTH WHICH MINTED PEGASI (in alphabetical order):

ALYZIA
AMBRACIA (on closure of the mint, see Note M, p. 206.)
ANACTORIUM
APOLLONIA
ARGOS AMPHILOCHICUM
? ASTACUS. The only type known has never been recorded in a Sicilian hoard. It is illustrated in *BMC Corinth* Plate XXXIII.10.
CORCYRA
? CORONTA. See Hoard No. 14, for example.
DYRRHACHIUM
? ECHINUS. The port of Thyrrheium, not to be confused with the more famous city of this name on the north coast of the Gulf of Malis. Only one type is known: see Hoard No. 14, for example.
LEUCAS

---

[1] O. E. Ravel, *The 'Colts' of Ambracia, Numismatic Notes and Monographs* No. 37 (1928), 5–6.
[2] O. E. Ravel, *Les 'Poulains' de Corinthe, Vol. 2: de 414 à 300 av. J.-C.*
[3] G. K. Jenkins, *CPANS*, pp. 367–79.
[4] *The 'Colts' of Ambracia*, esp. pp. 64–80 and 129–49.

METROPOLIS. Only one type is known; see Hoard No. 14, for example.

STRATUS. Not in *BMC Corinth*. See O. E. Ravel, 'Notes on some rare and unpublished "Pegasi" of my collection', *NC* 6 (1926), 315–16. The Pegasus published here by Ravel was found in Sicily, but Pegasi of Stratus have not been recorded in Sicilian hoards.

THYRRHEIUM

CITIES IN SOUTH ITALY WHICH MINTED PEGASI (in alphabetical order):

? HERACLEA. Not in *BMC Corinth*. See O. E. Ravel, 'Rare and unpublished coins of Corinthian types', *NC* 15 (1935), 13. No Pegasi of Heraclea have been recorded in Sicilian hoards.

? HIPPONIUM. Not in *BMC Corinth*. See *SNG* 11.633 and O. E. Ravel, 'Ritrovamento di Pegasi', *Numismatica* 11 (1936), 3 and 5–6 (Magna Graecia *c.* 1935 hoard – No. 12 in my list). A Pegasus similar to that published by Ravel appears in *BMC Corinth* Plate XXXIX.2 under 'Uncertain Mints'.

LOCRI

? MESMA. Cf. *SNG* 11.659. See Hoard No. 6, for example.

RHEGIUM. The only type known has never been recorded in a Sicilian hoard. It is illustrated in *BMC Corinth* Plate XXIV.12.

TERINA. Not in *BMC Corinth*. See *SNG* v.1649 and Hoard No. 14.

CITIES IN SICILY WHICH MINTED PEGASI (in alphabetical order):

ERYX. Imitation Pegasi, not in *BMC Corinth*. See O. E. Ravel, 'Contribution à l'étude de la numismatique Corinthienne', *Aréthuse* 6 (1929), 3–5; O. E. Ravel, *NC* 6 (1926), 309–10; L. Breglia, *AIIN* 9–11 (1962–4), 40; *SNG* v.1718. Pegasi of Eryx have not been recorded in Sicilian hoards.

LEONTINI. See Hoard No. 23, for example.

SYRACUSE

HOARDS

1. CENTURIPE 1952
Burial: *c.* 340 (Jenkins)
73 Pegasi from a total of 88 silver coins.
See:
G. V. Gentili, *NSc* 8 (1954), 70–7.

G. V. Gentili, *AIIN* 1 (1954), 167 (summary account).
G. K. Jenkins, *CPANS*, pp. 372–5.
M. T. Currò Pisanò, *AIIN* 9–11 (1962–4), 229–30 (summary account).

2. LICATA 1926   Noe 618
Burial: *c.* 340, according to Jenkins, *CPANS*, pp. 372–3.
75 Pegasi from a total of 91 silver coins.

3. LEONFORTE (NISSORIA) 1952
Burial: *c.* 335–330 (Jenkins)
297 Pegasi from a total of 327 silver coins.
See:
G. V. Gentili, *NSc* 8 (1954), 58–70.
G. V. Gentili, *AIIN* 1 (1954), 167 (summary account).
G. K. Jenkins, *CPANS*, pp. 372–5.
M. T. Currò Pisanò, *AIIN* 9–11 (1962–4), 230 (summary account).

4. PIAZZA ARMERINA (before 1894)   Noe 814
Burial: mid 4th century?
The hoard is now dispersed, but is described as 'Pegasi – chiefly Corinthian' by Noe.

5. LEONFORTE 1895   Noe 612
Burial: 3rd quarter of 4th century according to Jenkins, *CPANS*, p. 375.
54 Pegasi from a total of 68 silver coins.

6. SICILY UNCERTAIN 1912/13
Burial: *c.* 310
The full contents of the hoard are not known, but 277 Pegasi have been recorded.
From: E. T. Newell, Manuscript in A.N.S. Library.

7. CESARÒ 1915/16
Burial: *c.* 310
145 coins from this hoard (144 of them Pegasi) are at Syracuse, but nothing is known of the other coins. Cesano believes that these 145 coins represent half the hoard (S. L. Cesano, 'Il medagliere del museo archeologico di Siracusa', *Studi di Numismatica* 1 (1940), 63). See: G. K. Jenkins, *CPANS*, p. 376.

8. SICILY UNKNOWN 1877
Burial: late 4th century
65 Pegasi.
See:
A. Tusa Cutroni, *AIIN* 3 (1956), 207 No. VI (summary account).
A. Tusa Cutroni, *AIIN* 5–6 (1958–9), 167–77.

9. ACIPLATANI 1905 Noe 9
Burial: 4th century
The full contents of the hoard are not known, but of the 47 coins
recorded, 40 are Pegasi.

10. CANICATTINI 1907
Burial: 4th–3rd century
3 Pegasi.
See: M. T. Currò Pisanò, *AIIN* 9–11 (1962–4), 223.

11. GIBIL GABIB 1928
Burial: 4th century
The full contents of the hoard are not known, but there are 9 Pegasi
among the 26 coins recorded.
See: M. T. Currò Pisanò, *AIIN* 9–11 (1962–4), 226 (summary account).

12. MAGNA GRAECIA *c.* 1935
Burial: late 4th century
58 Pegasi. The rest of the hoard was not recorded.
See: O. E. Ravel, *Numismatica* 11 (1936), 1–7.

13. MESSINA 1868 Noe 684
243 Pegasi were recorded. (This hoard was bought in Messina; we do
not know where it was originally buried.)

14. SICILY UNKNOWN (no date)
Burial: early 3rd century
169 Pegasi.
See: E. Pozzi, *AIIN* 5–6 (1958–9), 91–124.

15. SICILY UNKNOWN 1879
Burial: early 3rd century
26 Pegasi from a total of 32 silver coins.
See: A. Tusa Cutroni, *AIIN* 5–6 (1958–9), 178–85.

16. MEGARA HYBLAEA 1949
Burial: 3rd quarter of 4th century (Vallet and Villard)
33 Pegasi from a total of 47 silver coins.
See:
F. Villard, *MEFR* 63 (1951), 45–7.
G. Vallet and F. Villard, *Kokalos* 4 (1958), 104–5.
M. T. Currò Pisanò, *AIIN* 9–11 (1962–4), 228 (summary account).

17. TERRANOVA 1906   Noe 1096
Burial: late 4th century – early 3rd century
The contents of the hoard were not recorded, but Noe says that it numbered 1,200 coins or more. According to him, Orsi saw about 100 Pegasi.

18. TERRANOVA 1911   Noe 1097
Burial: late 4th century – early 3rd century
27 Pegasi.

19. SICILY UNKNOWN (no date)
Burial: late 4th century – early 3rd century
21 Pegasi from a total of 23 silver coins.
See: A. Tusa Cutroni, *AIIN* 3 (1956), 208 No. xiv (summary account).

20. NOTO 1916   Noe 745
Burial: late 4th century – early 3rd century
The contents of the hoard were not recorded, but Pegasi were present.

21. CANICATTINI 1917
Burial: late 4th century – early 3rd century
Of the 19 silver coins recorded, 18 are Pegasi.
See:
M. T. Currò Pisanò, *AIIN* 9–11 (1962–4), 225.
(Kraay suggests to me that No. 20 and No. 21 may really be the same hoard).

22. SYRACUSE (1820?)   Noe 1027
Burial: late 4th century – early 3rd century
The contents of the hoard were not recorded, but there were thousands of Pegasi present.

23. PACHINO 1957
Burial: *c.* 300
600 Pegasi from a total of 642 silver coins.
See:
A. di Vita, *AIIN* 5–6 (1958–9), 125–65.
G. V. Gentili, *AIIN* 5–6 (1958–9), 289–90 (summary account).
A. di Vita, *Kokalos* 4 (1958), 99 n. 59 (brief mention).
M. T. Currò Pisanò, *AIIN* 9–11 (1962–4), 231 (summary account).

24. AVOLA 1888   Noe 108B
Burial: late 4th century – early 3rd century
The hoard consisted of about 150 silver coins, but only 53 coins were
examined. Among these 53 were 31 Pegasi.
See: G. K. Jenkins, *CPANS*, p. 375.

25. CAPO SOPRANO (no date)
Burial: early 3rd century
79 Pegasi from a total of 89 silver coins.
See: M. T. Currò Pisanò, *AIIN* 9–11 (1962–4), 231 (summary account).

26. SICILY UNKNOWN (*c.* 1837)   Noe 970
Burial: late 4th century – early 3rd century
242 Pegasi from a total of 245 silver coins.

27. MEGARA HYBLAEA 1967
Burial: early 3rd century
468 Pegasi from a total of 515 silver coins.
(Hoard so far unpublished; numbers from Kraay's notes.)

28. FUSCO, SYRACUSE 1955
Burial: early 3rd century
16 Pegasi from a total of 21 silver coins.
See:
G. V. Gentili, *AIIN* 3 (1956), 101–9.
G. V. Gentili, *AIIN* 5–6 (1958–9), 284–5 (summary account).

29. CAMMARATA 1859   Noe 193
Burial: *c.* 300
The contents of the hoard were not fully recorded, but there seem to
have been about 150 Pegasi from a total of about 200 silver coins.

30. PALMA MONTECHIARO 1929   Noe 789
Burial: *c.* 300 (Jenkins and Lewis)
69 Pegasi from a total of 77 silver coins.
See:
A. Tusa Cutroni, *AIIN* 3 (1956), 209 No. xvii (this summary is marred by misprints, and should be compared with the original publication of P. Marconi, *NSc* 7 (1931), 404).
G. K. Jenkins and R. B. Lewis, *Carthaginian Gold and Electrum Coins* (London 1963), p. 56.

31. PALAZZOLO ACREIDE 1897   Noe 784
Burial: early 3rd century
454 Pegasi from a total of 460 silver coins.

32. PACHINO 1921   Noe 779
The contents of the hoard were not fully recorded. There were upwards of 100 silver coins, among which were several Pegasi.

33. CAMARINA 1928
Burial: *c.* 289 (Jenkins and Lewis)
83 Pegasi from a total of 92 silver coins.
See:
G. K. Jenkins and R. B. Lewis, *op. cit.,* p. 57 (first group).
M. T. Currò Pisanò, *AIIN* 9–11 (1962–4), 226 (summary account).

34. SCOGLITTI 1938
Burial: *c.* 289 (Jenkins and Lewis)
159 Pegasi from a total of 191 silver coins.
See:
G. K. Jenkins and R. B. Lewis, *op. cit.,* p. 57 (second group).
M. T. Currò Pisanò, *AIIN* 9–11 (1962–4), 227–8 (summary account).

ADDENDUM

It was only at a very late stage in the production of this book that I saw M. Thompson, O. Mørkholm, C. M. Kraay (eds.), *An Inventory of Greek Coin Hoards* (American Numismatic Society, New York 1973). I have therefore been unable to take into account Kraay's full list of all Sicilian hoards in this valuable work, which now replaces that of Noe. But I do add a comparative table for those seeking further information on the hoards listed by me:

Talbert	Kraay	Talbert	Kraay	Talbert	Kraay
No. 1 = No. 2131		No. 12 = No. 2148		No. 23 = No. 2151	
2	2130	13	2188	24	2169
3	2133	14	2187	25	2183
4	2139	15	2146	26	2144
5	2136	16	2135	27	2180
6	2147	17	2171	28	2179
7	2145	18	2198	29	2182
8	2149	19	2189	30	2153
9	2174	20 ⎫		31	2181
10	2175	21 ⎭ 2150		32	2186
11	2132	22	2170	33 ⎫ 2185	
				34 ⎭	

Kraay No. 2127 should also be taken into account (previously unpublished).

CHAPTER 10

Sicilian coinage

Sicilian silver coinage in the age of Timoleon

It is remarkable that during the Timoleontic period no Greek city in Sicily seems to have made any attempt to produce a silver coinage which would clash with Pegasi. Rather Syracuse, Leontini and Eryx[1] copied Pegasi instead of creating their own designs for a silver coinage; while those cities, like Gela, which would have had sufficient resources to issue silver coins of high value, appear to have continued using Pegasi, presumably because these were acceptable throughout the Greek zone of the island. Apart from Pegasi, the only coins of high value minted in a precious metal by a Greek city were the gold and electrum issues of Syracuse.[2]

The tiny silver issues made by Greek cities in the Timoleontic period were all of small denominations, and were presumably intended only for local use. There follows a list of those cities which are believed by numismatists to have made such silver issues during the Timoleontic period, but it should be stressed that the dating of the issues of some cities is highly doubtful.

Akragas	Kimiss... ?* n. 5
Camarina n. 1	Megara Hyblaea* n. 6
Campani* n. 2	Morgantina n. 7
Entella *ibid.*	Syracuse n. 8
Gela n. 3	Tauromenium
Imachara* n. 4	Tyndaris n. 9

(* denotes a city which is not thought to have issued coins before the Timoleontic period. The figures following refer to notes on pp. 192–4.)

[1] For the imitation Corinthian Pegasi issued by Eryx, see p. 172.

[2] On the electrum issues, see G. K. Jenkins, 'Electrum Coinage at Syracuse', in *Essays in Greek Coinage presented to Stanley Robinson*, ed. C. M. Kraay and G. K. Jenkins (Oxford 1968), pp. 145–62.

Evans has published a unique gold coin, which he believed to have been minted by Herbessus in Timoleon's time. But the attribution seems very doubtful (A. Evans, 'Select Sicilian and Magna-Graecian coins', *NC* 6 (1926), 18–19).

As might be expected, the number of silver coins found on excavation sites has been small, but tabulation of recorded finds suggests that Corinthian and Syracusan pieces were the only silver coins to circulate widely in the Greek zone of Sicily (see table below).

Silver

	Coins of:										
	C5	C5	C5	C4	C4	C4	C4	C5	C5	C4	
Site	Himera	Naxos	Akragas	Akragas	Corinth	Gela	Morgantina	Segesta	Syracuse	Syracuse	See
Gela: Predio Leopardi (1)	—	—	—	—	2	—	—	—	—	—	n. 10
N. side of Acropolis	—	—	1	—	—	—	—	—	—	—	n. 11
Ospizio per i vecchi	—	—	—	—	2	—	—	—	—	—	n. 12
C. Soprano fortifications	—	—	—	1	—	1	—	—	—	1	n. 13
Random finds at Spinasanta	—	—	—	—	—	—	—	—	—	1	n. 14
Hellenistic house at C. Soprano	—	—	—	1	—	—	—	—	—	—	n. 15
Sabucina	—	—	—	—	—	—	—	1	—	—	n. 16
Vassallaggi	1	1	1	—	1	—	—	—	1	1	n. 17
Morgantina	—	—	—	—	—	—	2	—	—	—	n. 18

The figures in the last column refer to notes on pp. 192–4.

In addition, one fourth-century electrum coin of Syracuse was found at Butera (p. 193 n. 19).

Sicilian bronze coinage in the age of Timoleon

The great variety of bronze coinage believed by numismatists to have been produced in the Timoleontic period is at first sight striking, but only the issues of Syracuse are of more than local significance. The large number of cities which produced types is an indication of Sicily's revival at this time, but the limited issues of the minor cities were an assertion of new-found independence, rather than a serious attempt to create a permanent local coinage. Such issues are of no economic importance. Certainly some of the minor cities had never felt the need to issue coins before, and never issued them again until Roman times; then some cities were not even prepared to mint their own pieces, but contented themselves with overstriking, a possible sign that they were mainly concerned with placing their name and symbol on coins which were of an already acceptable standard.[1] Overstrikes are even found on the second Zeus Eleutherios type of Syracuse, which in Gabrici's view might not have been issued until ten years after Timoleon's retirement or death in 337.[2] There can hardly have been an economic reason which made overstriking necessary; the practice was continued for purely political reasons, and was perhaps favoured by new Greek colonists who felt that the minting of coinage was the mark of an independent community.

There follows a list of those cities and groups (Tyrrheni, for example) which are believed by numismatists to have made bronze issues during the Timoleontic period. As in the case of the list above, it should be stressed that the dating of some issues is highly doubtful:

Abacaenum	Herbessus*
Adranum*	KAINON* n. 22
Aetna n. 2	Leontini
Agyrium	Messana
Akragas	Morgantina n. 7
Alaesa* n. 20	Mytistratus* n. 23
Camarina	Nacona n. 24
Campani* n. 21	Petra* n. 25
Catania	Silerae*
Centuripe*	Syracuse n. 8
Enna	Tauromenium
Entella n. 2	Tyndaris n. 9
Eryx	Tyrrheni
Gela n. 3	

(* denotes a city which is not thought to have issued coins before the Timoleontic period. The figures following refer to notes on pp. 192-4.)

[1] Overstrikes were made most frequently on coins of Syracuse: see B. V. Head, *NC* 14 (1874), 34-40. To his list may be added, for example, the coins of Herbessus recorded at *NC* 6 (1926), 19 and at *NSc* 10 (1956), 382; and the coins of Petra recorded at *NC* 8 (1948), 132.

[2] E. Gabrici, *Boll. Circ. Num. Nap.* 37 (1952), 13.

Finds of bronze coins on excavation sites seem to suggest that only Syracusan issues had anything more than a restricted local circulation. Two bronze coins of Adranum and two of Herbessus were most unusual finds at Morgantina, while the same is true of the bronze coins of Herbessus found at Gela,[1] the bronze coin of Nacona found at Heraclea Minoa,[2] and the bronze coin of Lipari found at Milingiana. (See table on pp. 184–5 below.)

Siculo-Punic coins seem to have circulated in the Greek zone on a sizeable scale. Strangely, such bronze coins form the largest group of coins found in the excavations at Morgantina,[3] while a certain number of Siculo-Punic silver[4] and bronze[5] pieces have been found at Megara Hyblaea. Fifteen Siculo-Punic silver coins were present in the Pachino 1957 hoard (No. 23 in my list of hoards), and there were about thirty such coins in the Cammarata 1859 hoard (No. 29 in my list). Yet the number of Siculo-Punic pieces found at Gela or in the hinterland of Gela and Agrigento is unexpectedly small.[6]

Coin types

I have deliberately omitted any consideration of the particular coin types issued by Sicilian Greek mints in the Timoleontic period. No acceptable classification of all the coins has yet been

[1] *NSc* 10 (1956), 382.

[2] *NSc* 12 (1958), 287.

[3] R. Ross Holloway, 'Monetary circulation', pp. 141–2. I have taken the anepigraphic Persephone head / free horse bronze coins to be Siculo-Punic. Jenkins notes that specimens of the same type have been recorded in Africa, and these finds strongly suggest a Siculo-Punic origin for the coins. Finds of Greek coins of this period in Africa are almost unknown. Ross Holloway suggests that the coins were an issue made by the alliance of Greek cities in Timoleon's time, but the absence of any legend and the fact that so many Greek cities minted their own coins make this idea seem rather unlikely. (G. K. Jenkins in *A Survey of Numismatic Research 1960–1965*, Vol. 1, *Ancient Numismatics*, ed. O. Mørkholm (Copenhagen 1967), pp. 90–1.)

[4] 10 and 34 Siculo-Punic silver coins were present in the Megara Hyblaea 1949 and the Megara Hyblaea 1967 hoards respectively (Nos. 16 and 27 in my list of hoards).

[5] For a hoard of 14 Siculo-Punic bronze coins found at Megara Hyblaea, see *MEFR* 66 (1954), 30.

[6] Cf. P. Orlandini, 'Una precisazione cronologica sulla comparsa delle monete puniche a Gela e nel suo retroterra', *AIIN* 9–11 (1962–4), 49–52.

made, while any new classification which disregards earlier and later issues would be valueless, and it is certainly not a task to be attempted by the historian alone.[1] Mention may be made in passing, however, of the long dispute over certain important Syracusan types.

In his study of the bronze coinage of Sicily[2] Gabrici isolated four Syracusan bronze series, which he dated to the second half of the fourth century B.C., each series being of a lower weight than the last. These series were as follows:

1. Litra with Obv./Head of Athena
        Rev./Star inside two dolphins
  Weight varying from 38.25 gr to 23.72 gr

2. Obv./Head of a soldier in Corinthian helmet
  Rev./Pegasus
  22.93 gr to 20.40 gr

3. Obv./Head of Zeus Eleutherios with long hair
  Rev./Free-running horse
  22.15 gr to 17.67 gr

4. Obv./Head of Zeus Eleutherios with short hair
  Rev./Thunderbolt
  17.66 gr to 12.85 gr

Gabrici dated the first of these four series to Timoleon's lifetime for various reasons, among them the point that Syracusan poverty would have prevented any heavy bronze issues before Timoleon's day. As a result of this dating Gabrici concluded

[1] The following works attempt a general classification of Timoleontic coinage:
A. Holm, *Geschichte des sicilischen Münzwesens bis zur Zeit des Augustus* (Leipzig 1898), esp. pp. 654–77. (This work is printed as pp. 543–741 of A. Holm, *Geschichte Siciliens im Alterthum*, Vol. 3.)
W. Giesecke, *Sicilia Numismatica* (Leipzig 1923), pp. 64–88 (unreliable).
E. Gabrici, *La monetazione del bronzo nella Sicilia antica* (reprinted from *Atti R. Accad. Palermo* 14, 1927), pp. 58–78.
S. Consolo Langher, *Contributo alla storia della antica moneta bronzea in Sicilia* (Milan 1964), pp. 159–203 (unreliable; the way in which Consolo Langher occasionally compels coins to fit the surviving historical evidence can lead her to rely too heavily on this evidence; cf. C. M. Kraay, *CR* 17 (1967), 212).
See further Note P, p. 208.
[2] E. Gabrici, *La monetazione del bronzo*, pp. 58–78.

Bronze

Site	Coins of:															See
	Akragas C5	Akragas C4	Gela C5	Gela C4	KAINON C4	Syracuse C5	Syracuse C4	Camarina C5	Camarina C4	Himera C5	Tauromenium	Lipari	Adranum C4	Herbessus C4	Morgantina C4	
Gela: Predio Leopardi (1)	25	—	—	2	—	—	5	2	—	—	—	—	—	—	—	n. 10
N. side of Acropolis	—	—	3	5	1	9	26	—	—	—	—	—	—	—	—	n. 11
Ospizio per i vecchi	1	8	—	—	—	—	6	—	—	—	—	—	—	—	—	n. 12
C. Soprano fortifications	1	—	—	3	—	—	8	—	—	—	—	—	—	—	—	n. 13
Random finds at Spinasanta	—	—	—	—	—	—	1	—	—	—	—	—	—	—	—	n. 14
Hellenistic house at C. Soprano	—	—	—	2	—	—	1	—	—	—	—	—	—	—	—	n. 15
Predio Leopardi (2)	—	3	—	2	—	—	43	—	—	—	—	—	—	—	—	n. 26
Piano Notaro (road)	—	3	—	3	—	—	2	—	—	—	—	—	—	—	—	n. 27
Piano Notaro (new hospital)	—	—	—	3	—	—	5	—	—	—	1	—	—	—	—	n. 28
Public baths	—	—	—	1	—	—	4	—	—	1	—	—	—	—	—	n. 29
Sacred building in Carrubazza area	—	—	1	—	—	—	2	—	—	1	—	—	—	—	—	n. 30
Sabucina	17	5	—	—	1	4	9	—	—	—	—	—	—	—	—	n. 16
Vassallaggi	27	6	—	—	1	1	2	—	—	—	—	1	—	—	—	n. 17
Gibil Gabib	1	2	—	—	3	2	3	—	—	—	—	—	—	—	—	n. 31
Gadira	—	—	—	—	—	4	9	—	—	—	—	—	—	—	—	n. 32
Manfria	—	—	—	—	—	—	36	—	—	—	—	—	—	—	—	n. 33

184

Site													Note
Castellazzo di Marianopoli	—	2	—	—	—	—	6	—	—	—	—	2	n. 34
Butera (necropolis of Piano della Fiera)	—	—	—	—	—	—	1	—	—	—	—	—	n. 35
Butera (Fontana Calda)	—	—	—	—	—	—	3	—	—	—	—	—	n. 36
M. Desusino	—	—	—	—	—	—	1	—	—	—	—	—	n. 37
Milingiana	—	—	—	—	1	—	—	—	—	—	—	—	n. 38
Helorus	—	—	—	—	—	—	1	—	—	—	—	—	p. 39
M. Raffe	—	—	—	—	—	—	1	—	—	—	—	—	n. 40
Capodarso	—	—	—	—	—	—	3	—	—	—	—	—	n. 41
Morgantina	—	38	—	11	—	—	161	—	2	2	—	21	n. 18
Hoards													
Milocca	93	23	—	—	—	1	19	1	—	—	—	—	n. 42
Siracusa 1912	—	—	—	—	—	—	14	—	—	—	—	—	n. 43
No findspot 1961	—	—	—	—	—	—	24	—	—	—	—	—	n. 44

The figures in the last column refer to notes on pp. 192–4

that the remaining three series of bronze coins must have been issued in the period after Timoleon's death.

Rizzo's examination of the style of the two Zeus Eleutherios issues[1] led him to attack some of Gabrici's conclusions. Rizzo agreed that Gabrici had placed the two issues in their correct order, but he also believed that the two issues were made during Timoleon's lifetime. In support of his belief he mentioned Timoleon's creation of an Amphipolia of Olympian Zeus; the attribution of gold and silver issues bearing the first Zeus Eleutherios head to Timoleon's lifetime; the spread of the Zeus Eleutherios type to other Greek mints in the Timoleontic period (that is, up to 317); and the revival of the type during the short period of freedom at Syracuse after Agathocles' death.[2]

Gabrici then reaffirmed his views unchanged,[3] and criticized Rizzo for determining the order of the Zeus Eleutherios issues on stylistic grounds, when the order could be fixed on the basis of declining weight. In the same article Gabrici went on to guess that the second Zeus Eleutherios issue must have been made at least ten years after Timoleon's retirement or death in 337 (p. 13).

The arguments used thus far by Gabrici and Rizzo were summarized by Breglia, who then cautiously added some comments of her own.[4] She suggested first (p. 199) that since the weights of Gabrici's series 2 and series 3 overlapped, these two series should perhaps be regarded as one. She added that if this idea were adopted, the general chronological problem would seem easier to resolve, because three changes of weight within the short space of Timoleon's years in Sicily appear more probable than four. Breglia next suggested (pp. 199–200) tnat there might be some value in the view of Head[5] and Giesecke,[6] who date Gabrici's series 1 before Timoleon's arrival in Syracuse.

---

[1] G. E. Rizzo, *Intermezzo: nuovi studi archeologici su le monete greche de la Sicilia* (Rome 1939), pp. 35–46.

[2] See P. Lederer, 'La coniazione del bronzo della quarta repubblica di Siracusa', *Numismatica e Scienze Affini* 4 (1938), 25–6.

[3] E. Gabrici, 'Divagazioni numismatiche', *Boll. Circ. Num. Nap.* 37 (1952), 10–13.

[4] L. Breglia, 'Divagazioni numismatiche e problema storico', *AIIN* 1 (1954), 196–200.

[5] B. V. Head, *HN²*, p. 178.

[6] W. Giesecke, *Sicilia Numismatica*, p. 64.

If this dating is followed also, then only two weight reductions remain in Timoleon's lifetime, a number which does not seem out of place in such a period of upheaval.

More recently the debate has been taken up by Consolo Langher.[1] She accepts Gabrici's order of Syracusan issues given above (Langher, p. 431), but she follows the idea of Head, Giesecke and Breglia that Gabrici's series 1 should be dated before Timoleon's arrival in Syracuse, and places the introduction of the series as early as 382 (pp. 429–30). She agrees with Breglia that Gabrici's series 2 and series 3 are really only one series (p. 433), and dates it to the years immediately before the battle of the R. Crimisus, because the Zeus Eleutherios type appears on coins of Aetna and Agyrium, both of which seem to have been destroyed by Timoleon soon after his great victory over the Carthaginians.[2]

Consolo Langher has re-stated her conclusions in a later publication too,[3] but these ideas were not favourably received by one reviewer at least.[4]

Having surveyed this complicated debate, the historian may doubt whether adequate evidence exists for the very precise dating of Syracusan issues within the Timoleontic period. Certainly one conclusion and one assumption seem seriously open to question.

First, the view of Consolo Langher that Gabrici's series 1 should be dated long before Timoleon's arrival in Syracuse seems to be invalidated by the frequent occurrence of such coins in the Timoleontic strata of excavation sites. In his review of all the coins found at Morgantina Ross Holloway expresses the opinion that: 'The Athene/star and dolphins and Athene/Hippocamp series seem well established as the major issues of the (Syracusan)

---

[1] S. Consolo Langher, 'Il *Sikelikon Talanton* nella storia economica e finanziaria della Sicilia antica', *Helikon* 3 (1963), 429–35.

[2] Pp. 431–2; this dating arises from a point made by L. Breglia, *AIIN* 1 (1954), 200.

[3] S. Consolo Langher, *Contributo alla storia della antica moneta bronzea in Sicilia*. See p. 189 for dating from coins of Aetna and Agyrium.

[4] C. M. Kraay, *CR* 17 (1967), 210–12, esp. p. 212. However G. Manganaro does support Consolo Langher's conclusions (*Kokalos* 14–15 (1968–9), 133–4).

mint in the earlier part of the Timoleontic period.'[1] This conclusion is confirmed by the frequent occurrence of these coins at Gela.[2]

Second, there seems to be small value in the assumption that Aetna and Agyrium can only have issued coins before Timoleon had expelled the Campanians from the former, and Apolloniades from the latter (D.S. 82.4). We know that Agyrium prospered after the departure of its tyrant (D.S. 83.3), while it would be strange if no settlers were sent to the fertile region of Aetna.[3] It is possible for both places to have issued coins at any time in the Timoleontic period; and it is far more likely that they copied Syracusan types in the period after their re-foundation by Timoleon, rather than in the earlier period, when they were held by opponents of Timoleon. The appearance of Zeus Eleutherios on these coins can hardly help to determine the date of the Zeus Eleutherios types issued at Syracuse.

Coins with the legend ΣΥΜΜΑΧΙΚΟΝ

A considerable amount has been written on the coins of Alaesa, but to small effect. Cavallaro[4] and Breglia[5] have distinguished four different legends on the coins:

[1] R. Ross Holloway, 'Monetary circulation', p. 142. M. Jessop Price would place these issues immediately before Timoleon's arrival in Sicily (review of S. Consolo Langher, *Contributo alla storia della antica moneta bronzea*, NC 7 (1967), 289).

[2] However, for more recent discussion of the dating of these Syracusan issues by A. Tusa Cutroni, with reference to finds at Himera and Motya, see A. Adriani and others, *Istituto di Archeologia, Università di Palermo: Himera I. Campagne di Scavo 1963-1965* (Rome 1970), pp. 364–5, and A. Ciasca and others, *Mozia – V, Consiglio Nazionale delle Ricerche* (Rome 1969), pp. 180–2 (cf. A. Tusa Cutroni, *AIIN* 15 (1968), 220–1).

[3] Justin (22.1.11) refers to a Syracusan campaign against the people of Aetna in the period between Timoleon's retirement and Agathocles' seizure of power. However it is possible that he and Diodorus (82.4) refer to the same campaign (cf. H. J. W. Tillyard, *Agathocles* (Cambridge 1908), p. 39). For the fertility of Aetna, see Strabo 6.2.3 and 8.

[4] The definitive treatment is that of G. Cavallaro, 'Le monete degli Alesini Siculi e della Symmachia', *Atti e Mem.* 8 (1934), 5–13. See also Cavallaro, 'L'ultimo rifugio degli Alesini Siculi', *Archivio Storico Siciliano* 54 (1934), 308–11.

[5] L. Breglia, 'La coniazione argentea di Alesa Arconidea', *Archivio Storico Siciliano* 2 (1947), 137–8.

1. ΣΥΜΜΑΧΙΚΟΝ
2. ΑΛΑΙΣΙΝΩΝ ΣΥΜΜΑΧΙ[ΚΟΝ
3. ΑΛΑ]ΙΣ[Ι]ΝΩΝ
4. ΑΛΑΙΣΑ[Σ

All four types are extremely rare.

Numismatists seem to agree that these coins were produced at some time during the Timoleontic period, but there appears to be no evidence which might help to fix their date with greater accuracy.

Cavallaro suggested that coins with the first two legends were minted at Alaesa, and that the alliance referred to is the one created by Timoleon (cf. D.S. 73.2); but in my opinion this second point is by no means as certain as many scholars have thought.[1]

Breglia (p. 138) rightly doubted Cavallaro's speculative ideas that coins with the third legend were minted for the various towns in Sicily called Alaesa (cf. D.S. 14.16.2), while coins with the fourth legend were minted by the principal Alaesa for its own use.

Bronze coins with the legend KAINON

It seems probable that there is no link between the ΣΥΜΜΑΧΙΚΟΝ and KAINON coins. This was the view of Cavallaro,[2] and it has been reinforced more recently by the fact that no finds of ΣΥΜΜΑΧΙΚΟΝ coins have so far been reported from the excavations conducted at Gela, at Morgantina, and at centres in the hinterland of Gela and Agrigento. Yet finds of coins with the legend KAINON suggest that these pieces circulated quite widely in Sicily and South Italy.[3]

There is general agreement that the KAINON coins should be dated to the Timoleontic period, but we do not know when they were issued within that period; who minted them; why they were produced anonymously; or how they came to circulate widely in Magna Graecia. Further, we do not know the noun to

[1] For example, Sordi, p. 57.
[2] *Atti e Mem.* 8 (1934), 18–19.
[3] Mr M. H. Crawford tells me that the Museum at Capua possesses a considerable number of KAINON coins, which were found locally.

which the adjective KAINON is intended to refer. The possibilities are endless, but since ancient readers of the legend presumably had nothing to help them interpret the word, it may be that the most obvious noun, 'new coin' or 'new coinage', is meant. Why the 'newness' of the coinage should be referred to so prominently remains another puzzle.

Gabrici's suggestion[1] that the KAINON coins were issues of the Anti-Agathoclean League formed by Akragas, Gela and Messana in 316 cannot be confirmed or refuted (cf. D.S. 19.70.2; 71.6; 102.1).[2]

Coins with the legend ΗΡΑΚΛΕΙѠΤΑΝ ΕΚ ΚΕΦΑΛΟΙΔΙΟΥ

De Miro strongly supports the idea that the Sicilian silver and bronze coins with a young Heracles and the legend ΕΚ ΚΕΦΑ-ΛΟΙΔΙΟΥ on the obverse, and a tossing bull and the legend ΗΡΑΚΛΕΙѠΤΑΝ on the reverse, were issued by colonists from Cephaloedium (= Cefalù) who settled at Heraclea Minoa in Timoleon's time.[3] He believes that citizens of Cephaloedium took advantage of the agreement between Timoleon and the Carthaginians, by which anybody was allowed to migrate from the Punic zone to the Greek zone (Plut. 34.2; cf. D.S. 19.2.8), and that they came to Heraclea Minoa. They re-named the city after Heracles, who is known to have been worshipped at Cephaloedium, and issued these coins bearing their new name. Although de Miro shows convincingly that the name of the city probably changed from Minoa to Heraclea in Timoleon's time, his opinion of the circumstances in which the coins were issued is hard to accept.

His view has been opposed by S. Consolo Langher, whose interpretation seems the more likely. She rightly suggests that de Miro's translation of the legend is doubtful, since it only makes sense when a verb is supplied. If the coins were issued by citizens of Cephaloedium who came south to colonize Heraclea, then the

[1] E. Gabrici, *MAN* 4 (1959), 141–3.

[2] All known KAINON coins are of bronze, except for one silver-plated example mentioned by Evans, 'Numismatic lights on the Sicily of Timoleon', p. 353 n. 1.

[3] For his full discussion, see *Kokalos* 4 (1958), 76–81.

legend must be translated: '(A coin issued by) Heracleots (who came) from Cephaloedium.' The verb 'came' has to be supplied here.

Langher also pays attention to the phrase ΕΚ ΚΕΦΑΛΟΙΔΙΟΥ and thinks it unlikely that settlers coming from Cephaloedium to Heraclea would take the trouble to record this purely historical information (and nothing else) on their coins. She therefore suggests that Cephaloedium was the place where the coins were issued, and that this fact was inscribed on the coins themselves for the reason that Cephaloedium was not the normal mint of the 'Heracleots'. Thus her translation gives considerable point to ΕΚ ΚΕΦΑΛΟΙΔΙΟΥ, and it does not require an extra verb: '(A coin issued) from Cephaloedium (by) Heracleots.' She dates the coins to the late fifth/early fourth centuries.[1]

The identity of the 'Heracleots' remains unknown, but confirmation of Langher's view that the coins were issued at Cephaloedium may be provided by a similar coin with the legend ΚΕΦΑΛΟΙΔΙΤΑΝ in the Pennisi collection. Jenkins suggests cautiously that this coin should be dated to the second half of the fourth century on stylistic grounds.[2]

[1] S. Consolo Langher, 'Gli ΗΡΑΚΛΕΙⲰΤΑΙ ΕΚ ΚΕΦΑΛΟΙΔΙΟΥ', *Kokalos* 7 (1961), 166–98. Her really important point, that these coins are not likely to have been minted at Heraclea Minoa, invalidates Sordi's speculative ideas on the circumstances in which the issues may have been made (Sordi, pp. 76–7).

[2] G. K. Jenkins, 'Coins of Punic Sicily', Part I, *Schweizerische Numismatische Rundschau* 50 (1971), 53–4 and Plate 21C.

NOTES TO TABLES IN CHAPTER 10

[1] For rare silver coins of Camarina, which were possibly minted at Syracuse, see G. K. Jenkins, 'Recent acquisitions of Greek coins by the British Museum', *NC* 19 (1959), 26.

[2] For silver coins, see B. V. Head, *HN²*, p. 130. Coins of Aetna, Campani, Entella and Nacona are discussed by A. Tusa Cutroni, 'I ΚΑΜΠΑΝΟΙ ed i ΤΥΡΡΗΝΟΙ in Sicilia attraverso la documentazione numismatica', *Kokalos* 16 (1970), 250–67.

[3] For the coinage of Gela in the Timoleontic period, see G. K. Jenkins, *The Coinage of Gela* (Berlin 1970), pp. 108–15.

[4] For this rare silver issue, which is perhaps datable to Timoleon's time, see E. Gabrici, 'Notes on Sicilian Numismatics', *NC* 11 (1931), 86; G. E. Rizzo, *Monete greche della Sicilia* (Rome 1946), p. 267; B. V. Head, *A guide to the principal coins of the Greeks* (revised by G. K. Jenkins, London 1965), p. 102, No. 32.

[5] This strange silver type has been included in the list because some scholars have dated it to the Timoleontic period. The type was first noticed by Evans, who believed that it was connected with the R. Crimisus and that it was issued in Timoleon's time (A. J. Evans, 'Contributions to Sicilian Numismatics II.8: On an alliance-coin of Western Sicily, with the altar of the Krimissos', *NC* 16 (1896), 140–3). However Giesecke (*Sicilia Numismatica* (Leipzig 1923), p. 74 n. 1) dated the coin to the mid third century B.C., while Gabrici, who discovered a second specimen, also believed Evans' idea to be wrong (*NC* 11 (1931), 87–8). Rizzo published a third specimen: in his view the legend ΚΙΜΙΣΣΑΙΩΝ showed that the coin was issued by a Sicilian city never mentioned in any literary source, while the coin's style and the theme referred to (OMONOIA) both suggest a Timoleontic date (*Monete greche*, p. 267).

[6] This rare silver issue should perhaps be dated to the Timoleontic period: see A. J. Evans, *NC* 16 (1896), 124–8; B. V. Head, *HN²*, p. 151.

[7] On the coinage of Morgantina in the Timoleontic period, see R. Ross Holloway, 'Monetary circulation in central Sicily to the reign of Augustus as documented by the Morgantina excavations', *Congresso Internazionale di Numismatica* Vol. 2: *Atti* (Rome 1965), 143–4.

[8] On the issues of Syracuse, see B. V. Head, 'On the chronological sequence of the coins of Syracuse', *NC* 14 (1874), 24–40, and my discussion, pp. 183–8 above.

[9] On the fourth-century coinage of Tyndaris, see S. Consolo Langher, 'Documentazione numismatica e storia di Tyndaris nel sec. IV A.C.', *Helikon* 5 (1965), 63–96. Timoleontic issues are covered on 81–9. The dating scheme proposed in this speculative article should be treated with caution, since it is closely linked with the uncertain ideas put forward by Langher in an earlier article; for comment on these ideas, see pp. 187–8 above.

[10] *MAL* 17 (1906), 418.

[11] *AIIN* 3 (1956), 228–31. There were twelve illegible bronze coins.

[12] *NSc* 14 (1960), 203; cf. *AIIN* 4 (1957), 204.

[13] *AIIN* 5–6 (1958–9), 304–5. There was one illegible silver coin.

[14] *AIIN* 5–6 (1958–9), 305.

[15] *NSc* 10 (1956), 352.

[16] C. Merighi, 'Nota sulla monetazione di alcuni centri greci o ellenizzati in provincia di Caltanissetta', *Arch. Cl.* 15 (1963), 99. It is possible that the total of fourth-century Syracusan bronze coins ought to be eleven, rather than nine, because there is no No. 26 nor No. 27 in Merighi's list. For Timoleontic coins found at Sabucina, cf. *Arch. Cl.* 17 (1965), 139.

[17] *Arch. Cl.* 15 (1963), 99–100. The list of finds at *AIIN* 4 (1957), 206, includes one fourth-century Corinthian stater.

[18] This is a record of all the coins datable between 344 and 317 found in excavations at Morgantina. See R. Ross Holloway, 'Monetary circulation', pp. 140–4. Unfortunately there are no publications of equal clarity which list the coin finds made at other Sicilian cities.

[19] *AIIN* 5–6 (1958–9), 305.

[20] See pp. 188–9.

[21] For a general discussion of fourth-century Campanian coinage in Sicily, see E. Gabrici, 'Problemi di numismatica greca della Sicilia e Magna Grecia', *MAN* 4 (1959), 99–110 and 156; and A. Tusa Cutroni, 'I ΚΑΜΠΑΝΟΙ ed i ΤΥΡΡΗΝΟΙ'.

[22] See pp. 189–90.

[23] On the coinage of Mytistratus, see G. Cavallaro, 'Mytistratum Sicana e le sue monete', *Atti e Mem.* 7 (1932), 14–37, esp. 17.

[24] On the coinage of Nacona, see G. Cavallaro, 'Note numismatiche-topographiche siciliane: Nacona elimica', *Bollettino di Numismatica* I, No. 3 (1929), 1–9, esp. 1–3; and A. Tusa Cutroni, 'I ΚΑΜΠΑΝΟΙ ed i ΤΥΡΡΗΝΟΙ'.

[25] Examples of the one issue which Petra is thought to have made in the second half of the fourth century are extremely rare, but the reading of the legend is not in doubt, according to Robinson (see *SNG* II.1164, and E. S. G. Robinson, 'Petra or Eryx?', *NC* 8 (1948), 131–3). G. de Ciccio argues unconvincingly against Robinson's attribution of the Lloyd Collection specimen to Petra (*Numismatica* 14 (1948), 1–4 and 15 (1949), 106–7).

[26] *MAL* 17 (1906), 420.

[27] *AIIN* 3 (1956), 231–2. There were two illegible bronze coins.

[28] *NSc* 14 (1960), 169–70; cf. *AIIN* 4 (1957), 203–4. There were two illegible bronze coins.

[29] *AIIN* 4 (1957), 205. There were five illegible bronze coins.

[30] *NSc* 10 (1956), 251–2.

[31] *Arch. Cl.* 15 (1963), 101. This list does not include the KAINON bronze, for which see *AIIN* 3 (1956), 235, and *NSc* 12 (1958), 404.

[32] *Arch. Cl.* 15 (1963), 100; cf. *AIIN* 4 (1957), 207.

[33] Of these 36 coins, 4 are excavation finds reported in *NSc* 12 (1958), 331; 32 form a hoard reported in *AIIN* 9–11 (1962–4), 265.

[34] *AIIN* 5–6 (1958–9), 305–6.

[35] *MAL* 44 (1958), 243.

36 *MAL* 44 (1958), 595.

37 *NSc* 12 (1958), 346.

38 *NSc* 12 (1958), 352.

39 *MAL* 47 (1966), 318.

40 *AIIN* 5–6 (1958–9), 305.

41 *Arch. Cl.* 15 (1963), 101.

42 P. Orsi, 'Ripostiglio di monete erose e di altri bronzi da Milocca (Caltanissetta)', *Atti e Mem.* 7 (1932), 38–46.

43 Unpublished hoard. See *AIIN* 9–11 (1962–4), 224 for brief description.

44 See *AIIN* 9–11 (1962–4), 231 for brief description. Part of an unpublished hoard, which was apparently not recovered complete.

The overwhelming majority of coins found at Scornavacche were Syracusan: see *Bollettino d'Arte* (1959), 362 n. 49.

ADDITIONAL NOTES

A (see p. 26)

Mention should be made of the extraordinary suggestion put forward by T. S. Brown on the identity of the Peripatetic biographer postulated by Westlake (Brown, *Timaeus of Tauromenium*, pp. 84–5). He draws attention to the statement of Clement of Alexandria, noticed long ago, that Θεόπομπος καὶ Ἔφορος καὶ Τίμαιος Ὀρθαγόραν τινὰ μάντιν ἀναγράφουσιν (*Strom.* 1.21.135). He regards it as remarkable that all three writers cited here mention Orthagoras, whereas at Plut. *Tim.* 4.6 Theopompus is said to mention Satyrus where Ephorus and Timaeus mention Orthagoras. Brown assumes that Clement and Plutarch refer to the same occasion, then supposes that a name has dropped out of Plutarch's text, and therefore proposes to emend it as follows: τῶν δὲ φίλων τὸν μάντιν, ὃν Σάτυρος μὲν * * Θεόπομπος, Ἔφορος δὲ καὶ Τίμαιος Ὀρθαγόραν ὀνομάζουσι. This, he considers, would give Satyrus as the name of the Peripatetic biographer; and he shows that a Satyrus who wrote biographies of political figures is known.

Brown's suggestion is too bold. It is possible that a name has dropped out of the text through a copyist's error, in the way that the name Crimisus may well have dropped out of Diodorus' narrative of Timoleon's great victory (for example at 79.5), but it is equally possible that an obscure name would catch a scribe's eye, and that he would take care over it. Then Clement had read some of Plutarch's work (see K. Ziegler, *Plutarchos von Chaironeia*, col. 311); and it may be that he obtained his information about Orthagoras from this passage, but read it carelessly or recalled it inaccurately. The mistake would be easy to make. Finally it is not likely that Plutarch would have written Θεόπομπος, Ἔφορος δὲ καὶ Τίμαιος, as Brown wishes. A more likely arrangement is perhaps the one adopted by Clement: Θεόπομπος δὲ καὶ Ἔφορος καὶ Τίμαιος. So a change would be required in two places, if the suggestion is admitted (the insertion of the gap for the name, and the change in the position of δὲ καί). Each additional change is bound to diminish Brown's chances of being right.

B (see p. 33)

Some further comments made by Hammond about the character of Diodorus' source for Group 3 require notice (*CQ* 32 (1938), 139). He regards the fact that before the Carthaginian invasion all the Sicilian states are represented as acceding to Timoleon as a suspicious exaggeration (D.S. 73.2). However I would follow Diodorus in believing that nearly all the states of Greek Sicily which were able to join Timoleon did actually do so, especially under the threat of a Punic invasion (see pp. 95 and 143 above). Similarly Hammond suspects that the Carthaginians' fear to embark for home after their defeat has been exaggerated (D.S. 81.2). But there seems no need to interpret the Carthaginians' fear as extravagant, when other passages of Diodorus show the extreme superstition of the Carthaginians (for example, 14.76.4 and 77.4; 20.14).

Nor is there any need to follow Hammond in regarding the Carthaginians' fear that Timoleon would invade Africa as extravagant, or as most probably projected into the past by an author who had experienced Agathocles' invasion. For according to Diodorus (11.24.4) the Carthaginians feared invasion after their defeat by Gelon at Himera in 480, whilst a similar fear is attributed to them after their defeat by Dionysius I at Syracuse in 396 (D.S. 14.76.2; cf. Hermocrates' remark about their fear of invasion by Athens at Thuc. 6.34.2; and the Athenians' fear of invasion from Sicily in 413, Thuc. 8.1.2). In the case of the passages of Diodorus cited above, it may well be that the Carthaginians' fear has been projected into the past by authors who remembered Agathocles' invasion, since in his account of that event Diodorus stresses how the Carthaginians had not expected an invasion of Africa, and how they were totally unprepared (for example, 20.3.2–3; 8.6; 9.3). On the other hand, it is not made quite clear whether it was because the very idea of an invasion of Africa had never entered their heads that the Carthaginians did not expect Agathocles' invasion, or whether it was because Punic ships were known to be blockading Syracuse (20.5.2). Diodorus' narrative, at one point at least, would seem to suggest the latter reason (20.9.3).

Lastly Hammond argues that Diodorus' source was acquainted with later events in Sicily because Agathocles is mentioned (16.83.2). Diodorus' source may well have been acquainted with such events, but I feel that it would be wiser to attribute the whole of chapter 83.2 to Diodorus himself, rather than to his source (as well as 82.5 and 83.3 on Agyrium).

C (see p. 47)

Sordi (p. 111) mentions a possible inconsistency in Diodorus' narrative in the fact that at 73.2, after gaining much booty from the devastation of the Punic sector, Timoleon ἔδωκε τοῖς μισθοφόροις εἰς πλείω χρόνον τοὺς μισθούς, yet nevertheless before the battle of the R. Crimisus Thrasius accuses Timoleon of ἐναποκυβεύων ταῖς τῶν μισθοφόρων ψυχαῖς, οὐδὲ τοὺς ὀφειλομένους μισθοὺς πολλοῦ χρόνου διὰ τὴν ἀπορίαν ἀποδεδωκώς (78.5). She regards this apparent inconsistency as a sign that a considerable interval elapsed between the plundering expedition to the Punic sector and the Crimisus campaign, and therefore she finds support for her dating of the battle of the R. Crimisus in 339.

The point is a fair one, but I do not think that too much emphasis should be laid upon it. The εἰς πλείω χρόνον of 73.2 and the πολλοῦ χρόνου of 78.5 are both very vague terms: they need not amount to more than a month or two. It is clear from Thrasius' speech that he and his companions were above all terrified of the odds against Timoleon's army, and they would most probably have been willing to magnify any little excuse in their desperation to escape from what they considered would turn out to be a massacre of the Greek army by the Carthaginians. It would be possible for these mercenaries to have been paid their *misthoi* in late 342, after gaining booty from the Punic sector, and then to have received no more *misthoi* between that time and June 341, when they made their complaint. Furthermore I suspect that the εἰς πλείω χρόνον of 73.2 need not amount to much, because it is most likely that Timoleon had to use the Punic booty to make more back payments than advance payments. As far as we know, this is the first sizeable gain of booty which he made, and by this time the pay of his original mercenaries could well have been seriously in arrears. Timoleon could have found little financial support in Syracuse (for Syracusan financial straits, see Plut. 23.6–8), and it must have been a considerable relief to him that his reinforcements came bringing some money with them (D.S. 69.4). So the most likely explanation of these points seems to be that Timoleon made up arrears of *misthos* to his mercenaries when he gained Punic booty in 342, and then added a modest advance payment. By June 341 there had been no further gain of booty, so that *misthos* was once again in arrears. Diodorus' narrative still makes good sense even if the battle of the R. Crimisus is placed in 341 rather than in 339.

On payment of mercenaries, see also pp. 56–7 and 67–8.

D (see p. 74)

N. Lojacono, 'Entella ed il Crimiso' (sect. 1, *L'Araldo di S. Margherita Belice* 1963, 2 pages of offprint; sect. 2, *ibid.* 1964, pp. 22–9). There is perhaps some value in mentioning this little-known study by Lojacono, which discusses not only the site of the battle of the R. Crimisus, but also the course of the fighting there. Although the section on the course of the fighting is useful, some points seem open to doubt. Lojacono's account implies that Timoleon was certain of a Punic plan to make for Entella, and that he therefore carefully chose a site for battle and then coolly took the enemy by surprise (sect. 2, p. 24). Certainly it would have been sensible of Timoleon to select an exposed river crossing at which to trap the Carthaginians (cf. D.S. 20.38.2–4; Plut. 31.3), but Plutarch's account of the campaign suggests that Timoleon marched to the Punic zone at great speed, happened on the invading force by accident, and then gave battle without any delay (cf. 25.6; 27.6).

There seems little support for Lojacono's idea (sect. 2, p. 25) that the Punic infantry was preceded not by war chariots, but by a group of 'carri', siege engines intended for the assault on Entella. It was normal for war chariots to precede a Punic army (cf. D.S. 20.10.6; 20.12.1–2), and Diodorus distinguishes the ἅρματα which took part in this battle (77.4; 80.2 and 5) from the σκευοφόρα, ζεύγη and ἅμαξαι which were later captured by the Greeks (80.5; but the ζεῦγος perhaps dedicated by Timoleon at Delphi would presumably have been a war chariot; see p. 50). Plutarch is even more explicit: he mentions how μηχαναί (25.1; cf. μηχάνημα at 13.6; 17.4) were transported to Sicily, and how τὰ ὑποζύγια were captured after the battle (29.1), but in his account these items of equipment are clearly distinguished from the ἅρματα or τέθριππα ἐκπληκτικῶς πρὸς ἀγῶνας κατεσκευασμένα (25.1; 27.4), which moved swiftly in front of the Punic infantry (27.8 and 10), and were later captured (29.2).

Despite his close examination of the various stages of the battle Lojacono does not discuss one problem which Plutarch's account leaves unsolved: how did Timoleon's infantry charge overcome the very large number of Punic war chariots or 'carri', after cavalry charges had failed to overcome them (Plut. 27.10; cf. G. Grote, *A History of Greece* (London 1869 ed.), Vol. 10, p. 456)? This is a crucial point, especially as it is known from Xenophon, for example (*Hell.* 4.1.18–19), that even a few chariots could wreak havoc when they charged men drawn up in the close formation adopted by Timoleon.

It is possible that at the R. Crimisus, as at Chaeronea in 86 B.C., there was little room for manoeuvre, and that the chariots may finally have driven into a position where they could not turn again and charge, with the result that they had to remain stationary and thus ineffective against Timoleon's phalanx (cf. Plut. *Sulla* 18.4–6). However Plutarch's account remains silent on this difficulty.

Finally Lojacono's Figures 2 and 3 (sect. 2, pp. 27–8) do not reproduce the later stages of the battle exactly as these are recorded by Diodorus at least. For while Lojacono represents the Greek infantry engaging the Punic phalanx in and around the river, with the Punic 'carri' some distance beyond the river, Diodorus (80.2) states that the Greek infantry, Punic infantry and Punic chariots all became entangled in the river itself.

E (see p. 110)

Plutarch refers to Mamercus as Μάμερκος throughout, whereas Diodorus calls him Μάρκος. Nepos calls him 'Mamercus', an agreement with Plutarch which might be taken as further evidence that the two authors had a common source. Polyaenus (5.12.2) uses the form Μάμερκος. F. Hiller v. Gaertringen has put forward the reasonable view that Μάρκος or Μᾶρκος is probably correct, on the grounds that in the list of Thearodokoi at Epidaurus there is a reference to Καττάναι· Ἄ[λ]κιππος Μάρκου (*IG* iv², 1.95, line 71). It is fairly certain that the Μάρκος referred to is the opponent of Timoleon and not some other Μάρκος. See F. Hiller v. Gaertringen, 'Marcus–Mamercus', *Wiener Studien* 46 (1928), 93–5. The relevant part of this inscription is discussed by G. de Sanctis, 'I Thearodokoi d'Epidauro', *Atti della Accad. Sc. di Torino* 47 (1911–12), 442–50. This article has been reprinted in G. de Sanctis, *Scritti Minori*, Vol. 1, pp. 171–9 (*Storia e Letteratura* 99, Rome 1966).

Although the testimony of the inscription is unassailable, the question cannot rest here: for if Marcus is the correct name, we should seek an explanation of why the longer Mamercus ever took its place. The appearance of the name Mamercus in three of our sources can hardly be the result of a casual slip for Marcus. And since the evidence which we have about Mamercus (especially Nep. 2.4) strongly suggests that he was an Italian, not a Greek, it seems sensible to conclude that Mamercus is the correct form of his name. It is the form Marcus which requires explanation.

F (see p. 113)

Westlake's section on relations between Mamercus and Timoleon (*Tyrants*, pp. 45–50) sets out nearly all the information about Mamercus known to us, but adds much speculation. It is interesting to suggest, as Westlake does, that Mamercus was intermediary in the negotiations between Dionysius and Timoleon (p. 46; cf. p. 25 n. 1), or that a small contingent from Catania may have fought at the battle of the R. Crimisus (p. 46), or that Mamercus directed most of the operations of the alliance formed against Timoleon after the battle of the R. Crimisus (p. 47), to take only three examples, but none of these ideas can be anything more than speculation. No evidence exists for any of them. The presence of so much speculation makes the section difficult to use, because of the constant need to distinguish between speculation and discussion of evidence.

Sordi (pp. 113–15) has put forward the view that the execution of Mamercus as referred to by Plutarch (ἔτι ζῶν ἀπαχθεὶς ἥνπερ οἱ λῃσταὶ δίκην ἔδωκε 34.7) is also referred to by Diodorus, when he mentions that Timoleon executed Postumius, an Etruscan pirate, who sailed into Syracuse with twelve ships, believing the city to be friendly to him (D.S. 82.3). Sordi's extraordinary idea that the two stories refer to the same incident, the execution of Mamercus, is cautiously accepted by Berve (*Gnomon* 35 (1963), 383; *Die Tyrannis*, Vol. 2, p. 665). But there seems to be no support whatsoever for the idea. The fact that Postumius was Etruscan and that Mamercus may have been one is of small significance: there were a number of Etruscans in Sicily at the time, as Sordi herself says (p. 115). Certainly this fact cannot serve as an argument for thinking Postumius and Mamercus to be the same man. Indeed such a conclusion could only be reached by a total disregard for all the evidence given to us by Plutarch and Diodorus. Plutarch gives a plausible and detailed account of Mamercus' death. When he says that Mamercus ἥνπερ οἱ λῃσταὶ δίκην ἔδωκε, he merely means that Mamercus suffered a gruesome death.

Diodorus' story of the execution of Postumius is also quite plausible. Timoleon wished to restore Sicilian prosperity by trade with mainland Greece, and he will therefore have opposed piracy. In these circumstances his summary execution of Postumius is understandable. That Postumius either misjudged Timoleon's attitude to piracy, or did not realize that Timoleon was controlling Syracuse at the time, is also understandable. As a somewhat similar case Ducrey cites the occasion when Aristonicus entered Methymna with five pirate ships, unaware that the city was in Macedonian hands. The pirate crews were executed immediately (Arrian, *Anabasis* 3.2.5; Curtius 4.5.18–21; P. Ducrey, *Le traitement des prisonniers de guerre dans la Grèce antique*, Ecole Française d'Athènes, Fasc. 17 (Paris 1968), p. 192). It is unbelievable that Diodorus should have confused the execution of Mamercus with that of Postumius. Even if he had done so, he would not have become so muddled as to portray Mamercus coming to Syracuse by sea with twelve ships, rather than by land as Timoleon's captive, which is Plutarch's version of events.

Sordi's suggestion has unfortunately been taken up and amplified by M.-P. Loicq-Berger, *Syracuse: histoire culturelle d'une cité grecque*, Collection Latomus Vol. 87 (Brussels 1967), 238–40. On the menace presented by piracy note Justin 22.1.14, and see Westlake, *CHJ* 7 (1942), 98.

G (see p. 124)

The expression πρὸς ἀλλοφύλους is a strange one. It may be translated literally 'against people of another race', but presumably it must come to mean 'against the Carthaginians' at Plut. 38.4, since a Corinthian *strategos* was not summoned to Syracuse for the wars against Acragas and Croton in the period after Timoleon's death (D.S. 19.3.1 and 3). But Syracuse does seem to have been at war with Carthage when Acestoridas was elected *strategos*, the only occasion on which we hear of this decree being put into effect (D.S. 19.4.3; cf. 5.4). The Syracusans' reasons for placing πρὸς ἀλλοφύλους rather than πρὸς Καρχηδονίους in the decree are not clear. It may be that they wished to make the decree's terms of reference as broad and as flexible as possible. Perhaps they envisaged the possibility of a war with foreign races other than the Carthaginians in the distant future. Timoleon himself had killed the Italian Mamercus (cf. Nep. 2.4), the Etruscan Postumius (D.S. 82.3) and the Campanians on Etna (D.S. 82.4), while the author of Ps. Dio Chrysostom 37.20 speaks of the Syracusans fighting πρὸς Καρχηδονίους καὶ τοὺς ἄλλους βαρβάρους τοὺς τὴν Σικελίαν καὶ τὴν Ἰταλίαν κατοικοῦντας, at the time when they melted down statues for money (cf. Plut. 23.7–8). But this idea is no more than speculation.

H (see p. 126)

Westlake's article 'The Purpose of Timoleon's Mission' (*AJP* 70 (1949), 65–75) proceeds on the assumptions, first that the substance of the Siceliot appeal to Corinth and the orders issued to Timoleon by the Corinthian government must have been closely parallel, and secondly that the orders issued to Timoleon by the Corinthian government were precise (p. 65). Both assumptions are open to question. The first presupposes that the Corinthian government will have accepted the exiles' claim to represent the government of Syracuse, instead of regarding them as rebels who wished to overthrow the established government of their city. The second assumption implies far closer links between the Corinthian government and Timoleon in Sicily than would appear to have been the case. Further, if Corinth had felt justified in attempting to re-establish peace and freedom in Sicily by direct interference in the internal affairs of her colony, she would have afforded Timoleon stronger support. With the small force he was given his chances of success were so slender that precise instructions would have been valueless: any success, however small, would have been surprising. Westlake's contention that Corinthian aid was sought against tyranny, not against Carthage (pp. 73–4), seems likely, but cannot be proved. It depends on his conjecture that the Carthaginians intervened in Sicily after the Syracusan exiles had set off to appeal to Corinth (p. 73). The only evidence is Diodorus' statement (67.1; cf. Plut. 2.1) that Carthage intervened a short time before Timoleon's voyage (βραχὺ πρὸ τούτων τῶν καιρῶν). We just cannot tell what Diodorus means by this period. But if the Carthaginians had intervened before the mission of the Syracusan exiles set off for Corinth, the mission might well have appealed for help against both the tyrants and Carthage.

J (see p. 143)

Sjöqvist seeks to show that Morgantina must have been one of the cities to join Timoleon in his campaign against Dionysius II. Morgantina may well have done so, but no evidence exists on the point. Sjöqvist suggests that Plutarch would have thought of Morgantina as a *polis* (cf. 13.2), assuming in his argument that both Plutarch and Diodorus attached a very exact meaning to *polis*. He seems to think that both authors would distinguish between πόλις μεγίστη (D.S. 90.1), πόλις μεγάλη (Plut. 35.2), πόλις, πόλις ἐλάττων (D.S. 83.3), and πόλις μικρά (Plut. 12.2), or πολίχνη (Plut. 11.5) or πολίχνιον (Plut. 12.5), but this is highly unlikely. *Polis* is a sufficiently vague term to cover Syracuse, Corinth and Carthage (Plut. 28.10), at one end of the scale, and Thurii (Plut. 16.4), Engyum (D.S. 72.3) and Centuripe (D.S. 82.4) at the other. Plutarch calls Tauromenium both *polis* (10.6; 10.8; 11.2) and πολίχνη (11.5) – even in the same chapter. Thus *polis* may be thought of as meaning variously 'city', 'town' or even 'place'. Although both Plutarch and Diodorus seem to distinguish between *polis* and φρούριον (Plut. 22.6; D.S. 69.4; 70.4), while Diodorus distinguishes between *polis* and χώρα (83.1), the authors' use of *polis* is not as exact as Sjöqvist would suggest (E. Sjöqvist, 'Timoleonte e Morgantina', *Kokalos* 4 (1958), 107–18, at 108–10 and 117).

Sjöqvist's suggestion should by no means be taken as proven, as has been done by S. Consolo Langher, 'Documentazione numismatica e storia di Tyndaris nel sec. IV A.C.', *Helikon* 5 (1965), 87 n. 92.

Equally doubtful is Sjöqvist's suggestion (*Kokalos* 4 (1958), 117–18) that the bronze coin of Morgantina, on the reverse of which there appears an eagle with a serpent, was minted after the battle of the R. Crimisus to celebrate the Greek victory and to show Morgantina's loyalty to Timoleon (cf. Plut. 26.6). Although the idea is an attractive one, we have nothing with which to link the coin and the omen, while it is perhaps strange that Morgantina should have chosen this particular emblem by which to commemorate the victory. See also A. J. Evans, 'Contributions to Sicilian Numismatics: 6: The Omen of the Krimisos on Coins of Herbessus and Morgantina', *NC* 14 (1894), 233–7.

K (see p. 150)

Di Vita's definite opinion (*Kokalos* 4 (1958), 83–90) that Camarina was not occupied between 405 and its revival by Timoleon would seem to invalidate Beloch's suggestion (*GG²* III.1, p. 587), followed by the Budé editors, that Καμάριναν be read for the Καλαυρίαν or Καλαβρίαν of the manuscripts at Plut. 31.2. In any event Beloch's suggestion requires Hicetas to take an extraordinary route on his way from Syracusan territory to Leontini. The conjecture of M. Sordi, Γαλερίαν (*Diodori Liber XVI*, pp. 116 and 143; cf. Ziegler's Γαλαρίαν in the Teubner text of Plut. *Tim.*) has the same weakness, if Galeria is sited at Gagliano sul Salso/Gagliano Castelferrato (Foglio 26), a matter itself uncertain. Similarly A. Tusa Cutroni assumes the place at Plut. 31.2 to be the Galeria of D.S. 67.3–4. She regards Galeria as a city occupied by Campanians (although this cannot be inferred with certainty from D.S.), and sees Timoleon as attacking it for that reason (cf. his treatment of the Campanians on Aetna at D.S. 82.4). ('I KAMΠANOI ed i TYPPHNOI in Sicilia attraverso la documentazione numismatica', *Kokalos* 16 (1970), 252 and 254 with n. 16). However, there is insufficient evidence to identify this place at Plut. 31.2: the account does not even state that it was definitely a city, while it was insignificant enough both for Timoleon to attack it with a small force, and for Hicetas to make no serious attempt to relieve it.

L (see p. 150)

A damaged mid third-century inscription from the sanctuary of Asclepius on Cos (cf. above, p. 150 n. 2) suggests that Coans took part in the Timoleontic restoration of Gela. But according to Plutarch it was Gorgos of Ceos who led the colonists brought to Gela (35.2). And since Ceos and Cos are so alike orthographically, it is tempting to argue that the ἐκ Κέω of Plutarch's text should be changed to ἐκ Κῶ, thus making Gorgos come from Cos. This change, advocated by a number of earlier scholars, has been pressed with particular force by Asheri, who stresses the additional point that whereas Dorian Cos can reasonably be expected to have taken part in the revival of Dorian Gela, it would be peculiar for Ionian Ceos to take part in the revival of a Dorian foundation.

For similar reasons Asheri questions the common belief that Ionian Elea in Lucania is the city referred to at Plut. 35.2 as taking part in the revival of Dorian Acragas. According to him, excavations have revealed no traces of Ionian influence in the fourth-century Acragas. He suggests therefore that Dorian Elea (or Elaia) in Epirus is meant, and discusses such meagre evidence as there is for contacts between Epirus and Acragas, including the bronze lamella *SGDI* 1340, on which see below.

Independently of Asheri, G. Manganaro, too, had suggested that Elaia in Epirus is meant at Plut. 35.2: he wished to follow the manuscript which reads 'Ελαίας (rather than 'Ελέας), and he believed that colonists from this Epirote city decided to sail to Sicily after the ravaging of their territory by Philip of Macedon in 342 (cf. Demosthenes 7.32).

For the text of the Cos inscription, see R. Herzog and G. Klaffenbach, *Asylieurkunden aus Kos*, pp. 23–4. For a full discussion see J. Seibert, *Metropolis und Apoikie*, pp. 135–8. To Seibert's list of publications may now be added G. Manganaro, 'Città di Sicilia e santuari panellenici nel III e II sec. A.C.', *Siculorum Gymnasium* 17 (1964), 41–4; G. Manganaro, 'Intervento' after P. Lévêque, 'De Timoléon à Pyrrhos', *Kokalos* 14–15 (1968–9), 155–6; D. Asheri, 'Note on the resettlement of Gela under Timoleon', *Historia* 19 (1970), 618–23; D. Asheri, 'I coloni elei ad Agrigento', *Kokalos* 16 (1970), 79–88.

Neither of Asheri's points can be considered definitely proved. It is a little strange that a scribe should write Κέω for Κῶ, although the difference would only be one extra stroke. Then if Plutarch had meant to refer to the little-known Elaia in Epirus at 35.2, it seems puzzling that he should not have clarified his meaning in order to prevent confusion with more famous cities of very similar name, especially when he has already mentioned how news of Timoleon's capture of Syracuse spread to Italy (21.6), and how many colonists later arrived from there (23.6). However, Asheri's point that Ionian cities would not normally take part in the revival of Dorian foundations is certainly a striking one.

There has been considerable uncertainty over the dating of a bronze lamella from Dodona, which records the Molossians' grant of *proxenia* to the people of Acragas. For example, Collitz (*SGDI*, Vol. 2, No. 1340) and Dittenberger (*SIG*³, Vol. 3, No. 942) dated it to the period immediately after Timoleon's restoration of Acragas, and they have been followed more recently by P. R. Franke (*Alt-Epirus und das Königtum der Molosser* (Erlangen 1954), 40; *Die antiken Münzen von Epirus* (Wiesbaden 1961), p. 276), by Lepore (*Kokalos* 10–11 (1964–5), 497 and 509), and by Lévêque (*Kokalos* 14–15 (1968–9), 139). This dating might suggest that there were trade links established between Epirus and Acragas soon after the latter's restoration. N. G. L. Hammond (*Epirus* (Oxford 1967), p. 571) prefers to see this grant of *proxenia* as an honour bestowed in recognition of the generous help afforded to Pyrrhus by the Acragantines in 278–276 (D.S. 22.10.1), and he conjectures that the three Acragantines mentioned on the lamella were envoys who brought news of Pyrrhus' success in Sicily. In my view both these suggested dates must remain conjectural when there exists no firm evidence with which to decide the question. Formal epigraphical criteria seem unable to help in this case where the letters on the lamella are formed by a series of punched dots. Hammond's suggestion is attractive, but there is no real link between the lamella and the narrative of Pyrrhus' Sicilian campaigns, while in any event the practice of connecting an isolated piece of epigraphical evidence with a convenient text may seem unsound. The opinion of Hammond and some of the other scholars cited above that it was rare for a whole city to be granted the privilege of *proxenia* seems open to doubt (see A. Wilhelm, *Attische Urkunden*, Vol. 5 (Vienna and Leipzig 1942), pp. 52–3).

M (see p. 162)

It has usually been assumed that the mint of Ambracia must have been closed in 338 on Philip's occupation of the city (cf. D.S. 17.3.3), and it is plain that Jenkins lays considerable weight on this assumption in his dating of Hoards Nos. 1–3 in my list. However only three cities – Ambracia, Corinth and Thebes – are known to have been garrisoned by Philip, and among these Corinth at least was clearly permitted to continue minting coins without restriction. In view of this fact it may be unwise to assume that Philip's occupation of Ambracia must have led to the immediate closure of the mint there. Jenkins certainly notes that the late fourth-century stage of coinage is missing at Ambracia (*CPANS*, p. 374), and it might therefore be best to imagine that she ceased issuing coins earlier than some of Corinth's other Western dependencies, rather than to assume that her mint must have been closed forcibly in 338. Pegasi of Ambracia continue to appear in limited quantities even in hoards buried as late as *c*. 289, but this may not be particularly significant (7 in Centuripe 1952 (No. 1 in my list); 5 in Licata 1926 (No. 2); 31 in Leonforte (Nissoria) 1952 (No. 3); 1 in Sicily Uncertain 1912/13 (No. 6); 1 in Sicily Unknown 1877 (No. 8); 2 in Magna Graecia *c*. 1935 (No. 12); 19 in Sicily Unknown (no date) (No. 14); 1 in Sicily Unknown 1879 (No. 15); 2 in Megara Hyblaea 1949 (No. 16); 9 in Pachino 1957 (No. 23); 5 in Sicily Unknown (*c*. 1837) (No. 26); 8 in Megara Hyblaea 1967 (No. 27)). Unspecified numbers of Ambracian Pegasi are also reported in Cesarò 1915/16 (No. 7); Gibil Gabib 1928 (No. 11); Palazzolo Acreide 1896 (No. 31); Scoglitti 1938 (No. 34).

Even if this caution over the date of Ambracia's last issues may partly undermine Jenkins' technical arguments for the dating of Hoards Nos. 1–3, there seems to be no doubt that the general dating of these hoards remains correct.

N (see p. 164)

Professor M. I Finley has suggested to me that the main centre for minting Pegasi might have been Syracuse, not Corinth. This idea is excellent in that it prevents us from forming the unlikely picture of raw silver (for example, that from the battle of the R. Crimisus) going from Sicily to Corinth, only to return again in the form of Pegasi. This lengthy and dangerous process would not have been necessary if dies for Corinthian Pegasi had been used at Syracuse. But there is no evidence for the use of dies in this way. Rather each city to mint Pegasi, including Corinth, seems to have put its name, fully or in abbreviated form, on each coin. That is not a definite proof that Pegasi with Corinthian dies cannot have been minted at Syracuse, but it does make such minting seem less likely. It would certainly be strange for Syracuse to mint some Pegasi marked with her own name and others marked with the koppa of Corinth. Finley's suggestion might gain support from certain Syracusan Pegasi, on which a koppa appears below the Pegasus. Such a type is illustrated by W. Giesecke (*Sicilia Numismatica* (Leipzig 1923), Plate 15.5 and 6), who dates it to the time of Dion (p. 65). This dating now seems unsatisfactory, since it is fairly clear that Syracuse did not mint Pegasi before Timoleon's time. It is possible that the koppa below the Pegasus denotes a Syracusan issue made on behalf of Corinth, but this explanation seems far-fetched. It is perhaps more likely that Syracusan engravers retained the koppa merely because they wished to make the closest possible copies of Corinthian types.

O (see p. 166)

In a number of articles Amorós argues from coin types that Syracusan influence on Emporion was great, especially during the fourth century B.C. (cf. 'Les dracmes Empuritanes', pp. 22–3; 'Les monedes Empuritanes', p. 65). Although the suggested similarities between the types of the two cities are not always very striking (cf., for example, 'Les monedes Empuritanes', Nos. 70, 75, 77), Amorós may be correct in his view that there was trade between Emporion and Sicily. That this trade came specifically from the Greek zone of the island is a more doubtful idea; certainly the proposition is not to be supported by Emporion's imitation of Syracusan coins, since such coins circulated freely in the Punic zone also. Then Amorós' idea that Syracusan coins were brought to Emporion by mercenaries serving in the Greek zone of Sicily ('D'un troballa', p. 17) cannot be substantiated by the existing evidence on mercenaries in Timoleon's time, whereas we know that Iberians fought for the Carthaginians on the Crimisus campaign (Plut. 28.11; D.S. 73.3; cf. Plut. 20.8). So it is perhaps more likely that Iberians in the Punic service brought Syracusan coins to Emporion.

Amorós has put forward his suggestions in:

'D'un troballa des monedes Emporitanes i la possible cronologia de les monedes d'Empuries', *Junta de Museus: Gabinet Numismatic de Catalunya*, Sèrie A, Núm. 1 (Barcelona 1933), 24 pages.

'Les dracmes Empuritanes', *ibid.* Sèrie A, Núm. 2, 51 pages.

'Les monedes Empuritanes anteriors a les dracmes', *ibid.* Sèrie A, Núm. 3 (1934), 66 pages.

Cf. also 'Apostillas al estudio de las monedas emporitanas', *Numisma* 12 (1954), 9–19.

P (see p. 183)

The coins of some cities are discussed by:

A. J. Evans, 'Numismatic lights on the Sicily of Timoleon' (pp. 349–55 of E. A. Freeman, *A History of Sicily from the Earliest Times*, Vol. 4, Oxford 1894).

G. E. Rizzo, *Monete greche della Sicilia* (Rome 1946), pp. 137, 257, 262–78.

The issues of the cities in the north-east of Sicily are reviewed by G. Tropea, 'Il settentrione greco della Sicilia dal 337 al 241', *Rivista di storia antica* (Messina) 5 (1901), 559–70, esp. 562–3, but this article is not of much importance.

The historian may feel that sometimes numismatists have disputed too long over matters which plainly cannot be resolved. One such matter seems to be the identification of the soldier with the thick beard and Corinthian helmet, who appears on Timoleontic *litrai* of Syracuse. When there exists no adequate evidence on the point, it seems valueless to spend time canvassing the claims of Archias, Timoleon, Archias in the guise of Timoleon, Adranus or Gelon (for the third of these, see C. T. Seltman, *Greek Coins* (London 1955), pp. 193–4; for the fourth, J. P. Six, *NC* 18 (1878), 124 n. 82, supported by S. Mirone, *Aréthuse* 4 (1927), 112–13; for the last, E. Gabrici, *Boll. Circ. Num. Nap.* 37 (1952), 9–10, who fancies that Plut. *Tim.* 23.7–8 supports his identification; S. Consolo Langher, *Helikon* 3 (1963), 430 n. 175, criticizes the idea). The head on the Syracusan coins bears no resemblance to that on a carnelian ringstone, which Babelon conjectured to be a portrait of Timoleon (see G. M. A. Richter, *The engraved gems of the Greeks, Etruscans and Romans: Part* 1: *Engraved gems of the Greeks and the Etruscans* (London 1968), pp. 162–3).

There are similar debates over the identification of the head on Timoleontic coins of Gela (see G. K. Jenkins, *The Coinage of Gela* (Berlin 1970), p. 114), and the *agon* on the reverse of certain Syracusan bronze coins (an issue made to commemorate the three-fold *agones* established in Timoleon's honour, according to P. Lederer, 'Eine verschollene Bronzemünze von Syrakus', *Transactions of the International Numismatic Congress* (London 1938), pp. 80–5).

BIBLIOGRAPHY

1. Literary and historical works

Aloisio, F., *Rocca di Entella: note storico-critiche* (Mazara 1940).

Ardizzone, T., 'Proagori in città Siceliote', *Kokalos* 13 (1967), 155–76.

Asheri, D., *Distribuzioni di terre nell'antica Grecia, Memoria dell' Accademia delle Scienze di Torino, Classe di Scienze morali, storiche e filologiche*, Serie 4a, No. 10 (1966).

Beloch, K. J., *Griechische Geschichte* (2nd ed., Berlin and Leipzig 1922).

Berve, H., *Das Alexanderreich auf prosopographischer Grundlage* (Munich 1926).

Die Herrschaft von Agathokles, Sitzungsberichte der Bayerischen Akademie der Wissenschaften (1952), Heft 5.

Review of H. D. Westlake, *Timoleon and his relations with tyrants*, *Gnomon* 25 (1953), 527–30.

Dion, Akad. der Wiss. in Mainz, Abh. der Geistes- und Sozialwiss. Kl. Nr. 10 (Wiesbaden 1956).

Review of M. Sordi, *Timoleonte, Gnomon* 35 (1963), 378–83.

Die Tyrannis bei den Griechen (Munich 1967).

Bousquet, J. 'Nouvelles Inscriptions de Delphes: III. Compte du IVe Siècle', *BCH* 62 (1938), 348–57.

Broneer, O., *Corinth*, Vol. 1 Part 4: *The South Stoa and its Roman Successors* (Princeton 1954).

'The Isthmian Victory Crown', *AJA* 66 (1962), 259–63.

Brown, T. S., 'Timaeus and Diodorus' Eleventh Book', *AJP* 73 (1952), 337–55.

Timaeus of Tauromenium (California 1958).

Cappellano, N. E., *Sulla venuta di Timoleonte in Sicilia* (Catania 1903).

Casson, L., 'Speed under sail of ancient ships', *TAPA* 82 (1951), 136–48.

Chambry, E. – see under R. Flacelière.

Chisesi, F., 'Entella, il Crimiso e la battaglia di Timoleone', *RAL* 5 (1929), 255–84.

Colquhoun, A. – see under G. Lampedusa.

van Compernolle, R., 'La clause territoriale du traité de 306/5 conclu entre Agathokles de Syracuse et Carthage', *Revue Belge de Philologie et d'Histoire* 32 (1954), 395–421.

Consolo Langher, S., 'Documentazione numismatica e storia di Tyndaris nel sec. IV A.C.', *Helikon* 5 (1965), 63–96.

Costanza, S., 'La synkrisis nello schema biografico di Plutarco', *Messana* 4 (1955), 127–56.

Costanzi, V., 'Dioclea', *ASSO* 16–17 (1919–20), 1–7.

de Crozals, J., 'Timoléon et la constitution de Syracuse au IVe siècle', *Annales de l'enseignement supérieur de Grenoble* 1 (1889), 335–415.

Drögemüller, H.-P., *Syrakus: Zur Topographie und Geschichte einer griechischen Stadt* (Heidelberg 1969 – *Gymnasium* Beihefte, Heft 6).

Ducrey, P., *Le traitement des prisonniers de guerre dans la Grèce antique*, Ecole Française d'Athènes, Fasc. 17, Paris 1968.

Dunbabin, T. J., *The Western Greeks* (Oxford 1948).

Edelstein, L., *Plato's Seventh Letter* (Philosophia Antiqua XIV, Leiden 1966).

Erbse, H., 'Die Bedeutung der Synkrisis in den Parallelbiographien Plutarchs', *Hermes* 84 (1956), 398–424.

Evans, A. J., 'Contributions to Sicilian Numismatics: 6: The Omen of the Krimisos on Coins of Herbessus and Morgantina', *NC* 14 (1894), 233–7.

di Fede, N., *Dionigi il Giovane* (Catanzaro 1949).

Finley, M. I, *A History of Sicily: Ancient Sicily to the Arab Conquest* (London 1968).

Fischer, C. T., *Diodori Bibliotheca Historica*, Vol. IV, *Libri XVI–XVIII* (Teubner, Leipzig 1906).

Flacelière, R. and Chambry, E., *Plutarque Vies* 4 (Budé, Paris 1966).

Fontana, M. J., 'Fortuna di Timoleonte: Rassegna delle Fonti Letterarie', *Kokalos* 4 (1958), 3–23.

Freeman, E. A., *A History of Sicily from the Earliest Times* (Oxford 1894).

Garufi, C. A., review of F. Chisesi, 'Entella, il Crimiso e la battaglia di Timoleone', *Archivio Storico Siciliano* 52 (1932), 445–8.

Ghinati, F., 'Synkletoi Italiote e Siceliote', *Kokalos* 5 (1959), 119–44.

Giuliano, L., *Storia di Siracusa antica* (Milan 1911).

Graham, A. J., *Colony and Mother City in Ancient Greece* (Manchester 1964).

Griffith, G. T., *The Mercenaries of the Hellenistic World* (Cambridge 1935).

'The Union of Corinth and Argos (392–386 B.C.)', *Historia* 1 (1950), 236–56.

Griffo, P., 'Sull'identificazione di Camico con l'odierna S. Angelo Muxaro a nord-ovest di Agrigento', *ASSO* 7 (1954), 58–78.

Hammond, N. G. L., 'The Sources of Diodorus Siculus XVI. 1: The Macedonian, Greek and Persian Narrative', *CQ* 31 (1937), 79–91.

'The Sources of Diodorus Siculus XVI. 11: The Sicilian Narrative', *CQ* 32 (1938), 137–51.

Herzog, R., and Klaffenbach, G., *Asylieurkunden aus Kos, Abhandlungen der Deutschen Akademie der Wissenschaften zu Berlin* 1 (1952).

Hiller von Gaertringen, F., 'Marcus–Mamercus', *Wiener Studien* 46 (1928), 93–5.

Holden, H. A., *Plutarch's Life of Timoleon* (Cambridge 1898).

Holm, A., *Geschichte Siciliens im Alterthum* (Leipzig 1874).

Hüttl, W., *Verfassungsgeschichte von Syrakus* (Prague 1929).

Jacoby, F., *Die Fragmente der Griechischen Historiker* (Leiden 1923–).

Kagan, D., *Politics and Policy in Corinth, 421–336 B.C.* (Ohio 1958).

Kahrstedt, U., *Griechisches Staatsrecht* Vol. 1: *Sparta und seine Symmachie* (Göttingen 1922).

Kent, J. H., 'The victory monument of Timoleon at Corinth', *Hesperia* 21 (1952), 9–18.

Kronenberg, A. J., 'Ad Plutarchi Vitas', *Mnemosyne* 5 (1937), 303–14.

di Lampedusa, G., *Two stories and a memory*, trans. A. Colquhoun (London 1966).

Larsen, J. A. O., 'Demokratia', *Classical Philology* 68 (1973), 45–6.

Lauritano, R., 'Sileno in Diodoro?', *Kokalos* 2 (1956), 206–16.

Lenschau, T., 'Hiketas', *RE* 8 (1913), cols. 1594–6.

Lévêque, P., 'De Timoléon à Pyrrhos', *Kokalos* 14–15 (1968–9), 135–51.

Lindskog, C. – see under K. Ziegler.

Loicq-Berger, M.-P., *Syracuse: histoire culturelle d'une cité grecque, Collection Latomus* Vol. 87, Brussels 1967.

Lojacono, N., 'Entella ed il Crimiso' (sect. 1, *L'Araldo di S. Margherita Belice* 1963, offprint of 2 pages; sect. 2, *ibid.* 1964, pp. 22–9).

Luria, S., 'Zum Problem der griechisch-karthagischen Beziehungen', *Acta Antiqua* 12 (1964), 53–75.

Mack Smith, D., *Mediaeval Sicily*; *Modern Sicily* (London 1968).

Manganaro, G., 'Tre tavole di bronzo con decreti di *proxenia* del Museo di Napoli e il problema dei proagori in Sicilia', *Kokalos* 9 (1963), 205–20.

Manni, E., 'Da Ippi a Diodoro', *Kokalos* 3 (1957), 136–55.

'Sileno in Diodoro?', *Atti Accad. Palermo* 18 (1957/8), 81–8.

'Agatocle e la politica estera di Siracusa', *Kokalos* 12 (1966), 144–62.

Mazzarino, S., *Introduzione alle guerre puniche. Saggi e Ricerche XIII* (Catania 1947).

Meister, K., *Die sizilische Geschichte bei Diodor von den Anfängen bis zum Tod des Agathokles: Quellenuntersuchungen zu Buch iv–xxi* (Munich 1967).

Meloni, P., 'Il soggiorno di Dionisio II a Locri', *Studi Italiani di Filologia Classica* 25 (1951), 149–68.

Milns, R. D., 'Alexander's pursuit of Darius through Iran', *Historia* 15 (1966), 256.

Momigliano, A. D., *The Development of Greek Biography* (Harvard 1971).

Mossé, C., *La fin de la démocratie athénienne* (Paris 1962).

'Intervento' after P. Lévêque, 'De Timoléon à Pyrrhos', *Kokalos* 14–15 (1968–9), 151–2.

Musti, D., 'Ancora sull' "Iscrizione di Timoleonte"', *La Parola del Passato* 87 (1962), 450–71.

Navarra, G., *Città sicane, sicule e greche nella zona di Gela* (Palermo 1964).

Neumann, C., 'A note on Alexander's march-rates', *Historia* 20 (1971), 196–8.

Pace, B., *Arte e civiltà della Sicilia antica*, Vol. I (Milan 1935).

Pais, E., 'A proposito della legislazione di Diocle siracusano', *Studi Italiani di Filologia Classica* 7 (1899), 75–98.

Palm., J., *Über Sprache und Stil des Diodoros von Sizilien* (Lund 1955).

Parke, H. W., *Greek Mercenary Soldiers* (Oxford 1933).

Pomtow, H., 'Ein sicilisches Anathem in Delphi', *Ath. Mitt.* 20 (1895), 483–94.

Rizza, G., 'Leontini: Campagne di scavi 1950–1951 e 1951–1952: La necropoli della Valle S. Mauro; le fortificazioni meridionali della città e la porta di Siracusa', *NSc* 9 (1955), 281–376.

Rose, V. (ed.), *Aristotelis qui ferebantur librorum fragmenta* (Teubner, Stuttgart 1967 repr.).

Russell, D. A., 'On reading Plutarch's *Lives*', *Greece and Rome* 13 (1966), 139–54.

de Sanctis, G., 'Diocle di Siracusa', *Studi Italiani di Filologia Classica* 11 (1903), 433–55.

'I Thearodokoi d'Epidauro', *Atti della Accad. Sc. di Torino* 47 (1911/12), 442–50.

Scritti Minori (*Storia e Letteratura* 99; Rome 1966).

Sartori, F., 'Proagori in città Siceliote', *Kokalos* 7 (1961), 53–66.

Scheele, M., ΣΤΡΑΤΗΓΟΣ ΑΥΤΟΚΡΑΤѠΡ: *Staatsrechtliche Studien zur griechischen Geschichte des 5. und 4. Jahrhunderts* (Leipzig 1932).

von Scheliha, R., *Dion: die platonische Staatsgründung in Sizilien* (*Das Erbe der Alten* xxv; Leipzig 1934).

Seibert, J., *Metropolis und Apoikie: Historische Beiträge zur Geschichte ihrer gegenseitigen Beziehungen* (Würzburg 1963).

Sinclair, R. K., 'Diodorus Siculus and the writing of history', *Proceedings of the African Classical Associations* 6 (1963), 36–45.

Sjöqvist, E., 'Timoleonte e Morgantina', *Kokalos* 4 (1958), 107–18.

Solmsen, F., review of L. Edelstein, *Plato's Seventh Letter, Gnomon* 41 (1969), 29–34.

Sordi, M., *Timoleonte* (Palermo 1961).

Diodori Siculi Bibliothecae Liber Sextus Decimus: Introduzione, testo e commento (Florence 1969).

Stadter, P. A., *Plutarch's Historical Methods: An analysis of the 'Mulierum Virtutes'* (Harvard 1965).

Stier, H. E., 'Timoleon', *RE* 2.vi a (1936), cols. 1276–91.

Stroheker, K. F., *Dionysios I: Gestalt und Geschichte des Tyrannen von Syrakus* (Wiesbaden 1958).

Szabó, M., 'Zur Frage des Keltischen Fundes von Isthmia', *Acta Antiqua* 16 (1968), 173–7.

T.C.I. *Carta Automobilistica* 1 : 200,000, Fogli 25, 26, 27 (Milan 1966).

T.C.I. *Guida d'Italia: Sicilia* (Milan 1968).

Tillyard, H. J. W., *Agathocles* (Cambridge 1908).

Timmerman, A. G., *De Dionis et Timoleontis Vitis Capita Quaedam* (Amsterdam dissertation published at Leiden, 1893).

Trevelyan, G. M., *Garibaldi and the Thousand* (London 1909).

Tusa, V., 'Aspetti storico-archeologici di alcuni centri della Sicilia Occidentale', *Kokalos* 4 (1958), 151–62.

'L'Anfipolia a Solunto', *Kokalos* 9 (1963), 185–94.

Uggeri, G., 'La Sicilia nella "Tabula Peutingeriana"', *Vichiana* 6 (1969) 11–55'

'Sull' "Itinerarium per maritima loca" da Agrigento a Siracusa', *Atene e Roma* 15 (1970), 107–17.

Voit, L., 'Zur Dion-Vita', *Historia* 3 (1954/5), 171–92.

Walbank, F. W., *A Historical Commentary on Polybius* Vol. 2 (Oxford 1967).

'The historians of Greek Sicily', *Kokalos* 14–15 (1968–9), 476–97.

Warmington, B. H., *Carthage* (London 1964).

Welles, C. B., *Diodorus Siculus* Vol. viii (Loeb, London 1963).

Wentker, H., *Sizilien und Athen* (Heidelberg 1956).

Westlake, H. D., 'The Sources of Plutarch's Timoleon', *CQ* 32 (1938), 65–74.

Westlake, H. D., 'Phalaecus and Timoleon', *CQ* 34 (1940), 44-6.

'Timoleon and the reconstruction of Syracuse', *CHJ* 7 (1942), 73–100.

'The Purpose of Timoleon's Mission', *AJP* 70 (1949), 65–75.

Timoleon and his Relations with Tyrants (Manchester 1952).

'The Sicilian Books of Theopompus' *Philippica*', *Historia* 2 (1953/4), 288–307.

Review of M. Sordi, *Timoleonte*, *CR* 12 (1962), 268–70.

Essays on the Greek Historians and Greek History (Manchester 1969).

Woodhead, A. G., review of G. Navarra, *Città sicane, sicule e greche nella zona di Gela*, *JHS* 87 (1967), 188–9.

Ziegler, K., *Die Überlieferungsgeschichte der vergleichenden Lebensbeschreibungen Plutarchs* (Leipzig 1907).

and Lindskog, C., *Plutarchi Vitae Parallelae* Vols. II.ii–III.ii (Teubner, Leipzig 1915–35).

Plutarchos von Chaironeia (Stuttgart 1949).

Plutarchi Vitae Parallelae Vols. I.i–II.i (Teubner, Leipzig 1957–64).

2. Archaeological and numismatic material

Adamesteanu, D.–see under P. Orlandini.

'Vasi figurati di Manfria', in *Istituto di Archeologia dell'Università di Catania: Scritti in onore di Guido Libertini* (Florence 1958), pp. 25–34.

Adriani, A. and others, Istituto di Archeologia, Università di Palermo: *Himera* I. *Campagne di Scavo 1963–1965* (Rome 1970).

Amorós, J., 'D'un troballa des monedes Emporitanes i la possible cronologia de les monedes d'Empuries', *Junta de Museus: Gabinet Numismatic de Catalunya* Sèrie A Núm. 1 (Barcelona 1933), 24 pages.

'Les dracmes Empuritanes', *ibid.* Sèrie A Núm. 2, 51 pages.

'Les monedes Empuritanes anteriors a les dracmes', *ibid.* Sèrie A Núm. 3 (1934), 66 pages.

'Apostillas al estudio de las monedas emporitanas', *Numisma* 12 (1954), 9–19.

Breglia, L., 'La coniazione argentea di Alesa Arconidea', *Archivio Storico Siciliano* 2 (1947), 135–51.

'Divagazioni numismatiche e problema storico', *AIIN* 1 (1954), 196–200.

'Prospetto unitario della Monetazione nella Sicilia antica', *AIIN* 9–11 (1962–4), 31–46.

Cavallaro, G., 'Note numismatiche-topographiche siciliane: Nacona elimica', *Bollettino di Numismatica* 1, No. 3 (1929), 1–9.

'Mytistratum Sicana e le sue monete', *Atti e Mem.* 7 (1932), 14–37.

'Le monete degli Alesini Siculi e della Symmachia', *Atti e Mem.* 8 (1934), 3–19.

'L'ultimo rifugio degli Alesini Siculi', *Archivio Storico Siciliano* 54 (1934), 308–23.

Cesano, S. L., 'Il medagliere del museo archeologico di Siracusa', *Studi di Numismatica* 1 (1940), 9–68.

Christ, K., 'Historische Probleme der griechisch-sizilischen Numismatik', *Historia* 3 (1954–5), 385–95.

'Literaturüberblicke der griechischen Numismatik – Sizilien', *JNG* 5–6 (1954–5), 183–228.

Ciasca, A. and others, *Mozia – v, Consiglio Nazionale delle Ricerche* (Rome 1969).

de Ciccio, G., 'Di un tetradramma inedito di Catania e di un hemiobolo di argento e la litra di bronzo di Eryx', *Numismatica* 14 (1948), 1–4.

'Ancora della litra di bronzo di Eryx', *Numismatica* 15 (1949), 106–7.

Consolo Langher, S., 'Gli ΗΡΑΚΛΕΙѠΤΑΙ ΕΚ ΚΕΦΑΛΟΙΔΙΟΥ', *Kokalos* 7 (1961), 166–98.

'Il *Sikelikon Talanton* nella storia economica e finanziaria della Sicilia antica', *Helikon* 3 (1963), 388–436.

Contributo alla storia della antica moneta bronzea in Sicilia (Milan 1964).

'Documentazione numismatica e storia di Tyndaris nel sec. IV A.C.', *Helikon* 5 (1965), 63–96.

Cosman, A. C., *Demosthenes' Rede tegen Zenothemis (Oratie XXXII) met Inleiding en Commentaar* (Leiden 1939).

Currò Pisanò, M. T., 'La consistenza del medagliere di Siracusa per quanto riguarda la monetazione grecosiceliota', *AIIN* 9–11 (1962–4), 217–39.

Evans, A. J., 'Numismatic lights on the Sicily of Timoleon' (pp. 349–55 of E. A. Freeman, *A History of Sicily from the Earliest Times*, Vol. 4, Oxford 1894).

'Contributions to Sicilian Numismatics II', *NC* 16 (1896), 101–43.

'Select Sicilian and Magna-Graecian Coins', *NC* 6 (1926), 1–19.

Gabrici, E., *La monetazione del bronzo nella Sicilia antica* (reprinted from *Atti R. Accad. Palermo* 14, 1927).

Gabrici, E., 'Notes on Sicilian Numismatics', *NC* 11 (1931), 73–90.

'Divagazioni numismatiche', *Boll. Circ. Num. Nap.* 37 (1952), 3–13.

'Problemi di Numismatica greca della Sicilia e Magna Grecia', *MAN* 4 (1959).

Gentili, G. V., 'Nissoria (Enna) – Ripostiglio di monete d'argento del V–IV secolo av. Cr.', *NSc* 8 (1954), 58–70.

'Centuripe (Enna) – Ripostiglio di monete d'argento del V–IV secolo av. Cr.', *ibid.* 70–7.

'Vita dei Medaglieri: Soprintendenza alle Antichità della Sicilia Orientale', *AIIN* 1 (1954), 166–9.

'Vita dei Medaglieri: Soprintendenza alle Antichità della Sicilia Orientale', *AIIN* 5–6 (1958–9), 284–95.

Giesecke, W., *Sicilia Numismatica* (Leipzig 1923).

Head, B. V., 'On the chronological sequence of the coins of Syracuse', *NC* 14 (1874), 1–80.

Historia Numorum (2nd ed., Oxford 1911).

A Guide to the Principal Coins of the Greeks (revised by G. K. Jenkins, London 1965).

Hirmer, M. – see under C. M. Kraay.

Holm, A., *Geschichte des sicilischen Münzwesens bis zur Zeit des Augustus* (Leipzig 1898).

Ingholt, H. – see under G. K. Jenkins.

Jenkins, G. K. – see also under B. V. Head and C. M. Kraay.

'A Note on Corinthian Coins in the West', *CPANS* (ed. H. Ingholt, New York 1958), 367–79.

'Recent acquisitions of Greek coins by the British Museum', *NC* 19 (1959), 23–45.

and Lewis, R. B., *Carthaginian Gold and Electrum Coins* (London 1963).

'Africa', in *A Survey of Numismatic Research 1960–1965*. Vol. 1, *Ancient Numismatics*, ed. O. Mørkholm (Copenhagen 1967), pp. 85–95.

'Electrum Coinage at Syracuse', in *Essays in Greek Coinage Presented to Stanley Robinson* (Oxford 1968), pp. 145–62.

The Coinage of Gela (Berlin 1970).

'Coins of Punic Sicily, Part 1', *Schweizerische Numismatische Rundschau* 50 (1971), 25–78.

Jessop Price, M., review of S. Consolo Langher, *Contributo alla storia della antica moneta bronzea in Sicilia*, *NC* 7 (1967), 287–9.

Kraay, C. M., and Hirmer, M., *Greek Coins* (London 1966).

Review of S. Consolo Langher, *Contributo alla storia della antica moneta bronzea in Sicilia, CR* 17 (1967), 210–12.

and Jenkins, G. K. (editors), *Essays in Greek Coinage Presented to Stanley Robinson* (Oxford 1968).

Greek Coins and History: Some Current Problems (London 1969).

Lederer, P., 'Eine verschollene Bronzemünze von Syrakus', *Transactions of the International Numismatic Congress* (London 1938), pp. 80–5.

'La coniazione del bronzo della quarta repubblica di Siracusa', *Numismatica e Scienze Affini* 4 (1938), 25–6.

Lewis, R. B. – see under G. K. Jenkins.

Manganaro, G., 'Intervento' after K. F. Stroheker, 'Sizilien und die Magna Graecia zur Zeit der beiden Dionysii', *Kokalos* 14–15 (1968–9), 133–4.

'Per la storia della circolazione della moneta attica nella Sicilia Orientale', in *La Circolazione della Moneta Ateniese in Sicilia e in Magna Grecia* (Istituto Italiano di Numismatica, Rome 1969), pp. 151–63.

Marconi, P., 'Palma Montechiaro (Agrigento) – Sequestro di tesoretto di monete greche e c.d. punico-sicule', *NSc* 7 (1931), 404.

Merighi, C., 'Nota sulla monetazione di alcuni centri greci o ellenizzati in provincia di Caltanissetta', *Arch. Cl.* 15 (1963), 97–101.

de Miro, E., 'Eraclea Minoa e l'epoca di Timoleonte', *Kokalos* 4 (1958), 69–82.

Mirone, S., 'Monnaies Historiques de la Sicile Antique (suite)', *Aréthuse* 4 (1927), 101–28.

Mørkholm, O. – see under G. K. Jenkins.

Noe, S. P., *A Bibliography of Greek Coin Hoards* (2nd ed.), *Numismatic Notes and Monographs* No. 78 (1937).

Orlandini, P. and Adamesteanu, D., 'Vita dei Medaglieri: Soprintendenza alle Antichità per le province di Agrigento e Caltanissetta: Gela', *AIIN* 3 (1956), 228–35; and *AIIN* 4 (1957), 203–7. Title as above, *AIIN* 5–6 (1958–9), 302–6.

'Una precisazione cronologica sulla comparsa delle monete puniche a Gela e nel suo retroterra', *AIIN* 9–11 (1962–4), 49–52.

Orsi, P., 'Ripostiglio di monete erose e di altri bronzi da Milocca (Caltanissetta)', *Atti e Mem.* 7 (1932), 38–46.

Pozzi, E., 'Gruzzolo di monete greche del museo archeologico nazionale di Napoli', *AIIN* 5–6 (1958–9), 91–124.

Ravel, O. E., 'Notes on some rare and unpublished "Pegasi" of my collection', *NC* 6 (1926), 305–21.

Ravel, O. E., *The 'Colts' of Ambracia*, Numismatic Notes and Monographs No. 37 (1928).

'Contribution à l'étude de la numismatique Corinthienne', *Aréthuse* 6 (1929), 1–20.

'Rare and unpublished coins of Corinthian types', *NC* 15 (1935), 1–15.

'Ritrovamento di Pegasi', *Numismatica* 11 (1936), 1–7.

Les 'Poulains' de Corinthe, Vol. 2: *de 414 à 300 av. J.-C.* (London 1948).

Richter, G. M. A., *The engraved gems of the Greeks, Etruscans and Romans:* Part 1: *Engraved gems of the Greeks and Etruscans* (London 1968).

Rizzo, G. E., *Intermezzo: nuovi studi archeologici su le monete greche de la Sicilia* (Rome 1939).

Monete greche della Sicilia (Rome 1946).

Robinson, E. S. G. (editor), *Sylloge Nummorum Graecorum*, Vol. 2: *The Lloyd Collection* (London 1933).

'Petra or Eryx?', *NC* 8 (1948), 131–3.

Ross Holloway, R., 'Monetary Circulation in central Sicily to the reign of Augustus as documented by the Morgantina excavations', *Congresso Internazionale di Numismatica*, Vol. 2: *Atti* (Rome 1965), pp. 135–50.

Seltman, C. T., *Greek Coins* (London 1955).

Six, J. P., 'Monnaies d'Hierapolis en Syrie', *NC* 18 (1878), 103–31.

Tod, M. N., *A Selection of Greek Historical Inscriptions*, Vol. 2 (Oxford 1948).

Trendall, A. D., *Red-figured vases of Lucania, Campania and Sicily: Book III, Sicilian* (Oxford 1967).

Tropea, G., 'Il settentrione della Sicilia dal 337 al 241', *Rivista di storia antica* (Messina) 5 (1901), 559–70.

Tusa, V., 'Libertinia, Rinvenimenti archeologici', *NSc* 13 (1959), 350–7.

Tusa Cutroni, A., 'Il Medagliere del Museo Nazionale di Palermo', *AIIN* 3 (1956), 205–12.

'Ripostigli monetali del Museo Nazionale di Palermo: I. Ripostiglio di sessantacinque stateri', *AIIN* 5–6 (1958–9), 167–77; 'II. Ripostiglio di trentadue monete d'argento', *ibid.* 178–85.

'I KAMΠANOI ed i TYPPHNOI in Sicilia attraverso la documentazione numismatica', *Kokalos* 16 (1970), 250–67.

Vallet, G. and Villard, F., 'Le repeuplement du site de Mégara Hyblaea à l'époque de Timoléon', *Kokalos* 4 (1958), 100–6.

di Vita, A., 'Camarina e Scornavacche in età timoleontea', *Kokalos* 4 (1958), 83–99.

'Pachino – Tesoretto monetale del IV–III sec. A.C. rinvenuto in Contrada "Coste Fondovia"', *AIIN* 5–6 (1958–9), 125–65.

Warren, J., 'The trihemidrachms of Corinth', in *Essays in Greek Coinage Presented to Stanley Robinson* (ed. C. M. Kraay and G. K. Jenkins, Oxford 1968), pp. 125–44.

Winter, F. E., 'The chronology of the Euryalos Fortress at Syracuse', *AJA* 67 (1963), 363–87.

3. Archaeological works

Surveys of excavations showing Timoleon's revival of Greek Sicily:

P. Orlandini, 'La rinascita della Sicilia nell'età di Timoleonte alla luce delle nuove scoperte archeologiche', *Kokalos* 4 (1958), 24–30.

There is a similar piece by the same author and with the same title in *Atti del Settimo Congresso Internazionale di Archeologia Classica*, Vol. 2, pp. 53–9 (Rome 1961).

Surveys of excavations in Sicily:

P. Griffo, 'Bilancio di cinque anni di scavi nelle Province di Agrigento e Caltanissetta', *Atti Accad. Agrigento* 3 (1953/4), 143–73. An important article, which in fact reviews archaeological work carried out between the end of the Second World War and 1954 at the following sites: Agrigento; Heraclea Minoa; Gela; Manfria; Butera, Priorato, Milingiana; M. Desusino and M. Bubbonia; unauthorized excavations at M. Raffe.

B. Neutsch, 'Archäologische Grabungen und Funde im Bereich der Soprintendenzen von Sizilien (1949–1954)', *Jahrbuch des Archäologischen Instituts* 69 (1954), 465–706.

P. Griffo, 'Aspetti archeologici della provincia di Caltanissetta', *Quaderni di Archeologia, Arte, Storia a cura della Soprintendenza alle Antichità di Agrigento* No. 4 (Agrigento 1955) (31 pages).

P. Griffo, 'Relazione sull'attività svolta della Soprintendenza alle Antichità di Agrigento, dal gennaio 1951 al dicembre 1954', *La Giara, Numero Speciale dedicato all'attività dell'Assessorato per la P. I. della Regione Siciliana 1951–55* (undated volume; 1956?), pp. 255–84: Agrigento, Heraclea Minoa, Gela, Manfria, Butera, M. Desusino.

L. Bernabò Brea and G. V. Gentili, 'Attività della Soprintendenza alle Antichità della Sicilia Orientale negli anni 1951–54', *ibidem* 375–440; p. 394 Scornavacche; pp. 418–22 Tyndaris; pp. 422–6 Alesa.

P. Griffo, *Sulle Orme della Civiltà gelese* (Agrigento 1958). (Many plates, together with 30 pages of text, which cover the same ground as P. Griffo, *Aspetti archeologici*.)

P. Orlandini, 'I nuovi scavi archeologici in Sicilia: Scoperte e Problemi', *Annali della Pubblica Istruzione* 5 (1959), 538–44, esp. 543–4.

P. Griffo, 'Recenti scavi archeologici nelle province di Agrigento e Caltanissetta: suoi riflessi culturali e turistici' (*Quinto Congresso del 190° distretto del Rotary Internazionale*, Naples 1959), pp. 249–62.

L. Bernabò Brea, 'La Sicilia Orientale', *ibidem* pp. 263–74.

W. Fuchs, 'Archäologische Forschungen und Funde in Sizilien von 1955 bis 1964', *Jahrbuch des Archäologischen Instituts* 79 (1964), 657–749 (East Sicily); 749–85 (West Sicily).

'Attività delle Soprintendenze (1960–1965): Sicilia', *Bollettino d'Arte* 51 (1966), 89–116.

Articles on the Greek cities, together with bibliographies, have appeared in *Enciclopedia dell'arte antica, classica e orientale* (7 volumes, Rome 1958–66).

Two good general guides to sites are:

M. Guido, *Sicily: An archaeological guide* (London 1967). The plan of Gela (fig. 24, p. 143) should be used with caution, since the scale is given wrongly, and the thick arrows in fact mark the western limit of the town until *c.* 340 B.C.

Guida d'Italia del Touring Club Italiano: Sicilia (Milan 1968).

Articles in *Sicilia* and *Le Vie d'Italia* have been included in the following list despite their general nature: they are almost always well arranged and well illustrated.

Tyndaris

N. Lamboglia, 'Gli scavi di Tindari (1950–52)', *La Giara* 2 (1953), 70–84, esp. p. 75.

F. Barreca, 'Tindari colonia dionigiana', *RAL* 12 (1957), 125–34.

F. Barreca, 'Tindari dal 345 al 317 a. Cr.', *Kokalos* 4 (1958), 145–50.

N. Lamboglia, 'Opus Certum', *Rivista di Studi Liguri* 24 (1958), 165.

F. Barreca, 'Precisazioni circa le mura greche di Tindari', *RAL* 14 (1959), 105–13 (reply to Lamboglia, above).

L. Bernabò Brea, 'Due secoli di studi, scavi e restauri del teatro greco di Tindari', *Rivista dell'Istituto nazionale d'archeologia e storia dell'arte* 13–14 (1964–5), 99–144, esp. 134–6 for dating.

Less detailed publications:

N. Lamboglia, 'Tindari: città sepolta della Sicilia', *Le Vie d'Italia* 57 (1951), 1457–63.

M. A. Mezquíriz, 'Cerámica ibérica en Tyndaris (Sicilia)', *Archivo español de arqueología* 26 (1953), 156–61, esp. p. 157 on the walls.

M. A. Mezquíriz, 'Excavaciones estratigráficas de Tyndaris', *Caesaraugusta* 5 (1954), 85–99.

R. Ross Holloway, 'Tyndaris: last colony of the Sicilian Greeks', *Archaeology* 13 (1960), 246–50.

Megara Hyblaea

F. Villard, 'Mégara Hyblaea: I. Les Fouilles de 1949', *MEFR* 63 (1951), 7–52, esp. 32 (layout of city), 43–5 (fourth-century pottery), 50 (historical conclusion).

(The following articles are all by F. Villard and G. Vallet in *MEFR*.)

'Report on 1950', Vol. 64 (1952), 7–38, esp. 16.

'Report on 1951', Vol. 65 (1953), 9–38, esp. 12–13 (conclusions from finds).

'Report on 1952', Vol. 66 (1954), 13–38, esp. 30 and 38.

'La forteresse Hellénistique', Vol. 70 (1958), 39–59.

'Un temple dorique du IVe siècle', Vol. 74 (1962), 61–78, esp. 73–5 (possible dating), and 75–7 (possible identification of the divinity).

MEFR: Suppléments 1 (Paris 1966), 'Mégara Hyblaea 4: Le temple du IVe siècle', esp. 65 (final conclusion on date and dedication).

'Les problèmes de l'agora et de la cité archaïque', Vol. 81 (1969), 7–35, esp. 12 (stressing humble nature of the Timoleontic city).

F. Villard and G. Vallet, 'Le repeuplement du site de Mégara Hyblaea à l'époque de Timoléon', *Kokalos* 4 (1958), 100–6.

Less detailed publications:

J. Bayet, 'Les fouilles archéologiques de l'Ecole Française de Rome en Italie de 1946 à 1956: Mégara Hyblaea et Bolséna', *Etudes d'archéologie classique* 1 (1955/6), 21–38. Pp. 24–31 are devoted to Megara Hyblaea.

G. Vallet and F. Villard, 'Les fouilles de Mégara Hyblaea (1949–1959)', *Bollettino d'Arte* 45 (1960), 263–73, esp. 270.

Brief reports on the excavations have appeared in issues of *CRAI*, but the only important one of these is G. Vallet and F. Villard, 'Communication: Un temple dorique du IVe siècle à Mégara Hyblaea', *CRAI* (1960), 98–105.

Camarina, Scornavacche and Castiglione

(All the articles are by A. di Vita.)

'Due matrici della stessa serie da Scornavacche e da Selinunte', *ASSO* 7 (1954), 79–88.

'Recenti scoperte archeologiche in provincia di Ragusa', *Archivio Storico Siracusano* 2 (1956), 30–44, esp. 36–41 (Scornavacche).

'Camarina e Scornavacche in età timoleontea', *Kokalos* 4 (1958), 83–99.

'Breve rassegna degli scavi archeologici condotti in provincia di Ragusa nel quadriennio 1955–1959', *Bollettino d'Arte* 44 (1959), 347–63.

Helorus

Various authors, 'Eloro', *MAL* 47 (1966), 203–340, esp. 310–18.

A. D. Trendall, 'Archaeology in South Italy and Sicily, 1964–66', *Archaeological Reports for 1966–67* 13, p. 44.

Morgantina

R. Stillwell and E. Sjöqvist, 'Excavations at Serra Orlando – Preliminary Report', *AJA* 61 (1957), 151–9.

E. Sjöqvist, 'Preliminary Report 2', *AJA* 62 (1958), 155–64, esp. 158–9 (sanctuary of Demeter and Kore).

E. Sjöqvist, 'Timoleonte e Morgantina', *Kokalos*, 4 (1958), 107–18. Only pp. 111–16 (on the sanctuary of Demeter and Kore) are relevant. On the speculative idea that Morgantina was a *polis* which supported Timoleon at an early stage (pp. 108–10), see pp. 202–3. On the bronze coins of Morgantina with an eagle and serpent motif (pp. 117–18), see p. 203.

R. Stillwell, 'Preliminary Report 3', *AJA* 63 (1959), 167–73, esp. 170 (city wall).

E. Sjöqvist, 'Preliminary Report 4', *AJA* 64 (1960), 125–35, esp. 126–8 (city wall and Necropolis III); 133 (sanctuary of Demeter and Kore).

R. Stillwell, 'Preliminary Report 5', *AJA* 65 (1961), 277–81, esp. 278 (shops on west side of agora).

E. Sjöqvist, 'Preliminary Report 6', *AJA* 66 (1962), 135–43, esp. 135–6 (agora); 138 (theatre); 142 (area V).

R. Stillwell, 'Preliminary Report 7', *AJA* 67 (1963), 163–71, esp. 170 (area V).

R. Ross Holloway, 'A tomb group of the fourth century B.C. from the area of Morgantina', *AJA* 67 (1963), 289–91.

E. Sjöqvist, 'Preliminary Report 8', *AJA* 68 (1964), 137–47, esp. 142–3 (Chthonian sanctuary).

R. Stillwell, 'The theater of Morgantina', *Kokalos* 10–11 (1964–5), 586.

R. Stillwell, 'Preliminary Report 9', *AJA* 71 (1967), 245–50, esp. 249 (West Hill).

H. L. Allen, 'Preliminary Report 10', *AJA* 74 (1970), 359–83, esp. 362 (street grid plan) and 363–4 (theatre).

For discussion of the view that modern Serra Orlando is ancient Morgantina:

K. Erim, Morgantina, *AJA* 62 (1958), 79–90.

E. Sjöqvist, 'Serra Orlando – Morgantina', *RAL* 14 (1959), 39–48. On the Timoleontic city, see p. 44.

Sjöqvist's article was challenged by:

M. T. Piraino, 'Morgantina e Murgentia nella topografia dell'antica Sicilia orientale', *Kokalos* 5 (1959), 174–89.

A reply appeared:

E. Sjöqvist, 'Perché Morgantina?', *RAL* 15 (1960), 291–300. On the Timoleontic city, see p. 298.

Less detailed publications:

C. Falcone, 'Città segreta', *Sicilia* 16 (1956), 38–42.

R. Stillwell, *Archaeology* 9 (1956), 221; 10 (1957), 286–7; 12 (1959), 133–4; 13 (1960), 220–1; 16 (1963), 60–1.

E. Sjöqvist, 'Gli scavi di Morgantina – Serra Orlando', *Atti del Settimo Congresso Internazionale di Archeologia Classica* (Rome 1961), Vol. 2, pp. 61–7. For the fourth-century city, see p. 66.

Gela

P. Griffo, 'Le recenti scoperte archeologiche di Gela', *ASSO* 1 (1948), 181–4. (Brief preliminary report on the discovery of the fortifications at C. Soprano. Here Griffo dates the original stone part of the fortifications to the fifth century, and the later brick part to the time of Timoleon (p. 184). He has consistently adhered to this dating scheme in later publications, although it has been challenged by Orlandini, who argues that the fortifications were only begun in the Timoleontic period. I accept Orlandini's dating. Griffo has never defended his scheme in detail, but see *Sulle Orme della Civiltà gelese*, p. 17.)

P. Griffo, 'Novità a Capo Soprano', *ASSO* 4 (1951), 281–6.

P. Griffo, *Attività archeologica a Gela: gli scavi delle fortificazioni greche in località Capo Soprano* (Agrigento 1953) (23 pages).

P. Orlandini, 'Vasi fliacici trovati nel territorio di Gela', *Bollettino d'Arte* 38 (1953), 155–8 (fourth-century vases from Manfria and Gela).

P. Orlandini, 'Due graffiti vascolari relativi al culto di Hera a Gela', *RAL* 9 (1954), 454–7.

P. Orlandini and D. Adamesteanu, 'Gela – ritrovamenti vari', *NSc* 10 (1956), 203–401. Not all the finds are datable to the fourth century, but note 236–41 (cistern); 242–52 (sacred building); 252–63 (archaic building restored in fourth century); 264–73 (wells and cisterns); 343–54 (house at C. Soprano).

D. Adamesteanu, 'Osservazioni sulla battaglia di Gela del 405 A.C.', *Kokalos* 2 (1956), 142–57, esp. 150 and 156–7.

P. Orlandini, 'Storia e topografia di Gela dal 405 al 282 A.C. alla luce delle nuove scoperte archeologiche', *Kokalos* 2 (1956), 158–76, esp. 163–8.

D. Adamesteanu, 'Fotografia aerea ed i problemi archeologici della Sicilia', *SIFET* 2–3 (1957), 76–85, esp. 79–81.

G. Schmiedt, 'Applicazioni della fotografia aerea in ricerche estensive di topografia antica in Sicilia', *Kokalos* 3 (1957), 18–30, esp. 28–9.

P. Orlandini, 'Tipologia e cronologia del materiale archeologico di Gela dalla nuova fondazione di Timoleonte all'età di Ierone II', *Arch. Cl.* 9 (1957), 44–75 (Parte I), 153–73 (Parte II), esp. 48–74 (description of three phases in material found at Gela; material datable to 339–*c.* 310); and 171–3 (conclusions).

P. Orlandini, 'Il gusto per l'imitazione dell'antico nella Gela del IV–III sec. A.C.', *Arch. Cl.* 10 (1958), 240–2.

P. Orlandini and D. Adamesteanu, 'Gela – nuovi scavi', *NSc* 14 (1960), 67–246.

P. Orlandini, 'Materiale archeologico gelese del IV–III sec. A.C. nel museo nazionale di Siracusa', *Arch. Cl.* 12 (1960), 57–70. See esp. conclusions on 69–70. Orlandini revises his classification of *Arch. Cl.* 9 (1957), and now distinguishes between an *età di Timoleonte* (339–*c.* 320) and an *età di Agatocle* (*c.* 320–*c.* 300).

P. Orlandini, 'La terza campagna di scavo sull'acropoli di Gela (rapporto preliminare)', *Kokalos* 7 (1961), 137–44.

D. Adamesteanu and P. Orlandini, 'Gela – L'acropoli di Gela', *NSc* 16 (1962), 340–408.

Less detailed publications:

L. Aliotta, 'Importanti risultati dei recenti scavi di Gela', *Scienza e Tecnica* 12 (1951), 114–16 (a thin piece despite its title).

D. Adamesteanu, 'Dalle foci del Danubio agli scavi di Gela', *Sicilia* 6 (1954), 12–14 (general article describing how Adamesteanu came to work at Gela).

P. Orlandini, 'Scavi, ricerche e scoperte nelle province di Agrigento e Caltanissetta', *Nuova Antologia* 470 (1957), 511–18.

D. Adamesteanu, 'Nouvelles fouilles à Géla et dans l'arrière-pays: à Géla (1re partie)', *Rev. Arch.* 49 (1957), 20–46.

P. Griffo, 'Il museo archeologico nazionale di Gela', *Bollettino d'Arte* 43 (1958), 342–6.

P. Griffo, 'Civiltà di Gela', *Le Vie d'Italia* 64 (1958), 1453–60.

J. L. de Bruyne, 'De nieuwste opgravingen in Gela', *Hermeneus* 30 (1958–9), 149–54.

P. Orlandini, 'Il nuovo museo nazionale di Gela', *Annali della Pubblica Istruzione* 5 (1959), 151–6.

V. Eftimie, 'Săpăturile de la Gela şi din teritoriul său', *Studii şi cercetări de istorie veche* 10 (1959), 175–82.

P. Orlandini, 'Gela rediviva: nowe wykopaliska muzeum w Geli', *Z Otchłani Wieków* (Wroclaw) 26 (1960), 39–49.

P. Griffo, *Gela: destino di una città di Sicilia* (Genoa 1963). For Timoleontic Gela, see pp. 185–6. Fine plan of the city on pp. 174–5.

P. Orlandini and D. Adamesteanu, *Guide to Gela* (Milan 1968).

Hinterlands of Agrigento and Gela

(All articles are by D. Adamesteanu, unless otherwise stated.)

'Grondaie a testa leonina nel territorio di Butera', *Bollettino d'Arte* 39 (1954), 259–61 (Adamesteanu revises his dating of the piece from Milingiana in *NSc* 12 (1958), 360–1, below).

'ΠΟΛΥΣΤΕΦΑΝΟΣ ΘΕΑ', *RAL* 9 (1954), 467–9 (an inscribed vase from Fontana Calda).

'"'ANAKTOPA" o sacelli?', *Arch. Cl.* 7 (1955), 179–86 (mainly devoted to M. Bubbonia).

'Due problemi topografici del retroterra gelese', *RAL* 10 (1955), 199–210 (on pp. 199–203 Adamesteanu describes the excavations at M. Desusino, and seeks to identify the site with ancient Phalarion).

'Monte Saraceno ed il problema della penetrazione rodio-cretese nella Sicilia meridionale', *Arch. Cl.* 8 (1956), 121–46, esp. 132–5.

'Le fortificazioni ad aggere nella Sicilia centro-meridionale', *RAL* 11 (1956), 358–72: 362 M. Saraceno and M. Bubbonia; 363–7 M. Desusino; 367–8 Gibil Gabib.

'Storia di un sarcofago', *Sicilia* 16 (1956), 3–9 (general article on Vassallaggi).

'Nouvelles fouilles à Géla et dans l'arrière-pays: l'arrière-pays (2e partie)', *Rev. Arch.* 49 (1957), 147–80 (not detailed).

'Butera – A Sicilian town through the ages', *Archaeology* 10 (1957), 166–73 (not detailed).

'Fotografia aerea ed i problemi archeologici della Sicilia', *SIFET* 2–3 (1957), 76–85: 80–2 M. Bubbonia; 81–4 M. Raffe.

'L'opera di Timoleonte nella Sicilia centro-meridionale vista attraverso gli scavi e le ricerche archeologiche', *Kokalos* 4 (1958), 31–68: Butera, M. Desusino, M. Bubbonia, M. Saraceno, Vassallaggi, Gibil Gabib, Manfria, Milingiana, Priorato.

'Butera, Piano della Fiera, Consi e Fontana Calda', *MAL* 44 (1958), 205–672.

'Scavi e scoperte nella provincia di Caltanissetta dal 1951 al 1957', *NSc* 12 (1958), 288–408: Manfria, M. Desusino, Milingiana; survey of farms in the area of M. Desusino and Milingiana; Priorato, Gibil Gabib.

Fasti Archeologici 13 (1960). Notes on: No. 2251 Balate; No. 2272 Castellazzo; No. 2288 Cozzo Mususino; No. 2423 Terravecchia.

P. Orlandini and D. Adamesteanu, 'Gela – nuovi scavi', *NSc* 14 (1960), 67–246: 239 Feudo Nobile; 243 Contrada Farello.

P. Orlandini, 'Sulle colline di Manfria', *Sicilia* 28 (1960), 52–5 (not detailed).

M. Bonavia, 'Le città sepolte di Caltanissetta', *Sicilia* 29 (1961), 2–6 (not detailed; mainly on Gibil Gabib and Sabucina).

P. Orlandini, 'L'espansione di Gela nella Sicilia centro-meridionale', *Kokalos* 8 (1962), 69–121. This article is not devoted to fourth-century developments, but 118–19 and Plate v give a useful summary of Greek centres in the hinterland of Gela.

'Note di topografia siceliota (Parte I)', *Kokalos* 9 (1963), 19–48: 26–31 M. Desusino; 32–5 Lavanca Nera; 38–9 Cozzo Mususino; 39–41 Castellazzo di Marianopoli.

P. Orlandini, 'Sabucina: (a) scoperte varie; (b) prima campagna di scavo (1962): rapporto preliminare', *Arch. Cl.* 15 (1963), 86–96, esp. pp. 92–6.

P. Orlandini, 'Nuovi graffiti rinvenuti a Gela e nel territorio di Caltanissetta', *RAL* 20 (1965), 454–60, esp. No. 10 (pp. 459–60), which may bear the name of a colonist brought to Sicily by Timoleon.

P. Orlandini, 'Sabucina: la seconda campagna di scavo (1964): rapporto preliminare', *Arch. Cl.* 17 (1965), 132–40.

P. Orlandini, 'Sabucina: la terza campagna di scavo (1966): rapporto preliminare', *Arch. Cl.* 20 (1968), 151–6.

G. V. Gentili, 'Piazza Armerina (Enna): Le anonime città di Montagna di Marzo e di Monte Navone', *NSc* 23 (1969), *Il Supplemento*.

Agrigento

P. Marconi, *Agrigento, topografia ed arte* (Florence 1929), esp. pp. 108–13, where Marconi puts forward the old view that there was almost no development in the city during the fourth century, except for the alterations made to the fortifications.

P. Marconi, 'Agrigento: studi sulla organizzazione urbana di una città classica', *Rivista del R. Istituto d'Archeologia e Storia dell'Arte* 2 (1930), 7–61, esp. pp. 38–9 (fortifications).

P. Griffo, 'Ultimi scavi e ultime scoperte in Agrigento', *Quaderni di Archeologia, Arte, Storia a cura della Soprintendenza alle Antichità, Agrigento* No. 3 (Agrigento 1946) (34 pages), esp. 7–9 (excavations in Rock Sanctuary) and 11–12 and 32–4 (excavations in San Nicola quarter).

P. Griffo, 'Interessi Agrigentini', *Akragas* 2 (1946), 43–9 (an outline of Griffo's plans for the development of the archaeological zone at Agrigento; cf. *Akragas* 3 (1947), 36–44).

P. Griffo, 'Topografia storica di Agrigento antica – note ed appunti', *Atti Accad. Agrigento* 2 (1948–52), 38–47 (this is not a detailed article, and it has little to say specifically on the fourth-century city; but see 40–4 in general).

P. Griffo, *Ripresa degli scavi in Agrigento: il quartiere ellenistico-romano presso S. Nicola* (Agrigento 1953) (14 pages). (Brief report of excavations up to that time, with plates and a plan. No very precise ideas on dating at this stage.)

E. de Miro, 'Il quartiere ellenistico-romano di Agrigento', *RAL* 12 (1957), 135–40, esp. 139.

G. Schmiedt, 'Applicazioni della fotografia aerea in ricerche estensive di topografia antica in Sicilia', *Kokalos* 3 (1957), 20–2.

G. Schmiedt and P. Griffo, 'Agrigento antica dalle fotografie aeree e dai recenti scavi', *L'Universo* 38 (1958), 289–308 (summarized by R. Grillo in *Bollettino dell'Istituto storico e di cultura dell'Arma del Genio* 25 (1959), 277–9).

P. Griffo, 'Ritorna alla luce l'antica Agrigento', *Le Vie d'Italia* 64 (1958), 734–44.

P. Griffo and F. Minissi, 'Completamento degli scavi del "Quartiere ellenistico-romano" di Agrigento e sistemazione turistica della zona archeologica relativa', *IV Settimana dei Musei Italiani* 10–20 Novembre 1960 (offprint of 11 pages); see esp. pp. 3–7.

P. Griffo, *Nuovissima guida per il visitatore dei monumenti di Agrigento: la zona archeologica e la città moderna* (Agrigento 1961).

G. Zuntz, 'Osservazioni sul "Santuario Rupestre" presso S. Biagio, Agrigento', *Klearchos* 5 (1963), 114–24, esp. 123. Now reprinted in G. Zuntz, *Opuscula Selecta* (Manchester 1972), pp. 69–77, with some additional comment.

E. de Miro, 'Agrigento: scavi nell'area a sud del tempio di Giove', *MAL* 46 (1963), 81–198, esp. 81–5 and 187–96.

E. de Miro, 'I recenti scavi sul poggetto di S. Nicola in Agrigento', *Cronache di Archeologia e di Storia dell'Arte* 2 (1963), 57–63.

G. Schmiedt, 'Le ricerche sull'urbanistica delle città Italiote e Siceliote', *Kokalos* 14–15 (1968–9), 401–2.

J. A. de Waele, *Acragas Graeca: die historische Topographie des griechischen Akragas auf Sizilien, 1. Historischer Teil, Archeologische Studiën van het Nederlands Historisch Instituut te Rome, deel III* ('s-Gravenhage 1971).

Heraclea Minoa

(All publications are by E. de Miro unless otherwise stated.)

'Eraclea Minoa (primi scavi e prime scoperte)', *Siculorum Gymnasium* 5 (1952), 54–67.

'Heraclea Minoa: Il teatro', *NSc* 9 (1955), 266–80, esp. 277–9 on the date of the theatre.

A. Scaturro, 'Torna alla luce Eraclea Minoa città sepolta da venti secoli', *Le Vie d'Italia* 62 (1956), 666–7.

'Heraclea Minoa – scavi eseguiti negli anni 1955–56–57', *NSc* 12 (1958), 232–87. For dating see pp. 242–3 (perimeter wall); 254–5 (theatre).

'Eraclea Minoa e l'epoca di Timoleonte', *Kokalos* 4 (1958), 69–82. The additional note on pp. 81–2, which takes into account developments during the 1959 excavations, is important for the dating of the perimeter wall.

P. Griffo, 'Una città greca di Sicilia: Eraclea Minoa', *Le Vie d'Italia* 65 (1959), 485–94.

L'antiquarium e la ʒona archeologica di Eraclea Minoa (Ministero della Pubblica Istruzione: *Itinerari dei Musei, Gallerie e Monumenti d'Italia*, No. 110, 1965).

'Il teatro di Heraclea Minoa', *RAL* 21 (1966), 151–68. See pp. 167–8 for dating.

P. Griffo, 'Eraclea Minoa', *Sicilia* 51 (1966), 61–8.

Index

231